THE NEW IMMIGRATION CHALLENGE

Due to shifting demographic trends and the increased need for workers, immigration continues to grow in many parts of the world. However, the increased diversity that immigration creates within societies is also associated with intergroup friction, perceived threat, and the rise of extremist right-wing nationalist movements, making it a central political issue that impacts societies globally. This book presents a psychological explanation of the immigration challenge in the twenty-first century and the ongoing backlash against immigrants by examining within nations and beyond national borders. It explains the relationship between immigration and national identity through an analysis of the intersection of globalization, deglobalization, and collective behavior. Addressing a crucial gap in existing literature, it applies a psychological perspective on immigration and offers new solutions to address the complex challenges facing minorities, asylum seekers, undocumented immigrants, and host society members.

FATHALI M. MOGHADDAM is Professor of Psychology at Georgetown University. His most recent works include *The Psychology of Revolution* (Cambridge, 2024) and *The Psychology of Assimilation, Multiculturalism, and Omniculturalism* (2024). He has been recognized for his research through a number of prestigious academic awards.

MARGARET J. HENDRICKS is an Asylum Officer with the US Citizenship and Immigration Services Agency. She is coeditor of *Contemporary Immigration: Psychological Perspectives to Address Challenges and Inform Solutions* (2022) and was previously awarded a Presidential Management Fellowship. She received her PhD in Psychology from Georgetown University.

RAIMUNDO SALAS-SCHWEIKART is a PhD from Georgetown University researching the intersection of psychology and immigration. He has worked in volunteer formation at Servicio Jesuita Migrantes (https://sjmchile.org/), focusing on intergroup relations and trust.

THE PROGRESSIVE PSYCHOLOGY BOOK SERIES

This book is part of the Cambridge University Press book series, Progressive Psychology, edited by Fathali M. Moghaddam. As the science of human behavior, psychology is uniquely positioned and equipped to try to help us make more progress toward peaceful, fair, and constructive human relationships. However, the enormous resources of psychology have not been adequately or effectively harnessed for this task. The goal of this book series is to engage psychological science in the service of achieving more democratic societies, toward providing equal opportunities for all. The volumes in the series contribute in new and unique ways to highlight how psychological science can contribute to making justice a more central theme in health care, education, the legal system, and business, combatting the psychological consequences of poverty, ending discrimination and prejudice, better understanding the failure of revolutions and limits on political plasticity, and moving societies to more openness. Of course, these topics have been discussed before in scattered and *ad hoc* ways by psychologists, but now they are addressed as part of a systematic and cohesive series on Progressive Psychology.

THE NEW IMMIGRATION CHALLENGE
A Psychological Exploration Toward Solutions

FATHALI M. MOGHADDAM
Georgetown University

MARGARET J. HENDRICKS
US Citizenship and Immigration Services Agency

RAIMUNDO SALAS-SCHWEIKART
Georgetown University

Shaftesbury Road, Cambridge CB2 8EA, United Kingdom

One Liberty Plaza, 20th Floor, New York, NY 10006, USA

477 Williamstown Road, Port Melbourne, VIC 3207, Australia

314–321, 3rd Floor, Plot 3, Splendor Forum, Jasola District Centre, New Delhi – 110025, India

103 Penang Road, #05–06/07, Visioncrest Commercial, Singapore 238467

Cambridge University Press is part of Cambridge University Press & Assessment, a department of the University of Cambridge.

We share the University's mission to contribute to society through the pursuit of education, learning and research at the highest international levels of excellence.

www.cambridge.org
Information on this title: www.cambridge.org/9781009412193

DOI: 10.1017/9781009412186

© Fathali M. Moghaddam, Margaret J. Hendricks, and Raimundo Salas-Schweikart 2026

This publication is in copyright. Subject to statutory exception and to the provisions of relevant collective licensing agreements, no reproduction of any part may take place without the written permission of Cambridge University Press & Assessment.

When citing this work, please include a reference to the DOI 10.1017/9781009412186

First published 2026

Cover Image: PeterPencil / DigitalVision Vectors / Getty Images

A catalogue record for this publication is available from the British Library

A Cataloging-in-Publication data record for this book is available from the Library of Congress

ISBN 978-1-009-41219-3 Hardback
ISBN 978-1-009-41216-2 Paperback

Cambridge University Press & Assessment has no responsibility for the persistence or accuracy of URLs for external or third-party internet websites referred to in this publication and does not guarantee that any content on such websites is, or will remain, accurate or appropriate.

For EU product safety concerns, contact us at Calle de José Abascal, 56, 1°, 28003 Madrid, Spain, or email eugpsr@cambridge.org

*This book is dedicated to our mothers:
Ashraf, Paula, and Viola*

Contents

List of Figures	*page* xi
List of Table	x
Preface	xi

1. Understanding the Immigration Challenge: A Psychological Examination toward Solutions — 1

PART I UNDERSTANDING THE NEW IMMIGRATION CHALLENGE: A PSYCHOLOGICAL PERSPECTIVE — 19

2. Threatened National Identity, Nationalism, and Patriotism — 25
3. The Challenges of Diversity: Lowered Trust, Fragmentation, and Intergroup Conflict — 43
4. The Deglobalization Era: The Psychology of Backlash against Immigrants and a Globalized Society — 65

PART II THE IMMIGRATION CHALLENGE AND NATIONAL IDENTITY — 87

5. Immigration and American Identity: The Undocumented Challenge — 93
6. Immigration and European Identity — 112
7. Immigration within the Global South: Case Studies in South America — 129

PART III TRADITIONAL AND NEW SOLUTIONS TO
MANAGING DIVERSITY   153

8   The Psychological Foundations of Multiculturalism
    and Assimilation   159

9   Building Commonality in Diverse Societies   180

10 Looking Ahead: The Future of Immigration, National
    Identity, and Deglobalization   199

Index   215

Figures

2.1	The continuum of material factors and psychological factors as shapers of behavior.	page 32
3.1	Trends in immigration by geographical region.	45
3.2	Country trend in generalized trust by geographical region.	47
7.1a	Analyzing regional immigration trends of women to South America from 1990 to 2020.	133
7.1b	Analyzing country-level immigration trends in South America from 1990 to 2020.	134

Table

7.1 Immigration in South America in 2020   *page* 131

Preface

We wrote this book in order to fill what we see to be an important gap: to provide an introductory text with a psychological perspective on the *New Immigration Challenge*, and the intersection of immigration, national identity, globalization, and deglobalization. Not only in the United States and Europe, but also in many non-Western countries, immigration has become a central political issue. This book is written in a style that makes it accessible to undergraduates. More broadly, this book is intended for students, researchers, and laypersons interested in better understanding the relationship between immigration and national identity in the global context, and particularly in relation to the deglobalization backlash. Students and teachers in courses focused on immigration, intergroup relations, ethnicity, advanced social psychology, and nationalism will find this book of particular interest.

CHAPTER I

Understanding the Immigration Challenge
A Psychological Examination toward Solutions

Immigration represents a major global challenge in the twenty-first century (Moghaddam & Hendricks, 2022). Of course, large-scale immigration has taken place in past centuries and backlash against immigrants is not new. However, a number of new developments have resulted in immigration becoming a more serious and complex challenge for numerous Western and also non-Western societies in the twenty-first century. This book explores the new immigration challenge from a *psychological perspective*, giving attention to the psychological experiences and processes underlying both immigration and the policies available for the integration of immigrants in host societies.

The challenge raised by immigration in the twenty-first century is new and perplexing in a number of ways. First, the availability of rapid mass transportation means that enormous numbers of people now move across national borders, regions, and continents at an extremely rapid pace – far faster than was previously possible. This means that large-scale intergroup contact between dissimilar groups can take place extremely rapidly – far more rapidly than even before. Second, climate change and environmental disasters are putting new pressures on increasing numbers of people to move to safer geographical regions, which in some cases are only found in *other countries and/or regions* of the world. This problem will become exacerbated over the next few decades, as environmental disasters accelerate. Third, many immigrants to North America and other immigrant-receiving countries (e.g., European countries, Australia, New Zealand) are now from Africa, Asia, and South America. That is, they are mostly non-White, often not Christian, linguistically and culturally more dissimilar, and also phenotypically different, from the majority populations of the host societies. The movements of hundreds of millions of "dissimilar others" across countries, regions, and continents are being fueled by a fourth factor: Shifting labor needs in North America and Europe, where the host populations have low birthrates, are aging, and are even in decline in some countries. In important respects, what we discuss as the new challenge of immigration is a result of the unstoppable force of demography, and the international dynamics it unleashes (Dao et al., 2021).

These developments are associated with a number of psychological experiences, and theoretical and empirical psychological studies of immigration have grown as a specialized field of research to examine these experiences (Birman & Bray, 2017; Cobb et al., 2019; Dovidio & Esses, 2001; Frisby & Jimerson, 2016; Hernandez, 2009; Jasso, 2014; Mahalingam, 2006; Okazaki et al., 2019; Torres et al., 2018; Verkuyten et al., 2019). Much of this literature is focused on acculturation or intergroup relations (Berry, 2001; see also Schwartz et al., 2020). Almost all of the psychological literature on immigration is in specialized journals or edited books. This book is designed to address the lack of introductory books on the psychology of immigration in a global context.

The new immigration challenge is associated with increased perceived threat among citizens in host societies; these citizens feel threatened by the sudden arrival of large numbers of dissimilar others in their homelands. An outcome of this perceived threat is backlash against immigrants, and also populist movements in support of authoritarian strongmen (Moghaddam, 2019). This is particularly unfortunate, because a substantial number of immigrants to Western countries are escaping authoritarian regimes (such as those in Iran and Venezuela). A related development involves deglobalization, a strong backlash against globalization broadly, associated with the strengthening of local identities, but also in many cases associated with ethnocentrism and extremist right-wing nationalist movements (Leblang & Peters, 2022). These trends are reflected in the success of extreme right-wing political parties in elections in France, Germany, Austria, and other European countries, and the popularity of anti-immigrant politicians in the United States, in the third decade of the twenty-first century.

The rise of extreme right-wing anti-immigrant political movements poses major challenges for societies with diverse populations, including those that have a history of receiving immigrants. This challenge arises at a time when economic disparities between social classes are increasing, but the gap between ethnic groups is decreasing – so that group-based inequalities are more based on social class and less based on ethnicity (Chetty et al., 2024). But rising social-class economic differences are being masked by controversies around immigration, and particularly the anti-immigrant attitudes of some working-class Whites in Western societies. Many working-class Whites see the economic gap between themselves and middle-class Whites increasing, but the economic gap between themselves and ethnic minorities decreasing (Chetty et al., 2024). We explore these and related developments from a psychological perspective, with a focus on trends in both Western and non-Western societies.

Our analysis is guided in particular by psychological research on groups and collective behavior (Brown & Pehrson, 2019; Moghaddam, 2008; Taylor & Moghaddam, 1994). This research has been strongly influenced by the major theories and empirical studies on intergroup relations, and especially the social identity tradition (e.g., Lindstam et al., 2021). We interpret identity to be central to the psychological processes underlying the interactions of immigrants and host society members, and to the perception of immigrants as threats to "our nation" and "our way of life."

Immigration has been examined from the perspective of economists, political scientists, sociologists, and various other disciplines (for example, see Bansak et al., 2021; Collier, 2013; Hollifield et al., 2014). However, no one discipline can present a complete picture of immigration. By giving priority to the psychological perspective in this book, we are adding in valuable and accessible ways to the picture of immigration already developed by researchers from other disciplines.

Global Backlash against Immigrants

The contemporary global rise in anti-immigrant sentiment can be tied to the fear that immigrants do not share the same identity as the native-born citizens; they tend to be different in terms of religion, language, core values, appearance, and other key characteristics. Hence, they are perceived by host populations as not sharing the same identity. Increasing diversity in societies is in large part because of demographic trends around the world (which are linked with migration and climate change, Hugo, 2011): Western societies have birth rates lower than 2.1 percent, which means that unless they import millions of people from abroad, they will decline in population levels. On the other hand, the countries with high birth rates and the ability to export labor to Western societies are in Africa, Asia, and South America. This pattern of demographic growth discrepancies has resulted in large numbers of refugees, asylees, and immigrants who are dissimilar to host society populations arriving in Western societies. Examples are the arrival of millions of Middle Eastern and North African Muslim immigrants in Europe, and millions of Hispanic immigrants in the United States.

Anti-immigrant sentiment is also linked to labor market competition. Local workers in economic sectors with a large immigrant labor force often perceive the arrival of immigrants as a direct threat to their material interests (Kunovich, 2013). Consequently, in Europe unsettled macroeconomic conditions, such as GDP contractions and increasing foreign-born workers, have led to an increase in anti-immigrant attitudes (Polavieja, 2016). Another source of anti-immigration attitudes is the perceived insufficiency of state resources. For example, Colombian citizens living near the Venezuelan border identify healthcare as an insufficiently provided public resource due to the increase of Venezuelan migration which, in turn, has been linked to an increase in anti-immigrant attitudes (Vega-Mendez & Visconti, 2021).

As the above example of Venezuelan migration in Colombia indicates, anti-immigrant sentiment is not limited to Western societies (Harris et al., 2017). For example, in South Africa there have been very strong negative reactions to immigrants and refugees from other African countries (Gordon, 2022). Also, the arrival of millions of Afghan refugees in Tehran, Isfahan, Mashhad, and other Iranian cities has resulted in anti-Afghan sentiments among Iranians (Ruhani, 2023). Another example is anti-Muslim sentiments in India, which have been stirred up by the "Hindu nationalist" leadership of Narendra Modi, resulting in Hindu extremists attacking Muslim migrants. (See Kim & Kim, 2021, for a discussion of the *Asian Barometer Survey* that reflects these trends.)

Thus, twenty-first century deglobalization serves as the larger context for anti-immigrant sentiments, in both Western and non-Western societies.

Managing Diversity and Identity in Society

Psychological research on immigration emphasizes a motivation to manage the diverse array of group identities that coexist in contemporary societies (Moghaddam, 2008, 2012, 2024). While there have been positive impacts from initiatives to welcome immigrants into host societies (e.g., Tropp et al., 2018), immigrant integration into host societies is challenging and often associated with feelings of uncertainty and threat (Bose, 2018). A number of studies suggest that trust is negatively associated with diversity (see the meta-analytic review by Dinesen et al., 2020). Thus, one interpretation for the decline in trust in Western societies is the increased diversity experienced by these societies. We argue that a solution to the apparent negative association between diversity and trust is the development of more constructive integration policies.

Over the past century, assimilation and multiculturalism have been the two main policies that have emerged for immigrant integration into society (Cabaniss & Cameron, 2018; Moghaddam, 2024). The objective underlying assimilation policy is to promote social cohesion and maintain one central identity by immigrants' adoption of the host culture, and abandonment of their heritage culture, language, and identity (Badea et al., 2018; Callens & Meuleman, 2017). In theory, through reduction of the differences between immigrants and native-born citizens, and increasing their perceived similarities, immigrants become equal members of the national ingroup (Moghaddam, 2024).

However, in reality native-born citizens often do not see immigrants as belonging to the host society – as sharing the same collective identity as themselves. This is particularly true when immigrants are phenotypically different from the host population, such as in terms of skin color and other physical characteristics. Further, psychological research on intergroup relations has shown that it is impossible to eliminate all differences between groups of people (Moghaddam, 2008, 2012, 2024). Assimilation into the host culture does not stop discrimination against immigrants, especially if they are perceived as belonging to an ethnic minority group (Cabaniss & Cameron, 2018; Moghaddam & Perreault, 1992). For this reason, many immigrants who perceive discrimination tend to strengthen their ties with their native culture and identity instead of acculturating to the host culture and identity. Identifying with their native community has long been suggested to provide a protective buffer against discrimination (Crocker & Major, 1989; Moghaddam & Perreault, 1992; Tajfel, 1981). For example, in the United States context, Schildkraut et al. (2019) found that Latino immigrant and citizen participants who felt unwelcome in the state they lived in were more likely to identify as Latino than American.

In part due to this perceived outsider status within the host society, immigrants and ethnic minorities tend to prefer multiculturalism as an integration policy (Moghaddam & Breckenridge, 2010; Ward et al., 2018), possibly because ethnic minorities have stronger multicultural identities than the majority. For example, Roth and Mendez (2020) found that in Bolivia, Indigenous students had a stronger multicultural identity than non-Indigenous students. Through multicultural policies, immigrants can maintain their native culture while still integrating into the host culture. The idea is to promote diversity within the host society and the celebration of cultural differences (Levrau & Loobuyck, 2018; Moghaddam, 2012).

However, highlighting and celebrating the differences between groups can sometimes cause more division in society, rather than achieving integration and cohesion. As group boundaries are highlighted and strengthened (for example, by focusing on and even manufacturing new intergroup differences), discrimination against immigrants and ethnic minorities may increase due to their separation and greater perceived gap from the majority identity (Kauff et al., 2013). For example, Mashuri et al. (2013) found that in the Netherlands immigrants who chose to assimilate were perceived by native-born citizens as less threatening. The native-born citizens were more willing to help these immigrants adapt to society. In general, this perceived threat from immigrants is associated with greater preference for assimilation policies among host society members (Badea et al., 2018).

Immigration is not just a potential threat at the individual level, but also a potential collective threat at a national level (Young et al., 2018). Research has shown that native-born citizens with strong national identification are more threatened by immigrants and more likely to support assimilation policies (Badea et al., 2018). Wojcieszak and Garrett (2018) found that priming Americans with an existing anti-immigrant bias to think about their national identity significantly increased their bias against immigrants, compared to Americans who did not have this preexisting bias against immigrants (see also Lucas et al., 2014). These findings are in line with research suggesting that individuals with high ingroup identification will strengthen their group loyalty when they perceive threat from outgroup members (e.g., Dovidio et al., 2016).

Some psychological interventions have focused on finding commonalities and connections, a "common group identity," that members of both groups share in order to reduce the negative bias that forms toward a perceived outgroup (Gaertner & Dovidio, 2014). In line with this, omniculturalism has been suggested as a policy for managing diversity with the goal of uniting ethnically diverse societies through giving highest priority to shared similarities and values shared by all groups (Moghaddam, 2024). In this policy, group differences are acknowledged, but priority is given to cross-cultural similarities to create an equal and diverse community (Levrau & Loobuyck, 2018; Moghaddam, 2012, 2024). The main focus is on how humans are similar and share common characteristics, rather than how they are different. A representative sample of Americans showed support for this "common group" approach to managing diversity (Moghaddam & Breckenridge, 2010). Related to this, Li and Brewer (2004) found that when a common goal and shared interests were the focus, a unified American national identity could be reinforced without having to reduce tolerance for diversity. A challenge is that when national identity was based on similarity of identity, tolerance for diversity decreased.

A central theme in this book, then, is to explore paths toward more effective integration of immigrants, refugees, and asylees through critical assessments of different policies. In addition to the traditional policies of assimilation and multiculturalism, the alternative new policy of omniculturalism is also considered. The larger context for these discussions is the development of national identities in relation to deglobalization.

Book Contents

1 The New Immigration Challenge in Global Context

Immigration continues to be seen as a major force of disruption and change in the twenty-first century, both in historically immigrant-receiving societies such as the United States and in areas of the world – such as the European Union (EU) and the United Kingdom (UK) – which have not traditionally been seen as destinations for immigrants. Public opinion toward immigrants has become increasingly divisive in recent decades and attempts by governments to place restrictions on immigrants have become highly controversial. On the one hand, businesses, education systems, and liberal groups tend to welcome more immigration but, on the other hand, some widely popular nationalist politicians have pushed back against immigration. The contemporary global rise in anti-immigrant sentiment can be tied to the fear that immigrants do not share the same identity as the native-born citizens, and that immigrants use scarce resources badly needed by host populations. The reaction from host society populations has added to the backlash against globalization. This introductory chapter highlights the major themes discussed in the book (immigration, identity, globalization, deglobalization), and provides a framework through psychological theories and diversity management policies (Moghaddam, 2008, 2012, 2024) to help readers better understand the impact that immigrants have on national identity in societies around the world, as well as the global backlash against immigration.

Part I: Understanding the New Immigration Challenge: A Psychological Perspective

The three chapters in Part I explore psychological aspects of immigration in the context of globalization. These psychological aspects include threatened national identity arising from the perceived threat of large-scale immigration (Chapter 2), lower trust and other challenges arising from increased diversity (Chapter 3), and the emergence of a deglobalization movement, associated with ethnocentrism and extremist (sometimes violent) right-wing nationalism (Chapter 4).

2 Threatened National Identity, Nationalism, Patriotism

In Chapter 2 we examine the psychological processes underlying national identity, from basic cognitive processes involving categorization to affective and identification processes associated with nationalism and patriotism. Categorization is a universal cognitive process, with important consequences for intergroup relations. Examples of these consequences are the minimization of differences within groups, and the exaggeration of differences between groups. Categorization is also associated with stereotyping, as in the case of national and ethnic stereotypes. Particularly since the nineteenth century, the nation state has served as a highly important source of social identity, with individuals being socialized (through families, schools, sports events, and various international competitions) to show loyalty, dedication, and favoritism toward the national ingroup. Nationalism can transform to a sense of national superiority and dominance over other nations; whereas patriotism is seen as a healthier love of country (although their relationship with political orientation is not straightforward, Hanson & O'Dwyer, 2019). The centrality of the nation in personal and social identity becomes more important during times of threat, such as threats created by wars, or by large-scale migration of dissimilar others into the homeland. Such perceived threats can lead healthy feelings of nationalism to become transformed into less constructive and more ethnocentric populist movements, which create opportunities for authoritarian leaders to grab the spotlight.

3 The Perils of Diversity: Lower Trust, Disunity, and Intergroup Conflicts

Research shows that, on the one hand, increasing diversity in major societies is inevitable; on the other hand, diversity is associated with a number of perils. In the United States and many other societies, the level of trust reported by people has been declining, and research points to increasing diversity as a possible causal factor. People tend to show more trust toward others who they see as more similar to themselves. Also, increasing diversity has been associated with increasing prejudice, discrimination, and intergroup conflicts more broadly. Research in these domains and possible solutions (e.g., increased intergroup contact suggested by psychological science) are critically discussed and assessed. Finally, it is argued that psychological insights could inform effective policies aimed at managing diversity and enhancing trust in increasingly diverse societies.

4   *The Deglobalization Era: The Psychology of Backlash against Immigrants and a Globalized Society*

Chapter 4 explores how rising perceived threats associated with globalization have led to a backlash, discussed in the newly emerging literature on "deglobalization." The roots of this deglobalization movement were already evident in *fractured globalization*, "... the tendency for sociocultural disintegration to pull in a local direction at the same time that macroeconomic and political systems are set up to accelerate globalization" (Moghaddam, 2008, p. 13). On the one hand, identity needs tend to pull people to the local level, but on the other hand, economic forces are pushing people toward the global level. This sets up competing trends: For example, at the same time that integration into the EU is ongoing, there is Brexit taking the UK out of Europe, and Scottish nationalism and Irish nationalism pushing to get Scotland and Northern Ireland out of the UK. The backlash against globalization is in part a reaction to perceived threats "against our group, our way of life, our culture, our language, our values, and everything about us" in the face of perceived large-scale "invasions" (examples of such perceived invaders are Mexicans "invading" the United States, Muslims "invading" Europe, Westerners "invading" Islamic societies, and so on).

Part II: The Immigration Challenge and National Identity

National identity is the main theme of the three chapters in Part II. Immigrants are an unknown outsider element that can present a threat to the majority-endorsed national identity – particularly if they are believed to be too different to become integrated and truly belong to society. Thus, a major challenge of managing and maintaining the identity of a nation is controlling immigration. Immigrants are often labeled as "other," "undeserving," and seen as separate from the rest of society. The following three chapters delve into this conflict between national identity and immigration, and inclusivity versus exclusivity.

5 *Immigration and American Identity*

Chapter 5 examines national identity and immigration in the United States, with specific attention to undocumented immigration. Approximately 11 million undocumented immigrants live across the United States. These undocumented immigrants present major challenges for the United States government authorities. First is the challenge to the nation's ability to successfully manage immigration. The second challenge is perhaps of greater psychological importance: The ability to manage American identity. Undocumented immigrants represent a loss of control over national identity, and the threat of the United States being overtaken by "un-American" people. They present a major challenge to a nation's ability to successfully manage immigration to, and the identity of, the country. American identity was founded not from people coming from a common place and bloodlines but for a common purpose. Yet recent studies and public opinion polls have shown these shared ideals (e.g., individualism, hard work, liberty, equality of opportunity, and rule of law) are not so common across the United States. There is polarization and division in beliefs regarding America's history, present, and future. This chapter concludes with discussion of a recent research study exploring the extent that differences in beliefs regarding American identity relate to differences in beliefs regarding undocumented immigrants.

6 *Immigration and European Identity*

The experiences and challenges of developing a European identity are the central focus in Chapter 6. In addition to developing the EU as an integrated economic system, the challenge has been to develop a "European identity," so that the approximately 450 million people in the EU will feel that they are part of the same unit. Given the long history of wars within Europe, and the strong identities and fierce rivalries of the European nation states, achieving a European identity has been an uphill battle. One obstacle is demographic: The low birth rate of European countries has resulted in a need for imported labor, but the only available labor force is from non-Western societies, where birth rates are much higher. The result is large-scale importation of populations that are dissimilar to the European hosts, in terms of religion, language, phenotype, and other key characteristics. In reaction to this "invasion," extremist right-wing nationalism is on the rise in Europe, and the likes of the

French extremist (anti-EU) politician Marie Le Pen have gained large-scale popular support and become "mainstream" (Japan is among a number of other non-Western countries that also have a low birthrate, need immigrants, but find it difficult to absorb them, as a newspaper headline suggests: "Japan Needs Foreign Workers. It's Just Not Sure It Wants Them to Stay," Rich & Notoya, 2024). However, despite the threat of anti-EU right-wing extremism, evidence from the Eurobarometer suggests that a sense of European identity is growing stronger in Europe, particularly among younger Europeans.

7 Immigration within the Global South: Case Studies of Low-Income Countries

Chapter 7 uses South America as a case study for migration in the Global South. Most of the literature on immigration focuses on immigration flows to countries in the Global North (including Australia and New Zealand). However, at the global level, most immigration actually occurs within the Global South. Thus, there is a gap in research regarding immigration in the Global South. (See the discussions in Smith-Castro et al., 2021.) This is not surprising since the countries with the greatest resources for research are in the Global North. This chapter reviews and compares cases from Global South countries to bridge the knowledge gap regarding immigration within this region. Special attention will be given to how national identity, and economic and political contextual differences shape varying responses to immigration in the Global South. Additionally, we examine how religious fundamentalism, secular nationalism, and rising economic growth influence policy responses to immigration. For example, one of the case studies examines the evolution of identity and immigration in the context of Chile, a country that has experienced major changes in government in recent years. Immigration to Chile has grown rapidly since 2010 following years of closed borders and mass emigration in which many Chileans left the country under the Pinochet dictatorship. Today, approximately 70 percent of immigrants have arrived from neighboring countries in Latin America and share cultural commonalities with the Indigenous population in Chile. We discuss this recent increase in immigration and examine the impact this has on Chilean national identity. The discussion also centers on the interactive evolution of Chilean identity and the Indigenous people, given the current context of new demands for intergroup equality and dignity for minorities.

Part III: Traditional and New Solutions to Managing Diversity

The three chapters in Part III look to the future, by exploring different possibilities for how societies characterized by diversity can be better organized. The psychological foundations of the traditional approaches to managing diversity, including multiculturalism, are examined (Chapter 8). Next, psychological research is used to explore alternative approaches to managing diversity, based on a focus on human commonalities and universals (Chapter 9). In the final chapter, we look to the future of diversity and democracy, and examine how immigration can become a force for strengthening democracy, rather than representing threats and lowering trust (Chapter 10).

8 *The Psychological Foundations of Multiculturalism and Traditional Solutions to Managing Diversity*

Chapter 8 critically examines the traditional diversity management policies of assimilation and multiculturalism, as they evolved in historically immigrant-receiving societies. We identify and assess the psychological assumptions underlying multiculturalism and assimilation, in light of empirical evidence from psychological science. We also assess the public policy challenges of implementing both integration paradigms, highlighting the benefits and challenges to the identities of both host societies and immigrants. Multiculturalism and assimilation first developed in affluent Western countries, and were later exported to low-income societies. We discuss how these exported policies have evolved in low-income societies, and how their limitations have continued in the new contexts. The chapter will also discuss how South American countries managed migration by implementing policies based on assimilation and/or multiculturalism.

9 *Building Commonality through Families, Schools, and Communities*

In earlier chapters, we argued that a number of factors associated with globalization led to perceived threats to national identities, and a backlash that has been discussed under the term "deglobalization." Traditional solutions to diversity management, discussed in Chapter 9, have proven to be inadequate for solving twenty-first-century challenges. Our main goal in Chapter 10 is to critically assess an alternative new solution, with reference to research on the common group identity model, contact theory, and similarity-attraction research at the intergroup level. We argue that the alternative policy of omniculturalism is supported by psychological research and has high promise for managing diversity, because it gives priority to what is common to all human groups and individuals. Rather than highlighting and celebrating differences between human groups, omniculturalism prioritizes and celebrates intergroup similarities and the important ways in which all humans are similar to one another. The goal of developing common or "super-ordinate" identities (Gaertner & Dovidio, 2014) for humanity is discussed at the local level through families, schools, and communities, and globally in relation to climate change, maintaining peace, and other serious challenges faced by all humankind.

10 Looking Ahead: The Future of Immigration, National Identity, and Deglobalization

In the Afterword, we look to the future, particularly with an eye to how national identities can develop in ways that enhance rather than weaken democracy, despite the possibility of perceived threats from immigration. The authors critically analyze the challenge of building a common global identity in an era of deglobalization and polarized national identities.

Concluding Comment

Immigration is now a hotly contested and central political issue in many Western and non-Western societies. In this introductory book, we explore the challenge of immigration from a psychological perspective, highlighting the policy challenges confronting immigrant-receiving societies. Given the demographic and economic trends across the world, with declining and aging populations in most high-income societies, immigration will continue and probably even grow in the foreseeable future. This means that in the future most societies will become more diverse, and it will become even more important to better understand and manage immigration.

REFERENCES

Badea, C., Iyer, A., & Aebischer, V. (2018). National identification, endorsement of acculturation ideologies and prejudice: The impact of the perceived threat of immigration. *International Review of Social Psychology*, 31(1), 14. https://doi.org/10.5334/irsp.147

Bansak, C., Simpson, N., & Zavodny, M. (2021). *The economics of immigration*. Routledge. 2nd ed.
Berry, J. W. (2001). The psychology of immigration. *Journal of Social Issues, 57,* 615–631.
Birman, D., & Bray, E. (2017). Immigration, migration, and community psychology. In M. A. Bond, I. Serrano-Gracia, C. B. Keys, & M. Shinn (Eds.), *APA handbook for community psychology: Methods for community research and action for diverse groups and issues* (pp. 313–326). American Psychological Association.
Bose, P. S. (2018). Welcome and hope, fear, and loathing: The politics of refugee resettlement in Vermont. *Peace and Conflict: Journal of Peace Psychology, 24*(3), 320–329. https://doi.org/10.1037/pac0000302
Brown, R., & Pehrson, S. (2019). *Group processes: Dynamics within and between groups.* Wiley Blackwell. 3rd ed.
Cabaniss, E. R., & Cameron, A. E. (2018). Toward a social psychological understanding of migration and assimilation. *Humanity & Society, 42*(2), 171–192. https://doi.org/10.1177/0160597617716963
Callens, M. S., & Meuleman, B. (2017). Do integration policies relate to economic and cultural threat perceptions? A comparative study in Europe. *International Journal of Comparative Sociology, 58*(5), 367–391. https://doi.org/10.1177/0020715216665437
Chetty, R., Dobbie, W. S., Goldman, B., Porter, S., & Yang, C. (2024). *Changing opportunity: Sociological mechanisms underlying growing class gaps and shrinking race gaps in economic mobility* (Working Paper No. 32697). National Bureau of Economic Research.
Cobb, C. L., Branscombe, N. R., Meca, A., Schwartz, S. J., Xie, D., Zea, M. C., Molina, M. E., & Martinez, C. R., Jr. (2019). Toward a positive psychology of immigrants. *Perspectives on Psychological Science, 14,* 619–632.
Collier, P. (2013). *Exodus: How immigration is changing our world.* Oxford University Press.
Crocker, J., & Major, B. (1989). Social stigma and self-esteem: The self-protective properties of stigma. *Psychological Review, 96*(4), 608–630. https://doi.org/10.1037/0033-295X.96.4.608
Dao, T. H., Docquier, F., Maurel, M., & Schaus, P. (2021). Global migration in the twentieth and twenty-first centuries: The unstoppable force of demography. *Review of World Economics, 157,* 417–449.
Dinesen, P. T., Schaefer, M., & Sonderskov, K. M. (2020). Ethnic diversity and social trust: A narrative and meta-analytic review. *Annual Review of Political Science, 23,* 441–465.
Dovidion, J. F., & Esses, V. M. (2001). Immigrants and immigration: Advancing the psychological perspective. *Journal of Social Issues, 57,* 378–387.
Dovidio, J. F., Gaertner, S. L., Ufkes, E. G., Saguy, T., & Pearson, A. R. (2016). Included but invisible? Subtle bias, common identity, and the darker side of "we". *Social Issues and Policy Review, 10*(1), 6–46. https://doi.org/10.1111/sipr.12017

Frisby, C. L., & Jimerson, S. R. (2016). Understanding immigrants, schooling, and school psychology: Contemporary science and practice. *School Psychology Quarterly*, *31*, 141–148.

Gaertner, S. L., & Dovidio, J. F. (2014). *Reducing intergroup bias: The common ingroup identity model*. Routledge.

Gordon, S. (2022. Are foreigners welcome in South Africa? An attitudinal analysis of anti-immigrant sentiment in South Africa during the 2003–2018 period. In G. Houston, M. Kanyane, & Y. D. Davids (Eds.), *Paradise lost: Race and racism in post-apartheid South Africa* (pp. 245–268). Brill.

Hanson, K., & O'Dwyer, E. (2019). Patriotism and nationalism, left and right: AQ-methodology study of American national identity. *Political Psychology*, *40*(4), 777–795.

Harris, A. S., Findley, M. G., Nielson, D. L., & Noyes, K. L. (2017). The economic roots of anti-immigrant sentiment in the Global South: Evidence from South Africa. *Political Research Quarterly*, *7*, 228–241.

Hernandez, M. Y. (2009). Psychological theories of immigration. *Journal of Human Behavior in the Social Environment*, *19*, 713–729.

Hollifield, J. F., Martin, P. L., & Orrenius, P. M. (Eds.). (2014). *Controlling immigration: A global perspective*. Stanford University Press. 3rd ed.

Hugo, G. (2011). Future demographic change and its interactions with migration and climate change. *Global Environmental Change*, *21*, 521–533.

Jasso, G. (2014). The social psychology of immigration and inequality. In J. D. McLeod, E. J. Lawler & M. Schwalbe (Eds.), *Handbook of social psychology of inequality* (pp. 575–605). Springer.

Kauff, M., Asbrock, F., Thörner, S., & Wagner, U. (2013). Side effects of multiculturalism: The interaction effect of a multicultural ideology and authoritarianism on prejudice and diversity beliefs. *Personality and Social Psychology Bulletin*, *39*(3), 305–320. https://doi.org/10.1177/0146167212473160

Kim, H. H. S., & Kim, H. J. (2021). Understanding economic and cultural underpinnings of anti-immigrant attitudes: Multilevel evidence from the Asian Barometer Survey Wave IV (2014–2016). *International Journal of Public Opinion Research*, *33*, 377–396.

Kunovich, R. M. (2013). Labor market competition and anti-immigrant sentiment: Occupations as contexts. *International Migration Review*, *47*(3), 643–685. https://doi.org/10.1111/imre.12046

Leblang, D., & Peters, M. E. (2022). Immigration and globalization (and deglobalization. *Annual Review of Political Science*, *25*, 377–399.

Levrau, F., & Loobuyck, P. (2018). Introduction: Mapping the multiculturalism-interculturalism debate. *Comparative Migration Studies*, *6*(1), 13, s40878-018-0080-0088. https://doi.org/10.1186/s40878-018-0080-8

Li, Q., & Brewer, M. B. (2004). What does it mean to be an American? Patriotism, nationalism, and American identity after 9/11. *Political Psychology*, *25*(5), 727–739. https://doi.org/10.1111/j.1467-9221.2004.00395.x

Lindstam, E., Mader, M., & Schoen, H. (2021). Conceptions of national identity and ambivalence towards immigration. *British Journal of Political Science*, *51*(1), 93–114.

Lucas, T., Barkho, E., Rudolph, C., Zhdanova, L., Fakhouri, M., & Thompson, L. (2014). Political affiliation, collective self-esteem and perceived employability of immigrants: Inducing national identity polarizes host-nation employers. *International Journal of Intercultural Relations*, *39*, 136–151. https://doi.org/10.1016/j.ijintrel.2013.11.001

Mahalingam, R. (Ed.). (2006). *Cultural psychology of immigrants*.

Mashuri, A., Burhan, O. K., & van Leeuwen, E. (2013). The impact of multiculturalism on immigrant helping. *Asian Journal of Social Psychology*, *16*(3), 207–212. https://doi.org/10.1111/ajsp.12009

Moghaddam, F. M. (2008). *Multiculturalism and intergroup relations: Psychological implications for democracy in global context*. American Psychological Association.

(2012). The omnicultural imperative. *Culture & Psychology*, *18*(3), 304–330. https://doi.org/10.1177/1354067X12446230

(2019). *Threat to democracy: The appeal of authoritarianism in an age of uncertainty*. American Psychological Association.

(2024). *The psychology of multiculturalism, assimilation, and omniculturalism*. Springer Nature.

Moghaddam, F. M., & Breckenridge, J. (2010). Homeland security and support for multiculturalism, assimilation, and omniculturalism policies among Americans. *Homeland Security Affairs*, *6*(3), 1–14. https://www.hsaj.org/articles/82

Moghaddam, F. M., & Hendricks, M. J. (2022). *Contemporary immigration: Psychological perspectives to address challenges and inform solutions*. American Psychological Association.

Moghaddam, F. M., & Perreault, S. (1992). Individual and collective mobility strategies among minority group members. *The Journal of Social Psychology*, *132*(3), 343–357. https://doi.org/10.1080/00224545.1992.9924710

Okazaki, S., Guler, J., Haarlammert, M., & Liu, S. R. (2019). Translating psychological research on immigrants and refugees. *Translational Issues in Psychological Science*, *5*, 1–3.

Polavieja, J. G. (2016). Labour-market competition, recession, and anti-immigrant sentiments in Europe: Occupational and environmental drivers of competitive threat. *Socio-Economic Review*, *14*(3), 395–417. https://doi.org/10.1093/ser/mww002

Rich, M., & Notoya, K. (2024). Japan needs foreign workers. It's just not sure it wants them to stay. *The New York Times*, www.nytimes.com/2024/08/05/world/asia/japan-foreign-workers.html

Roth, E., & Méndez, A. (2021). Acculturation strategies and multicultural identity in Bolivia: Influences of a plural society. In V. Smith-Castro, D. Sirlopú, A. Eller, & H. Çakal (Eds.), *Intraregional migration in Latin*

America: Psychological perspectives on acculturation and intergroup relations (pp. 51–73). American Psychological Association.
Ruhani, A., Keshavarzi, S., Kızık, B., & Çakal, H. (2023). Formation of hatred emotions toward Afghan refugees in Iran: A grounded theory study. *Peace and Conflict: Journal of Peace Psychology, 29*, 355–364
Schildkraut, D. J., Jiménez, T. R., Dovidio, J. F., & Huo, Y. J. (2019). A tale of two states: How state immigration climate affects belonging to state and country among Latinos. *Social Problems, 66*(3), 332–355. https://doi.org/10.1093/socpro/spy008
Schwartz, S. J., Walsh, S. D., Ward, C., Tartakovsky, E., Weisskirch, R. S., Vedder, P., Makarova, E., Bardi, A., Birman, D., Oppedal, B., Benish-Weisman, M., Lorenzo-Blanco, E. I., Güngör, D., Stevens, G. W. J. M., Benet-Martinez, V., Titzmann, P. F., Silbereisen, R. K., Geeraert, N., & the Psychology of Migration Working Group (2020). The role of psychologists in international migration research: Complementing other expertise and an interdisciplinary way forward. *Migration Studies, 10*(2), 357–373. https://doi.org/10.1093/migration/mnz054
Smith-Castro, V., Sirlopú, D., Eller, A. D., Çakal, H., Gibbons, J., & Cumsille, P. (Eds.). (2021). *Intraregional migration in Latin America: Psychological perspectives on acculturation and intergroup relations*. American Psychological Association.
Tajfel, H. (1981). The achievement of group differentiation. In *Human groups and social categories: Studies in social psychology* (pp. 268–287). Cambridge University Press.
Taylor, D. M., & Moghaddam, F. M. (1994). *Theories of intergroup relations: International social psychological perspectives*. Praeger. 2nd ed.
Torres, S. A., Santiago, C. D., Walts, K. K., & Richards, M. H. (2018). Immigration policy, practices, and procedures: The impact on the mental health of Mexican and Central American youth and families. *American Psychologist, 73*, 843–854.
Tropp, L. R., Okamoto, D. G., Marrow, H. B., & Jones-Correa, M. (2018). How contact experiences shape welcoming: Perspectives from U.S.-born and immigrant groups. *Social Psychology Quarterly, 81*(1), 23–47. https://doi.org/10.1177/0190272517747265
Vega-Mendez, C., & Visconti, G. (2021). Does immigration increase concerns about the provision of public services? evidence from Colombia. *Revista Latinoamericana de Opinión Pública, 10*(1), 79–103. https://doi.org/10.14201/rlop.24089
Verkuyten, M., Wiley, S., Deaux, K., & Fleischmann, F. (2019). To be both (and more): Immigration identity multiplicity. *Journal of Social Issues, 75*, 390–413.
Ward, C., Gale, J., Staerklé, C., & Stuart, J. (2018). Immigration and multiculturalism in context: A framework for psychological research. *Journal of Social Issues, 74*(4), 833–855. https://doi.org/10.1111/josi.12301

Wojcieszak, M., & Garrett, R. K. (2018). Social identity, selective exposure, and affective polarization: How priming national identity shapes attitudes toward immigrants via news selection. *Human Communication Research*, *44*(3), 247–273. https://doi.org/10.1093/hcr/hqx010

Young, Y., Loebach, P., & Korinek, K. (2018). Building walls or opening borders? Global immigration policy attitudes across economic, cultural, and human security contexts. *Social Science Research*, *75*, 83–95. https://doi.org/10.1016/j.ssresearch.2018.06.006

PART I

Understanding the New Immigration Challenge
A Psychological Perspective

Introduction to Part I

The three chapters in Part I explore psychological processes central to immigration in the twenty-first century. At one level, immigration can be understood in purely objective economic terms (Bansak et al., 2020), by addressing the question: What are the economic benefits and costs of accepting immigrants into a country? From this materialist–rationalist perspective, people can assess the benefits of immigration objectively. The general consensus is that the overall economic benefits outweigh the costs for immigrant-receiving countries, and this is also the case for the United States as a whole, although not for all individual states that receive immigrants (Mackie & Blau, 2017).

However, the objective assessments of experts on the economics of immigration are very different from the subjective evaluations of ordinary people. In practice, what people think and feel about the benefits and costs arising from immigration are not explained well through a prism of rationality and objective facts. Indeed, how people behave in general is not explained well through rationality; in the words of the Nobel prize winner Daniel Kahneman, "Humans are not well described by the rational-agent model" (2011, p. 411). As elaborated in Chapter 2, reactions to immigration are much better explained by reference to emotions and subjectivity, and particularly to perceptions of threat represented by dissimilar others, rather than to objective assessments based on hard cold economic facts.

Not only are our reactions to immigrants based on subjective feelings, emotions, and assessments, but our understanding of "who we are" as opposed to "who they are" is also subjectively achieved. For example, consider the question of "who we are" and "who they are" in the context of the United States. The history of the United States demonstrates that in practice this is a land of immigrants; the people with the strongest claim to *not* being immigrants are the indigenous or Native Americans. Other than that, everyone else who lives in the United States is an immigrant or the descendent of immigrants. Also, the percentage of immigrants (i.e., foreign-born people) in the United States has never surpassed 15 percent; this peak was reached several times in the period between 1870 and 1910, and is close to being reached again in the 2020s (Esterline & Batalova, 2022); these are the objective facts. So, we might ask, if the percentage of foreign-born people in the United States has not surpassed previous levels, why has immigration become such as an extraordinarily controversial political issue in the early twenty-first century, and why is there such a strong backlash against immigration at this time?

In order to answer this question, we begin by noting that the political turmoil around the issue of immigration is not based on objective criteria and rationality; rather, it is based on biases against certain groups of immigrants, and in favor of other groups. When right-wing politicians attack immigrants and threaten to deport them, they are typically not referring to all immigrants, but to foreign-born people who are from Latin America, Africa, or Asia, but *not* those from Europe. Moreover, when the threat "We will deport them" is made, this is an act of defining who "we are," and who "we are not." It is a demarcation of boundaries. "Americans" are positioned by right-wing extremists as White and Christian, and everyone else – particularly Muslims, Mexicans, and various dissimilar others – as "non-Americans."

It may seem that from the perspective of right-wing extremists, no matter how long these dissimilar others remain the United States, they will never become part of the "American ingroup." But while the social categorization of the world is a universal feature of human behavior, the boundaries of categories are malleable and tend to shift over time (as discussed in Chapter 2). An example of shifting categories is "our nation" versus "foreigners." Over the last few centuries, the idea of "who we are" has changed for Americans, so that some of those who were excluded from the category of "Americans" in the past are now included. For example, Italian immigrants to the United States are among the Europeans who face less discrimination in the twenty-first century (as compared to Muslim and Mexican immigrants, for example), but were confronted by strong hostility during some past periods in American history (Simms, 2019).

One of the highly challenging continuities associated with immigration, as discussed in Chapter 3, is the negative association between diversity and trust: As diversity increases, the level of trust declines. This signals a serious problem, particularly for more democratic countries, as well as more broadly for the democratic movement around the world. Trust is a necessary and essential ingredient of democracy, particularly trust among citizens in their government, in institutions, in officials representing authority, in the police and other agents of the state security, as well as trust in other people in society. Harré (1999) argues that, "... democracy ... requires of its participants both individual responsibility in the exercise of their democratic rights and, falling in with that, a degree of interpersonal trust that makes possible the working of institutions of management that rely on discursive rather than authoritarian means for the resolution of differences" (p. 263). Citizens have a duty to participate in democratic governance, and their active participation (such as in elections) is less likely when they have a low level of trust in government. There are some signs that citizen participation is now lower in even the most well-established democracies. For example, the large Labour Party victory in the 2024 UK General Election was won with only just over a third (!) of the eligible UK citizens voting, and a 2024 poll found that 76 percent of people in the UK have little or no trust that the government will make decisions in the best interests of people in the UK (Wolf, 2024).

The makeup of the immigrants arriving in North America, Australia, New Zealand, and Europe is more diverse than it was prior to the Second World War. More of the new immigrants are from Africa, Asia, and South America, and more of them are non-White and non-Christian. These new immigrants have added to the diversity of North American, Australian, New Zealander, and European societies. The danger is that this increased diversity, which could accelerate over the coming decades, might contribute to further weakening of trust among the populations of these host societies. This is a serious challenge for democracy, which comes at a time of rising populism and authoritarianism (Moghaddam, 2019).

Immigration is taking place in the wider context of globalization, and this is discussed in Chapter 4. Just as there has been backlash against immigration, there has also been backlash against globalization. The so-called deglobalization movement is presented in the media as being associated with right-wing nationalism in European countries and of course in the United States, bringing to mind slogans such as "America First" and "Make America Great Again!" But the deglobalization movement also gained momentum early in the non-Western world, for example as reflected in the surge of radical Islam and the push against Westernization across the Islamic world from the 1950s. Clear signs of this can be found in the long and bloody revolution which forced the French out of Algeria (1954–1962), and the 1978–1979 Iranian revolution which toppled the pro-American Shah, and brought to power a vehemently anti-American and anti-Western regime. The Islamic regime in Iran is now allied with China and Russia, against the Western powers led by the United States.

From the perspective of Islamic – and also many other non-Western societies, globalization has always meant Westernization, and more specifically Americanization. Consequently, the efforts of non-Western countries to "deglobalize" have involved pushing away Western powers and Western cultures more broadly, and pushing Americans out of their territories more specifically. An extreme version of this is Osama bin Laden's insistence that Western powers must leave all Islamic lands, and his role in the tragic 9/11 attacks against targets in the United States. From this non-Western perspective, the hundreds of thousands of Westerners working in Islamic countries such as Saudi Arabia, Kuwait, and the United Arab Emirates, are all "unwanted immigrants" who are damaging the indigenous Islamic culture and should leave.

The demand that "Westerners must leave Islamic lands" made by extremists in Islamic countries echoes the call by extremist nationalists in Western countries for Muslims to leave Western countries. Just as Donald Trump, Marie Le Pen and other extremist right-wing nationalist politicians in Western countries have demanded the deportation of Muslims and some other groups of immigrants back to their "own countries," extremist Muslims in the Islamic world have called for the expulsion of Westerners (who they see as unwanted and unwelcome immigrants) from Islamic lands. Just as extremist right-wing nationalists in Western countries complain about Muslim immigrants "invading" and bringing along their foreign values, traditions, languages, cultures, and ruining the local Western cultures and ways of life, extremists in Islamic societies are reacting angrily against the "invasion" of Westerners with their "unwanted" gender roles, dress styles, liberal values, and "Hollywood culture" broadly. These extremist Muslims feel threatened particularly because of the global dominance of the English language, which is acting as a powerful vehicle for the "unwanted invasion" by Westerners and Western cultures (Salomone & Salomone, 2022).

Consequently, viewed in the context of globalization and deglobalization, the challenge of immigration and the backlash against immigration is not limited to Western societies; it also extends to numerous non-Western societies. The hundreds of thousands of Americans and other Westerners who for various reasons live and work in Islamic societies, and in other non-Western societies, are regarded by local extremists as "invaders" and "unwanted immigrants." Consequently, the psychological processes discussed in chapters in Part I should be considered in a global and not just a Western context.

REFERENCES

Bansak, C., Simpson, N., & Zavodny, M. (2020). *The economics of immigration*. Routledge.

Esterline, C., & Batalova, J. (2022). Frequently requested statistics on immigrants. Migration Policy Institute. https://www.migrationpolicy.org/sites/default/files/source_images/FRS2022-print_version_FINAL.pdf.

Harré, R. (1999). Trust and its surrogates: Psychological foundations of political process. In M. E. Warren (Ed.), *Democracy & trust* (pp. 249–272). Cambridge University Press.

Kahneman, D. (2011). *Thinking fast and slow*. Farrar, Straus and Giroux.

Mackie, C., & Blau, F. D. (Eds.). (2017). *The economic and fiscal consequences of immigration*. National Academies Press.

Moghaddam, F. M. (2019). *Threat to democracy: The appeal of authoritarianism in a time of uncertainty*. American Psychological Association.

Simms, N. (2019). The Italian-American image during the twentieth century. *The Histories*, 5(1), 4.

Salomone, R., & Salomone, R. C. (2022). *The rise of English: Global politics and the power of language*. Oxford University Press.

Wolf, M. (2024). British citizens should be asked to do more. *Financia*.

CHAPTER 2

Threatened National Identity, Nationalism, and Patriotism

Imagine if planet Earth were populated by Econs rather than humans (following Kahneman, 2011). Econs are not emotional. Unlike humans, Econs are not motivated by issues such as identity needs, national pride, and perceived threats from outgroups. Nor are Econs influenced by displacement of aggression and other types of irrational processes and factors which remain largely outside of their consciousness – a common characteristic of human beings. Econs make conscious choices that maximize their material resources. A world populated solely by Econs would behave rationally. In this rational world, surplus Econ labor would move to countries where it is most needed, so as to make maximum contributions to production and profits.

In a world populated by Econs, wherever and whenever the local population need additional Econ labor, they would import immigrant Econs from other parts of the world – even though the Econs that came from other regions would in various ways differ from the local Econs. The immigrant Econs would look different, speak different languages, practice different religions, and also arrive with cultures that differ from that of the majority of Econs in the host society. But local Econs would not give importance to these intergroup differences, because they problem-solve in rational ways toward the goal of maximizing efficiency, productivity, and profits. Local Econs would ignore intergroup differences. Immigrant Econs would not be seen as a threat; they would be welcomed because they are needed as part of the workforce of the host societies.

But humans are not Econs – far from it. Humans are not rational decision-makers, nor are they fully explained by rationalist causal models (Moghaddam, 2022). Despite the evidence that (particularly skilled) immigrants bring economic benefits to host societies (Borjas, 2019; Sherman et al., 2019), many in the host population do not look past the cultural, ethnic, religious, linguistic, phenotypical, and other differences between immigrants and the majority group population of the host society. Immigrants do not simply become integrated into the host society as individuals. Rather, immigrants are categorized on the basis of intergroup differences. Immigrants are stereotyped, treated primarily as group members, and behavior toward them is influenced by a wide variety of emotional and irrational factors, such as fears related to imagined ingroup identity threats, and the dread of collective ingroup decline. In this chapter, we examine the psychological processes underlying national identity, which lead humans to behave in many important ways very differently from Econs.

Econs would be able to treat immigrant Econs solely as individuals, with each individual evaluated as detached and independent. Econs would not – as do humans – automatically and routinely categorize the social world and perceive and evaluate immigrant Econs as group members based on stereotypes. Unlike for Econs, for humans categorization is a universal cognitive characteristic, as it is for many animals (Moghaddam, 2008, chapter 2). Humans categorize both social and nonsocial phenomena. In the first section of this chapter, we examine the basic cognitive process of categorization, as well as its serious consequences for social behavior. This is an important discussion and highly relevant to policies for managing intergroup relations, because the basic cognitive process of categorization and its consequences are an example of low *political plasticity*, concerned with how much, how fast, and in what ways behavior can (and cannot) be changed (Moghaddam, 2023). Low political plasticity underlies continuity in behavior across time and across groups.

In considering different possibilities for how relations between immigrants and the host society develop, we must consider the limitations set by political plasticity. In certain domains of cognition and action, such as social categorization and its consequences, political plasticity is low, which means there are hard limits on what we can change and how fast. In the second section, the focus is on national identity and how immigrants and refugees, especially if they are perceived as dissimilar to the majority group of the host society, can represent serious threats to national identity. In the third section, we critically review majority–minority relations from the perspective of psychological theories, distinguishing between theories that give priority to material factors as shapers of psychological experiences and theories that give priority to the psychological interpretation of material conditions.

Social Categorization and Its Consequences

Categorization is a basic cognitive process that for some time has been recognized by researchers as enabling information to be more efficiently assessed and used (Rosch & Lloyd, 1978). Categorization is useful when we need to process enormous volumes of information, but it can also be useful when we have too little information to use as a basis of decision making; imposing a category can lead us to make generalizations about a case for which we have too little information (Oakes & Turner, 1990). Given the varied and important advantages that categorization brings, it is not surprising that through evolutionary processes it has become a central cognitive characteristic of both animals and humans.

Research demonstrates that animals, such as mice, learn rule-based categorization and also generalize by applying the learned categories to new stimuli (Reinert et al., 2021). Research with human participants shows that there is some level of brain localization associated with different types of categorization tasks. For example, color naming and color categorization are associated with separate brain networks (Siuda-Krzywicka et al., 2021). This reflects the importance of categorization based on color in our evolutionary past. For example, categorizing food on the basis of color, to help correctly distinguish between edible food and poisonous food (when picking berries and fruits, for example), served as a crucial survival strategy for human and animal groups. Carolyn Mervis and Eleanor Rosch argued that "... categorization may be considered one of the most basic functions of living creatures" (1981, p. 341).

Research shows that social categorization appears early in individual human development. This research uses the length of time that infants gaze at faces belonging to different social categories (e.g., Black vs. White) as indicative of infants differentiating between groups (see Rhodes & Baron, 2019, for a review). Babies do not seem to notice human groups at birth, but by the age of three months they do differentiate between black and white faces (Bar-Haim et al., 2006) and also male and female faces within their own ethnic group (Quinn et al., 2008). By the end of the first year of life, infants are able to categorize faces on the basis of fairly complex characteristics, such as attractiveness and emotional expression (Kotsoni et al., 2001; Ramsey et al., 2004).

The very early development and universality of categorization lines up with the perspective of Immanuel Kant (1724–1804), and also with the more recent Gestalt viewpoint, that humans are born predisposed to structure their experiences in particular ways; for example, that hard-wiring within individuals leads people to experience space, time, and causation, in certain ways. Although we need to learn to tell time and measure distances using cultural products (such as clocks and measuring tapes), we do not need to learn that time passes and that some things are further away from us than others. Gestalt psychologists demonstrated that we are predisposed to structure the perceptual world influenced by factors such as similarity, proximity, continuation, and closure (Ellis, 1959). While categorization seems to fit with these pre-wired processes, it is not clear if and to what degree pre-wiring also accounts for the consequences of categorization.

Researchers have explored the consequences of both the categorization of social and nonsocial phenomena, and discovered intriguing continuities across the two. In studies that began in the 1950s, researchers have demonstrated that categorization *per se* of both nonsocial and social phenomena can result in the accentuation of between-group differences and the minimization of within-group differences (Campbell, 1956; Rothbart et al., 1997; Tajfel, 1959; Tajfel & Wilkes, 1963). The nonsocial phenomena used in these studies include lines that differed from one another in length by a constant ratio. The social phenomena used in these studies include the members of different ethnic, sex, age, and other groups. In the social arena, the crucial issue is how the mere cognitive act of categorization, such as on the basis of facial characteristics, can serve as a platform for stereotype construction (Hinton, 2020).

Social categorization has been shown to result in important perceptual and evaluative consequences. An example is the *outgroup homogeneity effect*, the tendency to perceive the outgroup as composed of interchangeable members, whereas the ingroup is perceived as composed of different individuals (Park & Rothbart, 1982). This results in a tendency to make comments such as, "Oh, those people all look the same to me." Research shows that biases in the differential processing of ingroup as opposed to outgroup faces emerge early in sensory perception (Hughes et al., 2019) and seem to remain outside conscious awareness. This is another domain where irrationality is a strong theme in human behavior.

Research using the minimal group paradigm also suggests that social categorization per se has consequences for intergroup bias (Tajfel et al., 1971). In these studies, participants first carried out a trivial task, such as dotestimation, and then were placed into groups "X" and "Y," ostensibly on the basis of how they carried out this trivial task. (Actually, they were randomly assigned to the two groups.) Next, the participants allocated points to the members of groups "X" and "Y" without knowing the identity of group members, without interacting with the members of groups "X" and "Y," and with knowledge that they would not receive any of the points they allocated (Taylor & Moghaddam, 1994). In other words, there was no functional reason to allocate points in a biased way.

However, the results of these studies showed a general tendency to favor the ingroup (Tajfel, 1978), and this occurred irrespective of whether the criterion for social categorization was objectively trivial or important (Moghaddam & Stringer, 1986).

In conclusion, social categorization, as far as it can be isolated as a factor, tends to lead to certain behavioral consequences for relations between groups, such as immigrants and host-society members. Some of these consequences, such as between-group differentiation, are common to the categorization of both nonsocial and social phenomena. Some other consequences, such as ingroup favoritism, are unique to the categorization of people. Such ingroup favoritism probably arises from socialization processes and culture broadly, in the context of norms that position ingroup bias as the correct (or incorrect) way to behave (Wetherell, 1982).

The universality of social categorization and some of its consequences have particularly important implications in the context of twenty-first-century societies, characterized as they are by increasing immigration and diversity.

Nationhood, Social Identity, and Perceived Threats

For much of the last ten thousand years or so, since humans began to live in larger settlements with stability and continuity, the most important criteria that served as the basis for social categorization were ethnicity and tribe – which served as an extension of kinship (Van den Berghe, 1987). However, in the last three thousand years, nationhood took on a more prominent role; for example, as in the case of the Roman Empire and the importance given to distinctions between citizens of Rome and others (Mathisen, 2006). The prominence of nationality as a basis for social categorization dramatically increased in the colonial era and the birth of the modern nation state, and has become of even greater importance in the twenty-first century. Bonikowski (2016) notes that, "... most nationalism research has long been preoccupied with exceptional moments of social transformation, such as the rise of the modern nation-state and more recent efforts by nationalist movements to realign existing state boundaries" (p. 428). However, in recent years researchers have given increasing attention to nationalism in everyday life and among everyday people rather than elites (e.g., Billig, 1995).

The research attention to how people experience nationalism in their everyday lives has coincided with populist movements across the globe, spearheaded by authoritarian strongmen (and in rare cases "strongwomen"). These authoritarian leaders promote far-right political movements that espouse particular forms of *blind patriotism*, involving uncritical support of all actions taken by the ingroup, rather than *constructive patriotism*, involving critical assessment of and loyalty to the ingroup (Staub, 1997). These ethnocentric populist movements are in some important respects reacting to perceived threats from immigrants, asylees, and refugees, depicted by far-right leaders as "an invasion." This is part of a larger strategy on the part of populist far-right leaders, exaggerating, highlighting, and focusing societal attention on (supposed) threats from dissimilar others, within and outside their nations (Moghaddam, 2019).

Threats from dissimilar others are depicted as potential destroyers of "our nation," "our way of life," and "our national identity." These threats are even more salient in the context of changing demographics in Western societies, where the numbers of minorities are rising faster than those of majorities (people with mixed-ethnicity parentage are the fastest growing group, Alba, 2020). When Whites who identify with their ethnic ingroup were reminded that non-White groups will outnumber Whites in the United States in the future, their support for Donald Trump increased (Major et al., 2018). Whites reminded of the declining relative size of the White population show a bias toward interacting with other Whites (Craig & Richeson, 2014), and express stronger identification with "White" rather than "American" (Abascal, 2015). Also, authoritarian leaders constantly invoke comparisons between "our country" and other nations (for example, through claims that "we are falling behind, I can lead our nation to be great again!"), and research demonstrates that comparisons of one's own nation with other nations is more likely to result in the derogation of other nations (Mummendey et al., 2001). Not only is identification with one's nation associated with positive evaluation of that nation, as predicted by social identity theory (Tajfel & Turner, 1979), but comparison of one's nation with other nations is more likely to result in bias against other nations.

Thus, the forecast that Whites in the United States are becoming a numerical minority is seen by the majority as a serious threat and has invoked various negative reactions toward non-Whites (Craig et al., 2018). This is despite empirical-based arguments that Latinos are actually integrating and labels such as "Latino threat" are misleading (Chavez, 2020), and that the rapid growth of Americans with *mixed* ethnicities is shaping the national future (Alba, 2020). The rapid increase in the numbers of mixed-ethnicity individuals might lead us to expect more openness on the part of Whites. After all, mixed-race others who are partly White could be perceived and recategorized as White. However, research evidence suggests that Whites are *less,* not more, likely to recategorize mixed race others – who could be perceived as White or Latino – as one of their White ingroup (Abascal, 2020; see Introduction in Part I and Part II for further discussion of recategorization).

But there is considerable complexity to White reactions to various minority threats, such as "Latino threat," "Muslim threat," and so on. A factor involved in this complexity is the size of the unit being considered (are the units different nations, or much smaller regions, or other?). For example, a study of majority reactions to immigrants in European countries showed that higher immigration was associated with more negative attitudes toward immigrants at the national level, but not in the regions with the highest numbers of immigrants (Weber, 2015). This suggests support for the contact hypothesis (Pettigrew, 2008): In regions with the highest number of immigrants, there was increased possibility of minority–majority contact and this led to increased liking. But not all Whites react to immigrants in the same way. In the United States context, living in a region with a larger immigrant population leads Republicans to be more supportive of immigration restrictions, but Democrats to be less supportive (Hawley, 2011). Also, a lot depends on who the minorities are. White opposition increases when the immigrants are Latino, and decreases when they are European (Brader et al., 2008). This reminds us, at the extreme level, of Donald Trump's desire to have more immigrants from places like Norway, rather than from "shithole" countries (Kirby, 2018).

Next, we turn to theoretical explanations of the experiences of Whites with immigration: Why do they feel threatened and what explains their reactions?

Theoretical Explanation of Majority Reactions to Immigration

All major societies will be more diverse in the future, in large part through the arrival of increasing numbers of immigrants, asylees, and refugees who are dissimilar to the host population. Research and everyday experiences suggest that large segments of the majority group in the host country, such as Whites in Western societies, will feel threatened by the arrival of these dissimilar others – who will mostly originate from non-Western countries. This perceived threat will result in negative attitudes and, sometimes, hostile actions toward the "outsiders." In order to better develop policies toward solving this problem, we need to first arrive at a fuller understanding of the psychological processes involved. Toward this goal, in this

| Material factors shape behavior | Psychological factors shape behavior |

Figure 2.1 The continuum of material factors and psychological factors as shapers of behavior.

section we discuss the main theories that explain majority reactions to minorities. (For reviews of the theories, see Moghaddam, 2008, 2024, chapters 2 and 3.)

We conceptualize the major theories applicable to majority–minority relations as lying on a continuum, at one extreme of which are situated theories that give more importance to material factors as drivers of behavior, and at the other extreme theories that give more importance to psychological factors as shaping behavior (see Figure 2.1).

In the terminology of traditional research methodology, the continuum depicted in Figure 2.1 shows at one extreme material factors serving as the independent variable(s), with psychological factors serving as the dependent variable(s), and at the other extreme psychological factors serving as the independent variable(s) and material factors serving as the dependent variable(s). For example, theories that assume material factors to serve as independent variable(s) and psychological factors as dependent variable(s) might argue that immigrants represent competition for jobs, housing, and other scarce resources, and this results in negative prejudice and discrimination against them. On the other hand, theories that assume psychological factors to serve as independent variable(s) and material factors as dependent variable(s) might argue that immigrants represent a challenge to the sacred values and traditions of the majority group, and this perceived threat results in them being excluded from job opportunities and other scare resources.

Materialist Theories of Intergroup Relations

The most important materialist account of majority–minority relations is provided by realistic conflict theory, best represented by Sherif's (1966) research. But it should be noted that Sherif did not reject the central role of psychological factors. For example, despite giving primacy to material factors as shapers of intergroup relations, Sherif also gave importance to the subjective experience of identification with a group, and this influenced later identity researchers (e.g., Tajfel & Turner, 1979). However, Sherif conceptualized identity and identification as shaped by material factors, not as independent drivers of behavior.

Sherif's realistic conflict account is supported through his classic empirical studies in summer camps. The participants in these studies were selected to be similar in key respects: They were all 11–12-year-old white male Protestants. In stage one, the boys arrived at the camp, got to know one another, and developed friendship patterns. In stage two, the boys were separated into two groups, making sure that those boys who had made closer friendships in stage one, were now separated into different groups (three sets of studies were conducted, and the arrangements were different in the 1954 "Robber's Cave" study, where the boys arrived separately in two groups and developed group cultures before they were allowed to directly interact). During stage three, the two groups engaged in intergroup competition, such as canoe races and tug-of-war. Two sets of changes came about, the first within, and the second between groups. Within groups, there emerged more aggressive leadership, as well as norms endorsing outgroup hostility. Between groups, hostile attitudes and actions toward the outgroup became dominant. In the fourth stage, in order to change intergroup relationships back to being peaceful, Sherif introduced *superordinate goals*, which are desired by both groups but can only be achieved when both the groups participate in the solution. For example, Sherif arranged for a truck bringing food to the summer camp to (ostensibly) break down, and all the boys in the two groups had to help pull the truck into the camp so they would have access to food.

From a realistic conflict perspective, the determining factor shaping relations between the two groups of boys was material factors. When the groups of boys were in competition with one another for material resource (i.e., prizes), they became hostile and aggressive toward the outgroup. When their material interests coincided (i.e., they all wanted food and helped to pull the food truck into their camp), they collaborated and became friends again. From this perspective, the arrival of large numbers of immigrants and refugees represents a threat to the material interests of the host majority, particularly in areas such as employment, housing, health, and education resources. This material threat results in prejudice and discrimination against immigrants and refugees.

Resource mobilization theory provides another materialist account (McCarthy & Zald, 1977) that in some key respects complements the realistic conflict theory account. Resource mobilization theory argues that those who control important resources can instigate, mobilize, and even shape collective movements and relations between different groups. From this perspective, Sherif and his associates were able to control resources in the summer camp setting, and they were able to instigate, mobilize, and shape relations between the two groups of boys. Similarly, those who wield a high level of influence over key resources in the larger society (such as media outlets, political groups, education institutions, religious organizations, and so on) can influence majority–minority relations and the reception of immigrants and refugees in a country. For example, considerable material resources, including vast media empires (such as the ones controlled by Rupert Murdoch and his family), were used in the United States and the UK to launch anti-immigration campaigns, helping to bring about the 2016 win for President Trump in the United States and the win for the "leave" side in the Brexit referendum in the UK (Joppke, 2020).

Another materialist line of theoretical analysis applicable to immigration and particularly to the hostile reception of certain groups of immigrants and refugees, stems from more recent developments of evolutionary theory (Dawkins, 1989; Wilson, 1975). This new perspective interprets evolution as involving competition between gene pools, with the role of humans being carriers of genes. According to this view, evolutionary processes have led to humans being programmed to perpetuate and propagate the genes they carry. Toward this goal, individuals favor those they perceive as carrying similar genes, and show hostility toward those who they perceive as carrying competitor genes. This becomes clear when we consider how parents care and even sacrifice for their own children (who carry their genes), and how the victims of within-family killing and injury tend to be non-blood relatives, such as spouses (typically, spouses are genetically dissimilar) rather than blood relatives (Daly & Wilson, 1988).

The implication of the sociobiological (more recently relabeled as "evolutionary psychology") perspective is that the relationship between the host country majority group, such as Whites in Western societies, and immigrants and refugees will depend on the perceived genetic similarity of the newcomers to the hosts. The greater the perceived similarity, the more positive the reception. The implication is that President Trump's embrace of immigrants from countries like Norway and his rejection of immigrants from "shithole" countries is influenced by his perception of how genetically similar (or dissimilar) the different groups of immigrants are to his White ingroup. Evolutionary psychologists do not claim that this is a conscious bias. Rather, this bias arises from a "whispering within," a hard-wiring that remains outside conscious awareness.

On the one hand, the genetic-based account provided by evolutionary psychologists can be faulted for assuming that phenotype accurately indicates genotype; that by looking at other people, we can arrive at accurate assessments of their genetic makeup. Clearly, this is a false assumption. Phenotype does not accurately indicate genotype. On the other hand, if we reinterpret the evolutionary psychology claim to the idea that people show a preference for similar rather than dissimilar others, then this lines up with research on similarity-attraction, at both the interpersonal (Byrne, 1971) and intergroup levels (Osbeck et al., 1977; Salas-Schweikart et al., 2024). Similarity-attraction has been extensively studied at the interpersonal level and well established as a basis for friendship and romantic love (Berschied & Reis, 1998). Similarity-attraction is less researched at the intergroup level. However, in a field study conducted in Canada involving samples from Algerian, Indian, Jewish, Greek, English-Canadian, and French-Canadian populations, strong endorsement was found for the similarity-attraction hypothesis: The more people perceived the outgroup to be similar, the more they desired to interact with them (Osbeck et al., 1977; Salas-Schweikart et al., 2024). The similarity-attraction research leads to the prediction that immigrants and refugees will be received more favorably by the majority group of the host society if they are perceived to be more similar. In line with this, refugees from Ukraine, White and Christian, have received a far more positive reception in Europe than have Afghan refugees, who are non-White and Muslim (De Coninck, 2023).

Theories That Give Priority to Psychological Factors

In response to materialist accounts of majority–minority relations, theories that give priority to psychological factors in explaining majority–minority relations argue that it is not objective material conditions, but the *subjective interpretation* of material conditions, that shape intergroup behavior. In particular, these psychological theories have given importance to the themes of irrationality (following Freud, 1921[1955], 1930[1961]) and identity, with social identity theory (Tajfel & Turner, 1979) having by far the most expansive and extensive global influence. An illustrative example that brings irrationality and identity together is the experience of *false consciousness*, when individuals lack awareness of their group membership and group interests in relation to outgroups.

Consider the case of low-income Whites in the United States. Support from this voting block proved to be essential for the victory of Donald Trump in the 2016 presidential election (Morgan & Lee, 2018) – and the

2024 election. From an objective materialist perspective, it is puzzling why poor Whites would vote for a billionaire whose policies favor the rich, such as lower taxes for wealthy people and corporations (Kazin, 2016). Why would poor Whites not see their economics interests as more in-line with poor immigrants and refugees? Why would they not form an alliance with other low-income people, of all ethnicities, and demand better economic conditions and social support from the rich elite?

According to system justification theory (Jost, 2018), people are strongly influenced by the dominant ideologies in society, and these are largely shaped by the elite and tend to justify the existing group-based inequalities and the *status quo*. The White working class are influenced by dominant ideologies in the United States to ignore their own economic interests, to reject the poor from other ethnic groups (including immigrants and refugees), and to instead identify with Trump and others who favor a White Christian American identity. This pattern of identification and allegiance is irrational, in the sense that poor Whites are not giving highest priority to their own economic interests and their own "membership" in the working class. In essence, they are favoring the economic outgroup – the rich.

A complementary perspective on the plight of immigrants and refugees, and their relationship with poor Whites, is provided by the concept of *displacement of aggression*, when a person feels distressed but reacts aggressively not against the source of distress but against a more convenient target (Marcus-Newhall et al., 2000). Given the increasing concentration of wealth in Western societies, particularly in the United States and the UK (Piketty, 2014), the economic plight of the working class is becoming more difficult. But it is much easier to displace aggression onto "soft" targets such as immigrants and refugees, than to show aggression against the rich elite – who also shape governments and direct security and military forces. After all, the rich elite are guarded by armies of lawyers and security guards, but immigrants and refugees are soft targets.

Research on collective action demonstrates the extreme difficulties confronting people when they try to mobilize against perceived injustice as a group (Louis et al., 2020), in part because of the general preference of individuals to try to get ahead individually rather than collectively (Wright et al., 1990). Relative deprivation research suggests that an important condition for collective action is the experience of *fraternal deprivation*, feeling deprived because of the position of one's group in society, rather than feeling deprived because of one's individual position in the ingroup (Guimond & Dubé-Simard, 1983). However, a great deal depends on how one perceives the ingroup; poor Whites who support populist movements tend to see their ingroup as other Whites (including rich Whites), rather than other poor people of all ethnicities. Thus, they tend to exclude immigrants and refugees from their ingroup, because they are mostly non-White and often also non-Christian.

It is important to keep in mind that psychological theories are not claiming that the ruling elites are engaged in conspiratorial behavior; that they believe the political and economic system is unfair but continue to support it because it serves their interests. Far from it. The ruling elites are not engaged in a conscious conspiracy. The assumption underlying social identity theory, system justification theory, and other psychological theories is that the ideologies that justify the present group-based inequalities are accepted and adopted by both non-elites and elites.

This is also the case with justice theories and particularly Lerner's (1980) just world theory, which proposes that people are motivated to perceive the world as fair, a place where good things happen to good people and bad things happen to bad people. Thus, in this "just world" the rich are seen as more talented and hardworking, and deserving of their superior power and resources. On the other hand, the poor (including poor immigrants and refugees) are seen as lacking the talent, drive, and ability to succeed. In short, the rich and poor are seen as deserving of their respective positions in society.

In conclusion, then, psychological theories provide insights as to why humans do not behave like Econs. Rather than behave rationally to achieve maximum profits for everyone, humans give priority to developing an identity that makes them feel positive and distinct, and exclude others who they interpret as not just different but also inferior. In practice, these others are the more dissimilar outgroups, and in the context of Western societies this specifically includes immigrants and refugees from non-Western countries.

Concluding Comment

From a rational materialist perspective, the arrival of immigrants and refugees in countries that badly need additional labor – as is the case with North American and European countries, as well as Japan and a number of other non-Western countries – should be welcomed by host populations. But human behavior is often irrational and even destructive, such as in the area of intergroup relations. Dissimilar outgroups often represent threats to ingroup identity, particularly when the ingroup is based on nationhood.

Defense of national identity, national traditions, national values, national language, and even socially constructed notions of "national race" – underlie negative reactions to immigrants and refugees.

In developing programs for managing majority–minority relations, we must keep in mind the central role played by political plasticity in group and intergroup dynamics. Certain behaviors in this domain, such as social categorization, have low political plasticity and are very slow to change. For example, social categorization is a resilient and universal behavior. But while we are not able to change the act of social categorization, we can influence the contents and evaluations of social categories, which have higher political plasticity. Through programs that give priority to human commonalities rather than human differences, we can move people to adopt more inclusive ingroups. We further develop this theme in later chapters, particularly Chapter 8.

REFERENCES

Abascal, M. (2015). Us and them: Black–white relations in the wake of Hispanic population growth. *American Sociological Review, 80*, 789–813.

Alba, R. (2020). *The great demographic illusion: Majority, minority, and the expanding American mainstream*. Princeton University Press.

Bar-Haim, Y., Ziv, T., Lamy, D., & Hodes, R. M. (2006). Nature and nurture in own-race face processing. *Psychological Science, 17*, 159–163.

Berscheid, E., & Reis, H. T. (1998). Attraction and close relationships. In D. T. Gilbert, S. T. Fiske & G. Lindzey (Eds.), *The handbook of social psychology* (Vol. 2, 4th ed., pp. 193–281). McGraw Hill.

Billig, M. (1995). *Banal nationalism*. Sage.

Borjas, G. J. (2019). *Immigration and economic growth*. National Bureau of Economic Research, Working Paper 25836. www.nber.org/papers/w25836

Bonikowski, B. (2016). Nationalism in settled times. *Annual Review of Sociology, 42*, 427–449.

Brader, T., Valentino, N. A., & Suhay, E. (2008). What triggers public opposition to immigration? Anxiety, group cues, and immigration threat. *American Journal of Political Science, 52*, 959–978.

Byrne, D. (1971). *The attraction paradigm*. Academic Press.

Campbell, D. T. (1956). Enhancement of contrast as a composite habit. *Journal of Abnormal and Social Psychology, 56*, 350–355.

Chavez, L. (2020). *The Latino threat: Constructing immigrants, citizens, and the nation*. Stanford University Press.

Craig, M. A., & Richeson, J. A. (2014). More diverse yet less tolerant? How the increasingly diverse racial landscape affects white Americans' racial attitudes. *Personality and Social Psychology Bulletin, 40*, 750–761.

Craig, M. A., Rucker, J. M., & Richeson, J. A. (2018). Racial and political dynamics of an approaching "majority–minority" United States. *ANNALS of the American Academy of Political and Social Sciences, 677*, 204–214.

Daly, M., & Wilson, M. (1988). *Homicide*. Routledge.

Dawkins, R. (1989). *The selfish gene*. Oxford University Press. 2nd ed.

De Coninck, D. (2023). The refugee paradox during wartime in Europe: How Ukranian and Afghan are (not) alike. *International Migration Review, 57*, 578–586.

Ellis, W. D. (1959). *Source book of Gestalt psychology*. Harcourt, Brace.

Freud, S. (1921[1955]). Group psychology and the analysis of the ego. In J. Strachey (Ed. & Trans.), *The standard edition of the complete psychological works of Sigmund Freud* (Vol. 18, pp. 67–143). Hogarth Press.

(1930[1961]). Civilization and its discontents. In J. Strachey (Ed. & Trans.), *The standard edition of the complete psychological works of Sigmund Freud* (Vol. 21, pp. 64–145). Hogarth Press.

Guimond, S., & Dubé-Simard, L. (1983). Relative deprivation theory and the Quebec nationalist movement: The cognition –emotion distinction and the personal-group deprivation issue. *Journal of Personality and Social Psychology, 44*, 526–535.

Hawley, G. (2011). Political threat and immigration: Party identification, demographic context, and immigration policy preference. *Social Science Quarterly, 92*, 404–422.

Hinton, P. R. (2020). *Stereotypes and the construction of the social world*. Routledge.

Hughes, B. L., Camp, N. P., Gomez, J., Natu, V. S., Grill-Spector, K., & Eberhardt, L. (2019). Neural adaptation to faces reveals racial outgroup homogeneity effects in early perception. *Proceedings of the National Academy of Science, 116*, 14532–14537.

Joppke, C. (2020). Immigration in the populist crucible: Comparing Brexit and Trump. *Comparative Migration Studies, 8*, https://doi.org/10.1186/s40878-020-00208-y

Jost, J. T. (2018). A quarter century of system justification theory: Questions, answers, criticisms, and societal implications. *British Journal of Social Psychology, 58*, 263–314.

Kahneman, D. (2011). *Thinking fast and slow*. Farrar, Struas and Giroux.

Kazin, M. (2016). Trump and American populism: Old wine, new bottles. *Espirit*, Nov/Dec, 42–53.

Kirby, J. (2018). Trump wants fewer immigrants from "shithole countries" and more from places like Norway. www.vox.com/2018/1/11/16880750/trump-immigrants-shithole-countries-norway

Kotsoni, E., De Haan, M., & Jounson, M. H. (2001). Categorical perception of facial expression by 7-month-old infants. *Perception, 30*, 1115–1125.

Lerner, M. J. (1980). *The belief in a just world: A fundamental delusion*. Plenum Press.

Louis, W., Thomas, E., McGarty, C., Lizzio-Wilson, Amiot, C., & Moghaddam, F. M. (2020). The volatility of collective action: Theoretical analysis and empirical data. *Political Psychology, 41*, 35–74.

Major, B., Blodorn, A. & Major Blascovich, G. (2018). The threat of increasing diversity: Why many White Americans support Trump in the 2016 presidential election. *Group Processes & Intergroup Relations, 21*, 931–940.

Marcus-Newhall, A., Pederson, W. C., Carlson, M., & Miller, N. (2000). Displaced aggression is alive and well: A meta-analytic review. *Journal of Personality and Social Psychology, 78*, 670–689.

Mathisen, R. W. (2006). *Peregrini, Barbari*, and *Cives Romani*: Concepts of citizenship and the legal identity of barbarians in the later Roman empire. *The American Historical Review, 111*, 1011–1040.

McCarthy, T. D., & Zald, M. N. (1977). Resource mobilization and social movements: A partial theory. *American Journal of Sociology, 82*, 1212–1241.

Mervis, C. B., & Rosch, E. (1981). Categorization of natural objects. *Annual Review of Psychology, 32*, 89–115.

Moghaddam, F. M. (2008). *Multiculturalism and intergroup relations: Psychological implications for democracy in global context.* American Psychological Association.

(2022). *How psychologists failed: We neglected the poor and minorities, favored the rich and privileged, and got science wrong.* Cambridge University Press.

(2023). *Political plasticity: The future of democracy and dictatorship.* Cambridge University Press.

(2024). *The psychology of revolution.* Cambridge University Press.

Moghaddam, F. M., & Stringer, P. (1986). "Trivial" and "important" criteria for social categorization in the minimal group paradigm. *Journal of Social Psychology, 126*, 345–354.

Morgan, S. L., & J. Lee (2018). Trump voters and the white working class. *Sociological Science, 5*, 234–245.

Mummendey, A., Klink, A., & Brown, R. (2001). Nationalism and patriotism: National identification and outgroup rejection. *British Journal of Social Psychology, 40*, 159–172.

Oakes, P. J., & Turner, J. C. (1990). Is limited information capacity the cause of social stereotyping? In W. Stroebe & M. Hewstone (Eds.), *European review of social psychology* (Vol. 1, pp. 111–135). Wiley.

Osbeck, L., Moghaddam, F. M., & Perreault, S. (1977). Similarity and attraction among majority and minority groups in a multicultural context. *International Journal of Intercultural Relations, 21*, 113–123.

Park, B., & Rothbart, M. (1982). Perception of outgroup homogeneity and levels of social categorization: Memory for the subordinate attributes of ingroup and outgroup members. *Journal of Personality and Social Psychology, 42*, 1051–1068.

Pettigrew, T. F. (2008). Future directions for intergroup contact theory and research. *International Journal of Intercultural Relations, 32*, 187–199.

Piketty, T. (2014). *Capital in the twenty-first century* (Trans. A. Goldhammer). The Belknap Press of Harvard University Press.

Quinn, P. C., Uttley, L., Lee, K., Gibson, A., Smith, M., et al., (2008). Infant preference for female faces occurs for same – but not other – race faces. *Journal of Neuropsychology, 2*, 15–26.
Ramsey, J. L., Langlois, J. H., Hoss, R. A., Rubenstein, A. J., & Griffin, A. M. (2004). Origins of a stereotype: Categorization of facial attractiveness by 6-month-old infants. *Developmental Science, 7*, 201–211.
Reinert, S., Hübener, M., Bonhoeffer, T., & Goltstein, P. M. (2021). Mouse prefrontal cortex represents learned rules for categorization. *Nature, 593*, 411–417.
Rhodes, M., & Baron, A. (2019). The development of social categorization. *Annual Review of Developmental Psychology, 1*, 359–386.
Rosch, E., & Lloyd, B. B. (Eds.) (1978). *Cognition and categorization.* Erlbaum.
Rothbart, M., Davis-Stitt, C., & Hill, J. (1997). Effects of arbitrarily placed category boundaries on similarity judgements. *Journal of Experimental Social Psychology, 33*, 122–145.
Salas-Schweikart, R., Hendricks, M. J., Boychuck, M., & Moghaddam, F. M. (2024). Similarity-attraction across ethnic, religious, and political groups: Does celebrating differences or similarities make a difference?. *The Journal of Social Psychology*, 1–20.
Sherif, M. (1966). *Group conflict and cooperation: Their social psychology.* Routledge & Kegan Paul.
Sherman, A., Trisi, D., Stone, C., Gonazalas, S., & Parrott, S. (2019). *Immigrants contribute greatly to US economy, despite administration's "public charge" rule rationale.* Center for Budget and Policy Priorities, www.jstor.org/stable/resrep27232
Siuda-Krzywicka, K., Witzel, C., Bartolomeo, P., & Cohen, L. (2021). Color naming and categorization depend on distinct functional brain networks. *Cerebral Cortex, 31*, 1106–1115.
Staub, E. (1997). Blind versus constructive patriotism: Moving from embeddedness in the group to critical loyalty and action. In D. Bar-Tal & E. Staub (Eds.), *Patriotism in the lives of individuals and nations* (pp. 213–228). Nelson-Hall.
Tajfel, H. (1959). Quantitative judgement in social perception. *British Journal of Social Psychology, 50*, 16–29.
(Ed.) (1978). *Differentiation between social groups.* Academic Press.
Tajfel, H., & Turner, J. C. (1979). An integrative theory of intergroup conflict. In W. G. Austin & S. Worchel (Eds.), *The social psychology of intergroup relations* (pp. 33-47). Brooks/Cole.
Tajfel, H., Flament, C., Billig, M. G., & Bundy, R. F. (1971). Social categorization and intergroup behaviour. *European Journal of Social Psychology, 1*, 149–177.
Tajfel, H., & Wilkes, A. L. (1963). Classification and quantitative judgement. *British Journal of Psychology, 54*, 103–113.
Taylor, D. M., & Moghaddam, F. M. (1994). *Theories of intergroup relations: International social psychological perspectives.* Praeger. 2nd ed.

Van den Berghe, P. (1987). *The ethnic phenomenon*. Praeger.
Weber, H. (2015). National and regional proportion of immigrants and perceived threat of immigration: A three-level analysis in Western Europe. *International Journal of Comparative Sociology*, *56*, 116–140.
Wetherell, M. S. (1982). Cross-cultural studies of minimal groups: Implications for social identity theory and intergroup relations. In H. Tajfel (Ed.), *Social identity and intergroup relations* (pp. 207–240). Cambridge University Press.
Wilson, E. O. (1975). *Sociobiology: The new synthesis*. Harvard University Press.
Wright, S. C., Taylor, D. M., & Moghaddam, F. M. (1990). Responding to membership in a disadvantaged group: From acceptance to collective protest. *Journal of Personality and Social Psychology*, *58*, 994–1003.

CHAPTER 3

The Challenges of Diversity
Lowered Trust, Fragmentation, and Intergroup Conflict

The benefits of diversity are acknowledged by researchers in different disciplines. For example, psychologists have highlighted the advantages of having a diverse group of individuals when it comes to problem-solving. This leads to better management of group issues and improved performance in teams (Knippenberg et al., 2020; Phillips et al., 2011). Similarly, political science theorists have highlighted the importance of ethnic diversity in enhancing political representation for minority groups (Lončar, 2023). When members of minority groups see political representatives who share their identities, the political system becomes more credible to them. In this way, ethnic diversity can provide solutions to some of the challenges faced by contemporary societies.

But diversity also has its limitations. For example, Putnam (2007) argued that increased ethnic diversity can lead to decreased trust between neighbors. In line with this, a meta-analysis of 87 studies revealed that increased ethnic diversity decreases trust in neighbors, other people, members of the ingroup and outgroup, and the overall disposition to trust unknown people (i.e., generalized trust; Dinesen et al., 2020). Policymakers and politicians have also raised concerns that increased ethnic diversity, as driven by immigration, has given rise to the erosion of trust and, thereby, of social cohesion. For instance, former UK prime minister Tony Blair, former Denmark prime minister Anders Fogh Rasmussen, and French former president Sarkozy have argued that immigrants should adopt the culture and language of the host society in order to preserve trust and social cohesion (i.e., assimilation, Holtug, 2021). The association between declining trust and rising diversity is seen as particularly troubling (Putnam, 2007). Diversity in the social sciences and psychology is measured as a function of the group composition of a given country or region (Budescu & Budescu, 2012). When researchers measure societal diversity, they consider the different groups that constitute society in terms of language, culture, ethnicity, and/or religion. In this sense, immigrants increase diversity by adding linguistic, religious, ethnic, and/or cultural differences.

Neglecting the challenge posed by rising diversity increases the probability of growing problems such as increasing anti-immigrant sentiments. This is related to the problem of extremist authoritarian leaders, who use narratives that raise fear in a population by portraying the "dangers" posed by immigrants to society. In this chapter, we address these challenges of decreased trust associated with rising immigration. Immigration could result in cohesive multicultural societies if decreased trust and other challenges raised by ethnic diversity are appropriately addressed. This chapter explores examples of how psychological science can assist in addressing the issue of ethnic diversity and offer potential solutions to promote inclusivity. In doing so, the chapter will demonstrate the value of psychology for immigration and diversity management.

We begin the chapter by discussing the problem of decreasing trust in association with rising immigration. Next, we explore the different kinds of trust and the psychological concepts behind them. After that, we examine the consequences of a decline in trust, particularly the intergroup divisions that arise as a result. We then examine how the increase in diversity is linked to the decline of trust, using empirical evidence to explain this connection. Finally, we discuss psychological theories that can build trust in societies characterized by diversity.

Rising Immigration and Declining Trust

Immigration has risen globally since 1990. According to data from the United Nations, the number of immigrants in the world since the 1990s has almost doubled, surpassing an immigrant stock of 270 million people (Migration Data Portal, n.d.). Furthermore, an analysis that breaks down immigration patterns across different geographical regions, utilizing data from the United Nations Department of Economic and Social Affairs, Population Division (2020), reveals a consistent rise in the proportion of immigrants across nearly all regions. The only exceptions to this trend are Sub-Saharan Africa and South Asia, which constitute emigrating regions (see Figure 3.1). A consequence of this increasing number of immigrants is higher diversity in host societies.

However, immigration is not the only source of diversity within a country. Many countries have populations that differ in terms of ethnicity, language, religion, and other important group-based characteristics. For example, consider the population of India. The majority are Indo-Aryan

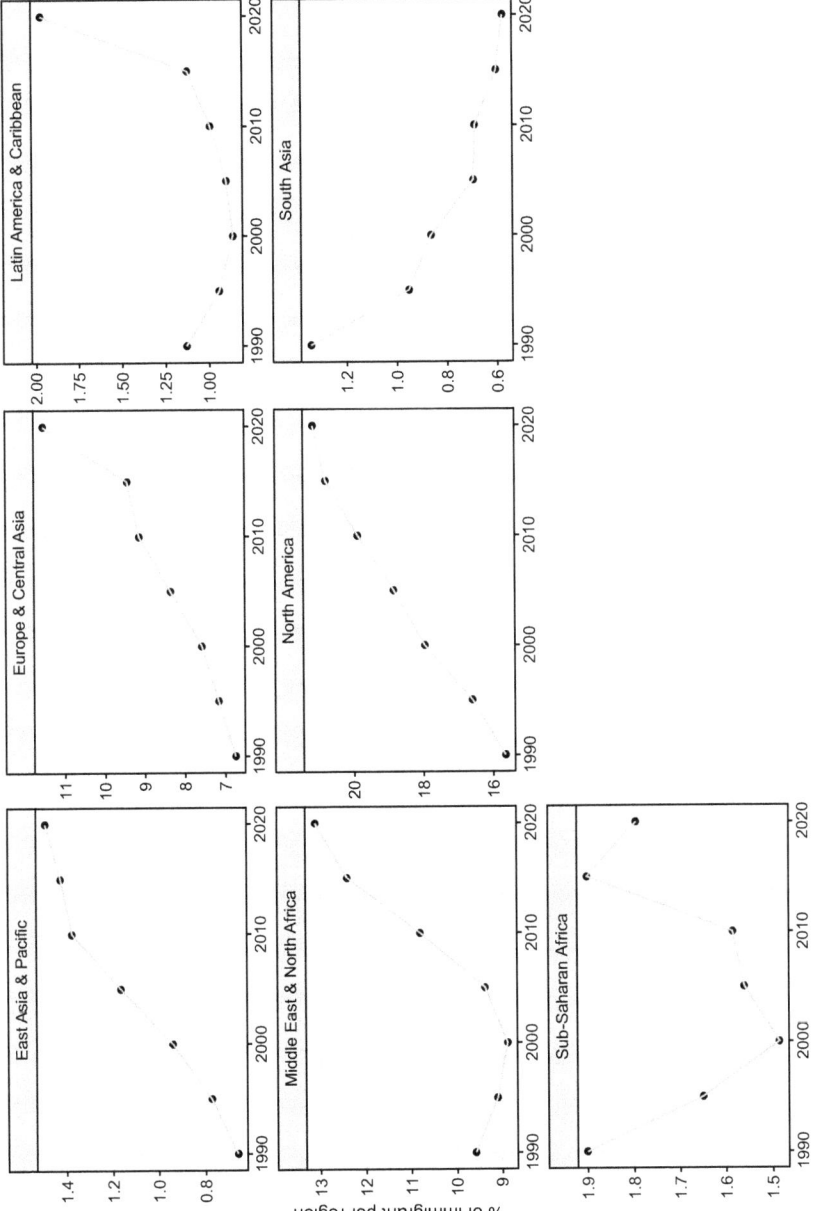

Figure 3.1 Trends in immigration by geographical region.
Source: United Nations Department of Economic and Social Affairs, Population Division (2020).

(72 percent) and Dravidian (25 percent) in terms of ethnicity. Hindi is the most commonly spoken language (43.6 percent), followed by Bengali and Marathi. Hinduism (79.8 percent) is the dominant religion, followed by Islam (14.2 percent) (Central Intelligence Agency, n.d.).

One of the challenges faced by India and other countries characterized by diversity is to create ways in which their different groups coexist peacefully. In the case of India, peaceful coexistence has been difficult after the gruesome conflicts around the time of independence from Great Britain (1947). The process of nation-building can lead to a (more or less) cohesive national identity in "new" countries (such as India) characterized by diversity, but immigration can be disruptive because it can introduce new forms of diversity (De Haas et al., 2020). Immigration often introduces new differences, particularly between the host population and recent immigrants, that pose additional challenges for new generations. One such challenge concerns trust.

In recent years, there has been a noticeable decline in trust across numerous countries. The trend can be seen in the data gathered by the World Value Survey (WVS) and European Value Study (EVS), which indicates a decrease in the overall percentage of people who trust "most people" when comparing the first and last wave of the EWVS/EVS data (Figure 3.2, black lines). For instance, while Denmark has seen an increase in trust levels to about 75 percent since 1980, Mexico has experienced a significant drop from 33 percent to 10 percent. The United States has also shown fluctuating levels of generalized trust, with lower levels observed in the 80s and early 90s. Overall, the measurement of generalized trust indicates a tendency toward declining trust, albeit with significant variations between and within countries.

The decline in trust is often associated with increasing ethnic diversity. Putnam (2007) highlights that as diversity measures increase, different indicators of trust tend to decrease. This trend is particularly relevant in the context of rising migration over time. The data from WVS and EVS further support this observation, showing that countries with higher levels of ethnic diversity tend to experience lower levels of generalized trust. While some countries like Denmark have managed to maintain or even increase trust levels, others like Mexico have seen a sharp decline. This suggests that the relationship between ethnic diversity and trust is complex and varies significantly across different contexts.

However, we must keep in mind that the relationship between declining trust and increasing diversity is correlational. As every undergraduate is repeatedly told, correlation does not mean causation. In line with this,

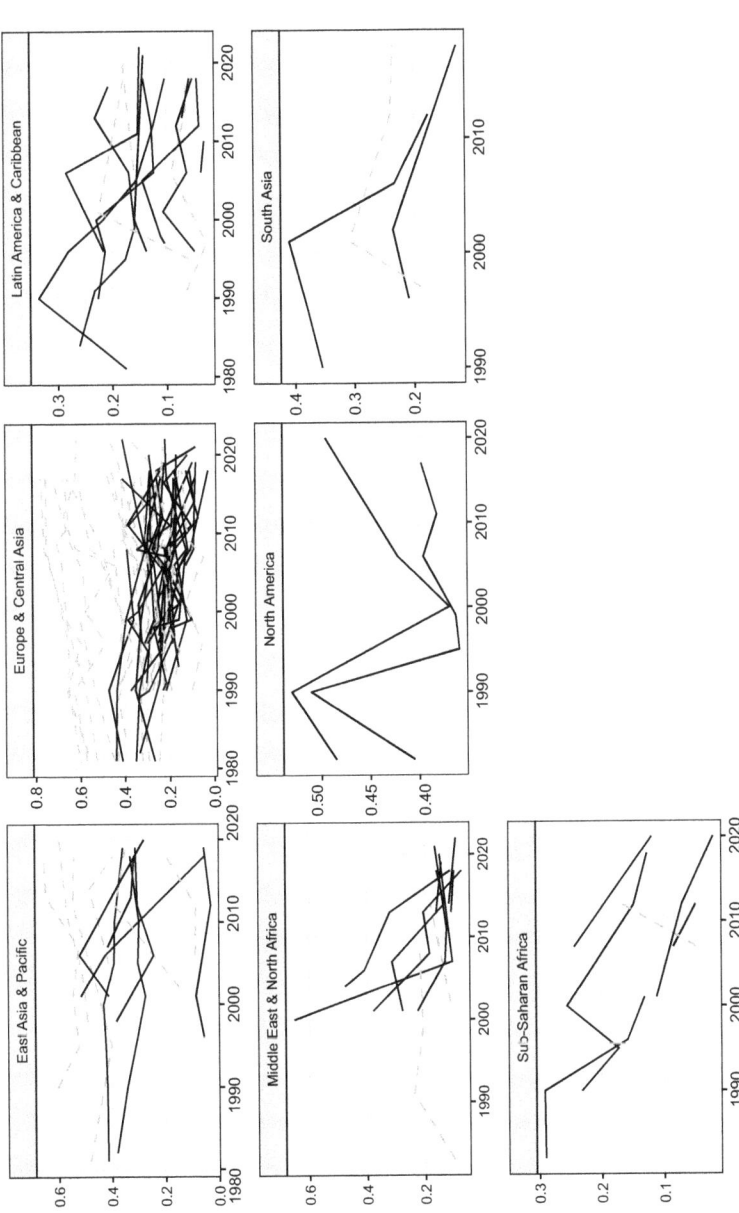

Figure 3.2 Country trend in generalized trust by geographical region.

Note: The countries with a decrease in generalized trust between the first and last survey measures are represented by black lines, while countries without a decline in trust are represented by grey lines. Countries with a single measurement in the integrated WVS/EVS survey are omitted. The author elaborated on the figure using the joint EVS/WVS dataset (2021).

Dawson (2019) argues that generalized trust can fluctuate, but will tend to revert to "default" levels formed in childhood. Thus, the current national decline could represent a transient variation. This interpretation could explain the shallowness of the slope of overall changes, as well as the variations in Canada and in the United States (Figure 3.2). Consequently, changes in the level of trust might not be caused by changes in diversity. By implication, while Figure 3.2 shows changes over time, we need to be careful in interpreting the significance of the changes and the possible causal role of diversity.

On the other hand, Dinesen et al. (2020) offer stronger support to link declining trust to diversity. In a meta-analysis, these researchers found a negative relationship between different types of trust (i.e., generalized trust, ingroup trust, and outgroup trust) and increased ethnic diversity. The persistent negative association between trust and diversity – across the studies drawn from different contexts – shows a robust finding: The declining trends of trust in the context of increased immigration (Dinesen et al., 2020; Putnam, 2007; Schmid et al., 2014). However, the wide variation also points to the need for a careful interpretation of the negative association. In effect, generalized trust is not only predicted by ethnic diversity, but by an array of individual and social factors. For example, parenting and effective government both influence generalized trust.

In summary, we have discussed the robust association between declining trust and increased ethnic diversity. But why does this matter – what are the real-world consequences of declining trust? In a later section, we explore how mistrust leads to fragmented societies, and the issues that arise in such societies.

A Psychological Understanding of Trust and the Relationship between Immigration and Declining Trust

Trust is a fundamental aspect of human relationships. This section explores the psychological understanding of trust. First, trust will be presented as a learned behavior influenced by past experiences and expectations. Next, trust will be presented as a multidimensional concept. Once we understand trust, we can comprehend how diversity, including cultural diversity, influences trust.

Trust has been the subject of rigorous investigation in psychology. Early research by Rotter (1967, 1971, 1980), conceptualized trust as a learned behavior that develops based on past experiences with others. Previous experiences shape a general expectation about whether to trust others. The research of Yamagishi and Yamagishi (1994) has also been highly influential, proposing the notion of *general trust* as the expectation of goodwill and benign intent. In addition, these authors distinguished general trust from *knowledge-based trust*. While the former refers to trust toward humanity in general, based on inferences from past experiences, knowledge trust refers to specific known individuals. According to these authors, it is different to trust a person based on a general expectation of people than based on knowledge about a particular person.

More recent developments in research on trust have provided further refinements. According to Rotenberg's (2010) model, trust is conceptualized by its bases, domains, and targets (hence, the theory is known as BDT). The bases for trust are honesty, positive emotions, and reliability. According to the BDT model, the foundation of trust lies in verified, consistent behavior. Therefore, trust encompasses affective and behavioral domains, namely, individual affects, the behaviors of others, and one's own behavior. Finally, trust as a behavior may be directed toward a group of people or to specific persons. Applying this complex framework of trust shows how trusting immigrants is more difficult than trusting native people. This is because in the absence of previous experiences, it is possible to predict weakened bases for trust since there is limited knowledge to judge the honesty and trustworthiness of immigrants, and there is scantly developed positive emotionality.

Various definitions of trust are used in the social sciences to capture trust regarding specific targets. *Generalized trust* (or social trust) is the trust that people have in an unknown and ordinary person (Uslaner, 2002). This type of trust is often measured by asking a single-item question about trust in the "majority of people," and it is often the type of question used to measure trust at the country level (Jennings & Stoker, 2004; Uslaner, 2017). Consequently, generalized trust involves the notion of a radius of trust with known people of the same moral community at the center and unknown others at the outermost position (Fukuyama, 1995).

Another important distinction of trust regards the ingroup and outgroup. *Ingroup trust* refers to the trust that members of a group have in other members of their own group (Kramer, 2018). It is based on the beliefs and expectations formed by previous interactions with group members with whom there is a shared identity. In our case, ingroup trust points to the trust among people of the host society. *Outgroup trust*, on the contrary, occurs when members of one group (i.e., people of the host society) trust members of an outgroup (i.e., immigrants) (Kramer, 2018).

Outgroup trust is the belief and expectation that members of the outgroup are likely to act in ways that are beneficial, favorable, or at least not harmful to the ingroup's interests.

Contextual factors are crucial to the development of trust in a relationship. If previous understandings of trust emphasized emotions, expectations, and behavior, recent research shows the interdependence of stable dispositions and context. Weiss et al. (2021, 2022) developed a concept of trust based on daily interactions. They consider trust as a hub connecting important features of the individual and the context. For example, according to this understanding, trust between immigrants and the host population is different in a workplace environment than in a brief exchange about weather in public transportation. Trusting an unfamiliar individual whom you first encountered in the public transportation system differs from trusting a colleague you just met. The working context provides a setting that frames the interaction in a different way than public transportation, where you might have brief exchanges with strangers who remain strangers.

The Consequences of Declined Trust: Social Fragmentation

Trust acts as a social lubricant, facilitating interactions among diverse individuals, including immigrants and nonimmigrants. Research shows that a lack of trust leads to fragmentation and a lack of social cohesion between individuals and groups (Hooghe, 2007; Keefer & Scartascini, 2022; Meer & Tolsma, 2014). Although trust is the "gateway" for interpersonal relationships and communal living, the mechanisms connecting trust, diversity, and social cohesion are complex.

First, trust is influenced by subjective biases. In this regard, the connection between trust, diversity, and social cohesion relies on subjective perceptions. Empirical studies have shown that increased *perceptions* of diversity and segregation negatively correlate with ingroup and outgroup trust (Van Assche et al., 2023). Individuals with lower levels of trust perceive higher levels of diversity and segregation. However, the same study found no meaningful association when compared with actual levels of diversity and segregation. In essence, people's subjective perceptions of diversity and segregation, rather than the actual levels of diversity and segregation, play a significant role in shaping social cohesion and fragmentation.

Second, trust can arise as a result of economic factors. In this vein, trust across diverse groups and social fragmentation are driven by economic incentives. Research has shown that due to low-paying jobs, immigrants often reside in low-income neighborhoods with family members who share the same financial background and ethnic group membership (De Haas et al., 2020). These financial and ethnic commonalities help to create tightly knit minority communities. These material conditions can shape divisions across immigrants and members of the host society, and also influence whether immigrants and host society members trust each other.

Third, trust is influenced by unintended policy outcomes. While multicultural policies aim to achieve social cohesion by creating a welcoming society that embraces diversity, Koopman (2010) has shown that in some cases, multicultural policies can have the unintended consequences of increased social fragmentation. He demonstrated that multicultural policies coupled with a generous welfare state that does not prioritize integration can lead to more significant social fragmentation, which, increases distrust across immigrants and members of the host society. Effectively, due to multicultural policies and by living in a segregated close-knit ethnic community, immigrants may not learn the language of the new society. In turn, this increases the difficulties for labor integration in society at large, which can lead to social fragmentation.

Next, we provide a more in-depth exploration of the relationship between declining trust and increased diversity.

Toward a Psychological Explanation of the Connections between Declining Trust and Increased Diversity

The first possible reason for the decline in trust regarding increased diversity is the host society's coexistence with different others. The proposition is that simply by "being around," immigrants have a detrimental effect on the host population's trust (Dinesen et al., 2020). This possible explanation rests on the idea that having people around who are different from one another influences trust. Related to this viewpoint, research has shown that people categorize individuals into groups, creating a distinction between those who belong to our group and those who belong to other groups (Tajfel et al., 1971; also see Chapter 2 in this text). This kind of ingroup/outgroup social categorization tends to lead to ingroup favoritism, and less cooperation with outgroup members (Balliet et al., 2014). Related to this, Voci (2006) has demonstrated how identity leads to higher trust toward ingroup members and lower trust toward outgroup members. The reverse behavior, the less favorable or negative treatment of the outgroup (i.e., outgroup derogation), has also found support. Trust decreases when outgroup members are perceived as threatening or when the ingroup is seen as harmed by the outgroup (Rotella et al., 2013; Voci, 2006; also, see Chapter 5 in this text for further discussion of ingroup favoritism).

A second possible explanation for declining trust due to increased diversity focuses on intergroup conflict over resources. The presence of different groups may lead to competition for scarce resources. Realistic conflict theory posits that material resources are a key determinant of intergroup relations (Moghaddam, 2008; Sherif, 1966). When immigrant and nonimmigrant populations compete for limited resources such as jobs, housing, and healthcare services, it leads to conflict and decreased trust. However, the resources are not necessarily only material. Members of the host population tend to exhibit more hostility toward immigrants when they perceive that their national symbols (such as religion, language, and identity) are at stake due to differences with immigrants at the symbolic level (McLaren & Johnson, 2007). In addition, immigrants enacting their identity symbols (e.g., non-Christian religious clothing) have been linked to increased intolerance in Germany (Erisen & Kentmen-Cin, 2017).

A third and fairly pessimistic theoretical explanation of the relationship between ethnic diversity and trust is presented by the "constrict theory" (Putnam, 2007). This theory suggests that ethnic diversity detrimentally influences ingroup and outgroup trust in part because of the uncertainty it creates about the norms of behavior. People in neighborhoods characterized by diversity become less sure of how they should behave and how they should interact with others, particularly those who are different from them. According to this perspective, an increase in ethnic diversity leads people to "hunker down" and stay more isolated. People lose social interaction, and as a consequence, trust is eroded. Consequently, people do not trust each other because of loosening social ties provoked by isolation.

The above explanations differ in how they account for the psychological mechanisms active in in real-life situations characterized by diversity. The first explanation suggests that psychological mechanisms like ingroup favoritism or outgroup aversion are activated by the presence of immigrants. The second explanation emphasizes the role of resource competition in undermining trust. The third explanation suggests that trust erosion is a result of weakened societal connections due to isolation. In the next section, we delve deeper into three psychological mechanisms underlying in the mentioned explanations. Specifically, we discuss how stereotypes and prejudices, intergroup contact, and perceived threats could play a role in the erosion of trust as a result of ethnic diversity.

Psychological Processes and the Trust–Diversity Relationship

Stereotypes, Prejudices, and Trust

Trust within diverse environments is intricately woven into the fabric of human relationships, shaped by psychological nuances that extend beyond individual experiences. In Chapter 2, we discussed the important role of categorization in shaping the relationship between immigrants and members of the host society. In this section, we delve into the pivotal role of stereotypes and prejudices in influencing the dynamics of trust within diverse societies. In effect, stereotypes and prejudices are embedded societal constructs that shape perceptions and attitudes toward social groups.

Stereotypes are defined as generalized beliefs about the characteristics of a particular group, while prejudices are negative attitudes toward a particular group, regardless of any experience with them (VandenBos, 2015). Indeed, empirical evidence has shown that stereotypes toward immigrants are strongly linked to national stereotypes present in culture (Timberlake et al., 2015). For instance, with reference to stereotypes in Canada, research indicates that Canadians perceive doctors with a Chinese accent as less competent than those with a standard English accent (Baquiran, 2020), leading to diminished trust.

Stereotypes and prejudices can significantly impact the formation and erosion of trust. Thus, understanding the connections between stereotypes, prejudices, and trust between different ethnic groups becomes imperative in fostering environments where trust can thrive. For instance, research has shown that stereotypes can foster collaboration between immigrants and natives. A study conducted in Spain found that adolescents with positive stereotypes about Moroccan immigrants were more likely to collaborate with them (Cuadrado et al., 2020).

One way in which stereotypes and prejudices can influence the relationship between intergroup relations and trust is by shaping perceptions of competence as an immigrant characteristic. For instance, whether the host society perceives immigrant doctors as a competent labor force has a significant impact on the attitudes of the host society (Louis et al., 2010). If the locals view immigrant doctors with suspicion and look down on the training they received abroad, it creates a sense of distrust between the host society members and the immigrant medical doctors (Baquiran, 2020; Louis et al., 2010).

Stereotypes can involve various domains in addition to competence. Lee and Fiske (2006) found that individuals tend to evaluate other people through stereotypes in two basic domains: How friendly (i.e., warm) and how capable (i.e., competent) they are. Using this perspective, Lee and Fiske (2006) discovered that Americans tended to perceive immigrants from Europe and Asia as having higher competence than warmth, and from Latin America as having higher warmth than competence. But how do competence and warmth stereotypes influence trust between the host population and immigrants? Cettolin and Suetens (2019) found that individuals had lower levels of trust if their counterpart was a non-Western immigrant, stereotyped as high on warmth and low on competence. In certain situations, trust can be built upon competence, specifically when knowledge or skill is a crucial aspect. One such example is when we place trust in physicians, which centers on our perception of their competence. Regarding warmth, evidence from multiple domains shows that higher perceptions of warmth increase trust. In effect, perceived warmth leads to increased trust with supervisors and public employees, and higher perceived warmth can even increase trust in government (Hansen, 2022; Oleszkiewicz & Lachowicz-Tabaczek, 2016).

Intergroup Contact, Trust, and Perceived Threat
Contact theory (Allport, 1954; Pettigrew & Tropp, 2006) has also been utilized to examine the correlation between ethnic diversity and trust. This theory suggests that contact between different groups can lead to a reduction in intergroup prejudice and an increase in cross-group prosocial attitudes, such as trust. Therefore, increasing contact between immigrants and nonimmigrants can result in a decrease in prejudice and an increase in trust between the two groups.

Contact theory opens the possibility that the relationship between ethnic diversity and trust is not always negative; it depends on the conditions of interactions between immigrant and nonimmigrant populations (Çakal et al., 2021; Hewstone et al., 2006). In the context of Ireland, increased contact between Protestants and Catholics led to greater outgroup trust (Hewstone et al., 2006), and in the context of Turkish immigration in Cyprus, higher intergroup contact between Turkish immigrants and Turkish Cypriots predicted higher intergroup trust between minority and majority group members (Çakal et al., 2021). Stolle et al. (2013) analyzed how ethnic diversity influenced the levels of trust in German neighborhoods. They discovered that Germans who had regular interactions with others who were immigrants or had immigrant parents did not exhibit a decline in their trust as the number of immigrants in their neighborhood increased.

But according to Allport (1954), in order to achieve positive outcomes from intergroup contact, certain strict conditions have to be met: The groups have to have equal status and shared goals, be in a cooperation group relationship, and be in an environment supportive of their intergroup cooperation. Only when these conditions are met can contact between groups have positive outcomes, such as increased trust (this topic is further discussed in Chapter 10 of this text). The conditions proposed by Allport in 1954 describe what might be an ideal for the integration process of immigrants into a new society. For immigrants to fully integrate, they must experience equality in their interactions with the native people, participate and collaborate with the goals of the new society, and receive support from the authorities. A qualitative investigation found that immigrants consider themselves to be integrated when they have "participatory ability" in different domains of society (Kyeremeh et al., 2021). In essence, the four conditions mentioned by Allport are echoed by immigrants in the expression "participatory ability."

In addition, quantitative experiments have tested Allport's (1954) first condition: Interacting under equal status. In effect, research has shown that contact interactions between groups that enjoy equal status promote prosocial behavior. Greene et al. (2023) designed an experiment in Mexico and tested whether contact in equal conditions correlated with higher tolerance across party members of opposed ideologies. Random pairs of participants of different political ideologies were invited to decide whether Mexicans valued friendship over professional success under equal and nonequal conditions. The results showed that communications in the equal condition – each participant's answers counted equally – resulted in higher degrees of tolerance compared to the unequal condition. Similar results were found at the societal level. Kende et al. (2018) extended the findings of Pettigrew and Tropp's (2006) meta-analysis by adding cultural-level measures of equality and hierarchy values. The researchers found that cultures that valued equality predicted that more contact was associated with lower prejudice. The idea proposed by Allport, that intergroup contacts require individuals to have equal standing, is also supported.

In summary, the "contact hypothesis " shows that increased diversity does not inherently lead to decreased trust. Empirical evidence supports this proposition, highlighting that increasing contact can mitigate the decreasing trust that can come about because of increased diversity. However, interactions need to occur under conditions of equality, shared goals, cooperation, and authority support in order for diversity not to result in lower trust. Therefore, the association between diversity and trust is not predetermined, but varying and contingent upon context and the qualitative aspects of intergroup engagements. Yet, one of the greatest challenges of diversity is that the differences may be perceived as threatening. The next section will explore the relationship between perceived threat, trust, and diversity.

Perceived Threat, Diversity, and Trust
Immigrants can elicit feelings of threat from the native population. Extensive research has shown the connection between perceived threat, intergroup relations, and negative outcomes for the outgroup. Riek et al. (2006) showed that intergroup threat predicts negative emotions (fear, anger, anxiety) that, in turn, translate into intergroup behavior and attitudes toward outgroup members. At a societal level, Carriere et al. (2022) show how threats can lead to the support of punitive actions toward outgroup members and the restriction of their civil liberties. Historical experience also attests to this, such as the case of the internment of Japanese immigrants in the United States during World War Two, when Japan was seen as a serious external threat by nonimmigrant Americans. Empirical studies support the view that both individuals and societies tend to have less trust in outgroups when they perceive them as threatening (Schmid et al., 2014; Zhu et al., 2021).

Viewed from an intergroup perspective, a threat is the ingroup's perception that the outgroup could in some way harm them (Stephan & Stephan, 2000). The nature of the threat can vary greatly, encompassing physical harm, harm produced by the deprivation of an essential resource, or symbolic harm caused by the outgroup's different values and/or culture (Stephan et al., 2005; Stephan & Stephan, 2000). Thus, perceived threat is divided into realistic and symbolic threats. Realistic threat refers to the perception that the outgroup poses a tangible and material risk to the well-being of the ingroup. Symbolic threat refers to the perception that the outgroup challenges or undermines the cultural identity, values, norms, or status of the ingroup.

The importance of realistic threat is supported by realistic conflict theory (Sherif, 1966), which posits that competition for material resources between groups leads to conflicts and a sense of menace that induces threat. Through his field studies, Sheriff (1966) showed that intergroup relations under resource scarcity increase competition due to material threat perception, leading to conflict and eroding trust between groups. For instance, this realistic conflict theory (Sheriff, 1966) interpretation explains how unemployed workers or individuals with lower education levels experience greater threats because of increasing immigration (Kunovich, 2013), and this leads to lower levels of trust toward outgroups.

The importance of symbolic threat is highlighted by social identity theory (Tajfel, 1974; Tajfel et al., 1971). According to the social identity perspective, the outgroup can induce a symbolic threat if it challenges the ingroup's positiveness or distinctiveness (Lemaine, 1974; Moghaddam, 2008; Turner et al., 1979). This symbolic outgroup threat relates to non-tangible resources of groups such as identity, values, and culture. Substantive research has shown that symbolic threat is at the core of symbolic racism. The pioneering research of Kinder and Sears (1981) showed that negative biases against minority ethnic groups contribute to the perception that members of the minority group pose a threat to the way of life and culture of the majority group. Later developments of symbolic racism have been applied to intergroup relations between natives and immigrants, showing that natives harbor anti-immigrant sentiments and decreased levels of trust in part as the result of symbolic threat (Esses, 2021; Rios et al., 2018; Wilkes & Wu, 2018).

Increasing levels of perceived threat and decreased trust contribute to social conflict and polarization. Indeed, research has shown that individuals experiencing symbolic and/or realistic threats suffer cognitive impairment; they have lower problem-solving skills and are less likely to cooperate with outgroup members (Rempel & Fisher, 1997; Weisel & Zultan, 2021). This reduced efficacy in solving common problems faced by all groups leads to supporting restricting civil liberties of the outgroup members (Carriere et al., 2022). In a similar vein, researchers have shown that individuals who experience threat and anger become polarized (Renström et al., 2023), with detrimental consequences for trust at the individual, intergroup, and institutional levels. The enormous common threat of global warming renders these findings particularly relevant and important.

In conclusion, perceived threats, whether realistic or symbolic, play a critical role in shaping intergroup relations and attitudes toward immigrants. Research indicates that these perceptions can lead to negative emotions, conflicts, and also decreased trust.

Concluding Comment

The connections between declining trust, rising immigration, and increasing ethnic diversity represent a challenge to contemporary societies. Trust is inherently linked to familiarity and shared experiences. In the context of immigration and increasing ethnic diversity, natives may lack the knowledge and familiarity necessary to extend trust to immigrants, impeding the integration process. Cultural differences in intergroup communication styles further exacerbate this challenge, as nonimmigrant individuals may struggle to interpret immigrant intentions and behaviors. Consequently, nonimmigrants may interact cautiously or even avoid interactions altogether with immigrants, perpetuating a cycle of mistrust and hindering social cohesion. Bridging this trust gap requires proactive efforts to foster understanding and familiarity between nonimmigrants and immigrants, emphasizing the importance of cross-cultural communication and shared experiences in building mutual trust and integration within diverse societies.

The current chapter has examined and revealed the dynamics encompassing situational, psychological, and societal influences that shape trust toward immigrants within diverse societies. A thematic argument is that exposure to ethnic diversity elucidates mechanisms through which increased diversity can lead to decreased trust. One line of argument is that the mechanism that best explains how trust declines relates to isolation; when diversity levels increase, people tend to isolate, which leads to decreased trust. However, an alternative viewpoint is that segregation arising out of material conditions (e.g., housing segregation based on wealth disparities) is key to explaining reduced levels of trust. In effect, segregation, either created by psychological perception or economic factors, leads to decreased trust. Either way, perceptions of the outgroup are central to the process leading to intergroup distrust. The importance of perception leads us to recognize the role of human psychology in the mechanism that leads to decreased trust in diverse settings.

As we have discussed, stereotypes and prejudices, intergroup contact, and perceived threats emerge as key psychological mechanisms influencing trust. Stereotypes and prejudices, deeply ingrained societal processes, can either foster collaboration or exacerbate distrust between nonimmigrants and immigrants. Intergroup contact offers a pathway to mitigate declining trust, but Allport (1954) stipulated that this positive outcome only occurs under conditions of equality, shared goals, cooperation, and authority support. However, more recent meta-analytic studies provide a more optimistic picture, suggesting that intergroup contact leads to positive outcomes irrespective of the conditions under which contact takes place (a view rejected by some critics, Moghaddam, 2024). Perceived threat, whether realistic or symbolic, significantly shapes intergroup relations, attitudes toward immigrants, and ultimately, trust levels.

Consequently, addressing the challenges posed by declining trust and increased diversity requires a psychologically informed policy. First, immigration policies should focus on fostering positive intergroup interactions, promoting equality, shared goals, and cooperation between host society populations and immigrants. Policy regulations regarding labor integration should avoid creating the perception that immigrants receive preferential treatment. Instead, such policy regulations should promote the notion that immigrant and native workers behave and are treated according to a common set of rules and contribute equally to the development of society. When necessary, interventions aimed at reducing stereotypes and prejudices through education, cultural exchange programs, and media campaigns can help cultivate more inclusive attitudes and foster trust. This is particularly when stereotypes and prejudices are a source of threat. In effect, intervention policies should aim to create inclusive environments that address both realistic and symbolic threats faced by immigrants and host society members, ensuring that their safety, dignity, and cultural identity are respected. For instance, policies could include anti-discrimination laws or programs that promote cultural understanding.

Finally, navigating the challenges of diversity requires a multifaceted approach that acknowledges the situational, psychological, and societal influences on trust. By adopting evidence-based policies informed by psychological insights, societies can harness the benefits of diversity while fostering greater trust, cohesion, and inclusivity for all members.

REFERENCES

Allport, G. W. (1954). *The nature of prejudice*. Addison-Wesley.

Balliet, D., Wu, J., & De Dreu, C. K. W. (2014). Ingroup favoritism in cooperation: A meta-analysis. *Psychological Bulletin, 140*(6), 1556–1581. https://doi.org/10.1037/a0037737

Baquiran, C. L. C. (2020). A doctor's foreign accent affects perceptions of competence. *Health Communication, 35*(6), 726–730. https://doi.org/doi.org/10.1080/10410236.2019.1584779

Budescu, D. V., & Budescu, M. (2012). How to measure diversity when you must. *Psychological Methods, 17*(2), 215–227. https://doi.org/10.1037/a0027129

Çakal, H., Halabi, S., Cazan, A.-M., & Eller, A. (2021). Intergroup contact and endorsement of social change motivations: The mediating role of intergroup trust, perspective-taking, and intergroup anxiety among three advantaged groups in Northern Cyprus, Romania, and Israel. *Group Processes & Intergroup Relations, 24*(1), 48–67. https://doi.org/10.1177/1368430219885163

Carriere, K. R., Hallahan, A., & Moghaddam, F. M. (2022). The effect of perceived threat on human rights: A meta-analysis. *Group Processes & Intergroup Relations, 25*(1), 247–279. https://doi.org/10.1177/1368430220962563

Central Intelligence Agency. (n.d.). *The world factbook: India*. Retrieved August 21, 2024, from www.cia.gov/the-world-factbook/countries/india/#people-and-society

Cettolin, E., & Suetens, S. (2019). Return on trust is lower for immigrants. *The Economic Journal*, *129*(621), 1992–2009. https://doi.org/10.1111/ecoj.12629

Cuadrado, I., López-Rodríguez, L., & Constantin, A. A. (2020). A matter of trust: Perception of morality increases willingness to help through positive emotions. *Group Processes & Intergroup Relations*, *23*(3), 462–480. https://doi.org/10.1177/1368430219838606

Dawson, C. (2019). How persistent is generalised trust? *Sociology*, *53*(3), 590–599. https://doi.org/10.1177/0038038517718991

De Haas, H. de, Castles, S., & Miller, M. J. (2020). *The age of migration: International population movements in the modern world*. Red Globe Press. 6th ed.

Dinesen, P. T., Schaeffer, M., & Sønderskov, K. M. (2020). Ethnic diversity and social trust: A narrative and meta-analytical review. *Annual Review of Political Science*, *23*(1), 441–465. https://doi.org/10.1146/annurev-polisci-052918-020708

Erisen, C., & Kentmen-Cin, C. (2017). Tolerance and perceived threat toward Muslim immigrants in Germany and the Netherlands. *European Union Politics*, *18*(1), 73–97. https://doi.org/10.1177/1465116516675979

Esses, V. M. (2021). Prejudice and discrimination toward immigrants. *Annual Review of Psychology*, *72*(1), 503–531. https://doi.org/10.1146/annurev-psych-080520-102803

EVS/WVS. (2021). *Joint EVS/WVS 2017-2021 Dataset (Joint EVS/WVS)* (Version 2.0.0) [Dataset]. World Values Survey Association. https://doi.org/10.14281/18241.14

Fukuyama, F. (1995). *Trust: The social virtues and the creation of prosperity*. Free Press.

Greene, K., Rossiter, E., Seira, E., & Simpser, A. (2023). Interacting as Equals: How contact can promote tolerance among opposing partisans. *SSRN Electronic Journal*. https://doi.org/10.2139/ssrn.4456223

Hansen, F. G. (2022). How impressions of public employees' warmth and competence influence trust in government. *International Public Management Journal*, *25*(6), 939–961. https://doi.org/10.1080/10967494.2021.1963361

Hewstone, M., Cairns, E., Voci, A., Hamberger, J., & Niens, U. (2006). Intergroup contact, forgiveness, and experience of "the troubles" in Northern Ireland. *Journal of Social Issues*, *62*(1), 99–120. https://doi.org/10.1111/j.1540-4560.2006.00441.x

Jennings, M. K., & Stoker, L. (2004). Social trust and civic engagement across time and generations. *Acta Politica*, *39*(4), 342–379. https://doi.org/10.1057/palgrave.ap.5500077

Holtug, N. (2021). *The politics of social cohesion: Immigration, community, and justice*. Oxford University Press. 1st ed. https://doi.org/10.1093/oso/9780198797043.001.0001

Hooghe, M. (2007). Social capital and diversity generalized trust, social cohesion and regimes of diversity. *Canadian Journal of Political Science*, *40*(3), 709–732. https://doi.org/10.1017/S0008423907070722

Keefer, P., & Scartascini, C. (2022). *Trust: The key to social cohesion and growth in Latin America and the Caribbean*. Inter-American Development Bank. https://doi.org/10.18235/0003792

Kende, J., Phalet, K., Van Den Noortgate, W., Kara, A., & Fischer, R. (2018). Equality revisited: A cultural meta-analysis of intergroup contact and prejudice. *Social Psychological and Personality Science*, *9*(8), 887–895. https://doi.org/10.1177/1948550617728993

Kinder, D. R., & Sears, D. O. (1981). Prejudice and politics: Symbolic racism versus racial threats to the good life. *Journal of Personality and Social Psychology*, *40*(3), 414–431.

Koopmans, R. (2010). Trade-offs between equality and difference: Immigrant integration, multiculturalism and the welfare state in cross-national perspective. *Journal of Ethnic and Migration Studies*, *36*(1), 1–26. https://doi.org/10.1080/13691830903250881

Kramer, R. M. (2018). Ingroup-outgroup trust. barriers, benefits, and bridges. In E. M. Uslaner (Ed.), *The Oxford handbook of social and political trust* (pp. 95–115). Oxford University Press.

Kunovich, R. M. (2013). Labor market competition and anti-immigrant sentiment: Occupations as contexts. *International Migration Review*, *47*(3), 643–685. https://doi.org/10.1111/imre.12046

Kyeremeh, E., Arku, G., Mkandawire, P., Cleave, E., & Yusuf, I. (2021). What is success? Examining the concept of successful integration among African immigrants in Canada. *Journal of Ethnic and Migration Studies*, *47*(3), 649–667. https://doi.org/10.1080/1369183X.2019.1639494

Lee, T. L., & Fiske, S. T. (2006). Not an outgroup, not yet an ingroup: Immigrants in the Stereotype Content Model. *International Journal of Intercultural Relations*, *30*(6), 751–768. https://doi.org/10.1016/j.ijintrel.2006.06.005

Lemaine, G. (1974). Social differentiation and social originality. *European Journal of Social Psychology*, *4*(1), 17–52. https://doi.org/10.1002/ejsp.2420040103

Louis, W. R., Lalonde, R. N., & Esses, V. M. (2010). Bias against foreign-born or foreign-trained doctors: Experimental evidence. *Medical Education*, *44*(12), 1241–1247.

Lončar, J. (2023). Evoking the resemblance: Descriptive representation of ethnic minorities. *Ethnicities*, 14687968231166 5. https://doi.org/10.1177/14687968231166514

McLaren, L., & Johnson, M. (2007). Resources, group conflict and symbols: Explaining anti-immigration hostility in Britain. *Political Studies*, *55*(4), 709–732. https://doi.org/10.1111/j.1467-9248.2007.00680.x

Meer, T. V. D., & Tolsma, J. (2014). Ethnic diversity and its effects on social cohesion. *Annual Review of Sociology*, *40*(1), 459–478. https://doi.org/10.1146/annurev-soc-071913-043309

Migration Data Portal. (n.d.. *International Data*. Retrieved December 11, 2023, from www.migrationdataportal.org/international-data

Moghaddam, F. M. (2008). *Multiculturalism and intergroup relations: Psychological implications for democracy in global context*. American Psychological Association. https://doi.org/10.1037/11682-000

(2024). *The psychology of multiculturalism, assimilation, and omniculturalism*. Springer Nature.

Oleszkiewicz, A., & Lachowicz-Tabaczek, K. (2016). Perceived competence and warmth influence respect, liking and trust in work relations. *Polish Psychological Bulletin, 47*(4), 431–435. https://doi.org/10.1515/ppb-2016-0050

Pettigrew, T. F., & Tropp, L. R. (2006). A meta-analytic test of intergroup contact theory. *Journal of Personality and Social Psychology, 90*(5), 751–783. https://doi.org/10.1037/0022-3514.90.5.751

Phillips, K. W., Kim-Jun, S. Y., & Shim, S.-H. (2011). The value of diversity in organizations: A social psychological perspective. In *Social psychology and organizations* (pp. 253–271). Routledge/Taylor & Francis Group. https://doi.org/10.4135/9781446250556.n9

Putnam, R. D. (2007). *E pluribus unum*: Diversity and community in the twenty-first century, the 2006 Johan Skytte prize lecture. *Scandinavian Political Studies, 30*(2), 137–174. https://doi.org/10.1111/j.1467-9477.2007.00176.x

Rempel, M. W., & Fisher, R. J. (1997). Perceived threat, cohesion, and group problem solving in intergroup conflict. *International Journal of Conflict Management, 8*(3), 216–234. https://doi.org/10.1108/eb022796

Renström, E. A., Bäck, H., & Carroll, R. (2023). Threats, emotions, and affective polarization. *Political Psychology, 44*(6), 1337–1366. https://doi.org/10.1111/pops.12899

Riek, B. M., Mania, E. W., & Gaertner, S. L. (2006). Intergroup threat and outgroup attitudes: A meta-analytic review. *Personality and Social Psychology Review, 10*(4), 336–353. https://doi.org/10.1207/s15327957pspr1004_4

Rios, K., Sosa, N., & Osborn, H. (2018). An experimental approach to intergroup threat theory: Manipulations, moderators, and consequences of realistic vs. symbolic threat. *European Review of Social Psychology, 29*(1), 212–255. https://doi.org/10.1080/10463283.2018.1537049

Rotella, K. N., Richeson, J. A., Chiao, J. Y., & Bean, M. G. (2013). Blinding trust: The effect of perceived group victimhood on intergroup trust. *Personality and Social Psychology Bulletin, 39*(1), 115–127. https://doi.org/10.1177/0146167212466114

Rotenberg, K. J. (2010). The conceptualization of interpersonal trust: A basis, domain, and target framework. In K. J. Rotenberg (Ed.), *Interpersonal trust during childhood and adolescence* (1st ed., pp. 8–27). Cambridge University Press. https://doi.org/10.1017/CBO9780511750946.002

Rotter, J. B. (1967). A new scale for the measurement of interpersonal trust1. *Journal of Personality, 35*(4), 651–665. https://doi.org/10.1111/j.1467-6494.1967.tb01454.x

(1971). Generalized expectancies for interpersonal trust. *American Psychologist*, *26*(5), 443–452. https://doi.org/10.1037/h0031464

(1980). Interpersonal trust, trustworthiness, and gullibility. *American Psychologist*, *35*(1), 1–7.

Schmid, K., Ramiah, A. A., & Hewstone, M. (2014). Neighborhood ethnic diversity and trust: The role of intergroup contact and perceived threat. *Psychological Science*, *25*(3), 665–674. https://doi.org/10.1177/0956797613508956

Sherif, M. (1966). *Group conflict and cooperation*. Routiedge and Kegan Paul.

Steele, L. G., Bostic, A., Lynch, S. M., & Abdelaaty, L. (2022). *Measuring Ethnic Diversity*. https://doi.org/10.1146/annurev-soc-030420-015435

Stephan, W. G., Lausanne Renfro, C., Esses, V. M., White Stephan, C., & Martin, T. (2005). The effects of feeling threatened on attitudes toward immigrants. *International Journal of Intercultural Relations*, *29*(1), 1–19. https://doi.org/10.1016/j.ijintrel.2005.04.011

Stephan, W. G., & Stephan, C. W. (2000). An integrated threat theory of prejudice. In S. Oskamp (Ed.), *Reducing prejudice and discrimination*. (pp. 23–45). Lawrence Erlbaum Associates Publishers.

Stolle, D., Petermann, S., Schmid, K., Schönwälder, K., Hewstone, M., Vertovec, S., Schmitt, T., & Heywood, J. (2013). Immigration-related diversity and trust in German cities: The role of intergroup contact. *Journal of Elections, Public Opinion & Parties*, *23*(3), 279–298. https://doi.org/10.1080/17457289.2013.809350

Tajfel, H. (1974). Social identity and intergroup behaviour. *Social Science Information*, *13*(2), 65–93. https://doi.org/10.1177/053901847401300204

Tajfel, H., Billig, M. G., Bundy, R. P., & Flament, C. (1971). Social categorization and intergroup behaviour. *European Journal of Social Psychology*, *1*(2), 149–178. https://doi.org/10.1002/ejsp.2420010202

Timberlake, J. M., Howell, J., Grau, A. B., & Williams, R. H. (2015). Who "they" are matters: Immigrant stereotypes and assessments of the impact of immigration. *The Sociological Quarterly*, *56*(2), 267–299. https://doi.org/10.1111/tsq.12076

Turner, J. C., Brown, R. J., & Tajfel, H. (1979). Social comparison and group interest in ingroup favouritism. *European Journal of Social Psychology*, *9*(2), 187–204. https://doi.org/10.1002/ejsp.2420090207

Uslaner, E. M. (2002). *The moral foundations of trust*. Cambridge University Press.

(2017). Trust. In F. M. Moghaddam (Ed.), *The Sage encyclopedia of political behavior* (1st ed., pp. 855–858). SAGE Publications, Inc.

Van Assche, J., Ardaya Velarde, S., Van Hiel, A., & Roets, A. (2023). Trust is in the eye of the beholder: How perceptions of local diversity and segregation shape social cohesion. *Frontiers in Psychology*, *13*, 1036646. https://doi.org/10.3389/fpsyg.2022.1036646

Van Knippenberg, D. V., Nishii, L. H., & Dwertmann, D. J. G. (2020). Synergy from diversity: Managing team diversity to enhance performance. *Behavioral Science*, *6*(1), 75–92. https://doi.org/10.1177/2379461520006000108

VandenBos, G. R. (2015). *APA dictionary of psychology*. American Psychological Association. 2nd ed.

Voci, A. (2006). The link between identification and in-group favouritism: Effects of threat to social identity and trust-related emotions. *British Journal of Social Psychology*, *45*(2), 265–284. https://doi.org/10.1348/014466605X52245

Weisel, O., & Zultan, R. (2021). Perceived level of threat and cooperation. *Frontiers in Psychology*, *12*, 704338. https://doi.org/10.3389/fpsyg.2021.704338

Weiss, A., Burgmer, P., & Hofmann, W. (2022). The experience of trust in everyday life. *Current Opinion in Psychology*, *44*, 245–251. https://doi.org/10.1016/j.copsyc.2021.09.016

Weiss, A., Michels, C., Burgmer, P., Mussweiler, T., Ockenfels, A., & Hofmann, W. (2021). Trust in everyday life. *Journal of Personality and Social Psychology*, *121*(1), 95–114. https://doi.org/10.1037/pspi0000334

Wilkes, R., & Wu, C. (2018). Trust and minority groups. In E. M. Uslaner (Ed.), *The Oxford handbook of social and political Trust* (pp. 231–250). Oxford University Press.

Yamagishi, T., & Yamagishi, M. (1994). Trust and commitment in the United States and Japan. *Motivation and Emotion*, *18*(2), 129–166. https://doi.org/10.1007/BF02249397

Zhu, N., Lu, H. J., & Chang, L. (2021). Trust as social investment: A life-history model of environmental effects on ingroup and outgroup trust. *Personality and Individual Differences*, *168*, 110303. https://doi.org/10.1016/j.paid.2020.110303

CHAPTER 4

The Deglobalization Era
The Psychology of Backlash against Immigrants and a Globalized Society

Children in the United States learn that "In 1492 Columbus sailed the ocean blue..." and consequently, opened up the world. Europeans came into contact with indigenous Americans, ushering in an era of exploration, conquest, and settlement into a once isolated continent. Of course, the world has always been globally connected; the exchange of goods, ideas, and people has been occurring for millennia (for example, the Silk Road trade route connecting Europe and Asia was established in 100 BCE). However, the Columbian Exchange brought more rapid expansion and growth of globalization to the world. Columbus and his group brought devastating diseases and mass colonization, but also opened up global trade routes (Pruitt, 2023). Throughout the last few centuries, the world has become more interdependent, sharing cultures, products and services, experiences, and crises (Diaz & Zirkel, 2012).

In 2008, the financial crisis in the United States brought on by the collapse of the housing market became a global crisis, leading to a global economic decline (Merle, 2018) and ushering in a call for deglobalization and drive to be less globally reliant. This "era of deglobalization" was further exacerbated by the COVID-19 pandemic, supply chain disruptions due to geopolitical instability, and refugee crises in Syria, Afghanistan, Ukraine, Palestine, and the continuous migration of Central American and Mexican immigrants entering the United States through the southern border. Driven by this fear of being globally reliant, protectionist policies have been enacted, such as the CHIPS and Science Act in the United States and the European Chips Act to increase production of US- and EU-made semiconductor chips, trade bans with Russia (S&P Global, n.d.), as well as proposals to strengthen border walls, limit the number of refugees and asylees, and increase deportations. The intermixing of cultures and peoples coupled with global crises has increased the "us versus them" mentality, and as a consequence immigrants are often seen as a threat and burden to the nation instead of an enhancement (Gelfand et al., 2011).

In this chapter we focus on the backlash against immigrants in response to globalization and increased calls for a return to national independence instead of global interdependence. The first part provides an overview of globalization, deglobalization, and re-globalization, and reviews the factors underlying the current drive for deglobalization across the world. In the second half of the chapter, we focus on the consequences of immigrants being perceived as a psychological and material threat to the host populations of nations such as the United States, those of the EU, and some non-Western countries.

Globalization, Deglobalization, and Re-globalization

At its core, globalization is the process of the world becoming more interconnected through the cross-border exchange of goods, services, money, people, information, and culture (Ariely, 2021). Globalization and migration bring many benefits to nations, including the spread of ideas, diversity, and shared knowledge (James, 2017). For many, globalization provides opportunities that can be or at least appear mutually beneficial. For example, immigrants often take essential jobs that native citizens shun. However, while fulfilling a need, these jobs are often low-pay, temporary, lack essential benefits, and do not lead to long-term residency or citizenship (e.g., gig economy jobs like TaskRabbit, Uber, DoorDash). Nor are these immigrants fully accepted as members of the host society, even as they become essential workers to keep the host society functioning.

For example, in preparation for the 2022 FIFA World Cup, Qatar brought in an estimated two million migrant laborers from South Asia – about 40 percent of Qatar's total population – to help with construction projects and other preparations for the games (Boundless Immigration, 2022). A year later, many of these workers have not been fully compensated for their labor and are stuck in Qatar without work, as the job market has slowed down post-World Cup (Human Rights Watch, 2023).

Canada, too, has a high immigrant population, with immigrants making up 25 percent of their population, which is high compared to other Western nations. (For example, immigrants make up 14 percent of the population in the United States and in the United Kingdom.) With a huge emphasis on economic immigration to aid their aging population and workforce, Canada is welcoming to immigrants entering the country on temporary work visas to fulfill much needed jobs (known as the Temporary Foreign Worker Program). However, many of these immigrants remain long-term residents who can reside in Canada indefinitely while never gaining citizenship and never fully integrating into society (Bongiorno, 2024; Levinson-King, 2022).

Further, the controversial mockumentary, *A Day Without a Mexican* (Arau, 2004), explored what would happen if all the people in California with Mexican heritage suddenly disappeared. The movie showed society falling apart as construction workers, people in the service industry, teachers, police officers, newscasters, etc., all vanished. Those left behind in a "California without people of Mexican heritage" realized how crucial this population was to the functioning of their society.

At the same time that immigrants are seen as thanklessly fulfilling essential societal roles, they are perceived by some people as taking jobs away from native citizens. By accepting these jobs at lower wages, immigrants are seen as driving income down and causing native citizens to lose out (Gordon, 2015; James, 2017). Further exacerbating this threat is the fear of losing out to people who are culturally different, resulting in changes in the identity of the nation and valued cultural traditions. Somewhat contradictory, globalization is both seen as introducing diversity into society while also threatening to create a culturally homogenous society, referred to as cultural globalization (Dahgrir, 2013).

The domination and influence of American culture (and the English language) throughout the world, known as Americanization, in particular has sparked protests and calls for cultural preservation in both Western and non-Western countries (Al-Rawashdeh, 2014; Daghrir, 2013). For example, in an attempt to curb the influence of Hollywood, many European nations have begun subsidizing European films and productions, and placing higher taxes and quotas on American films (Daghrir, 2013). In Sub-Saharan Africa, the introduction of Western ideals and values emphasizing individualism and autonomy have clashed with traditional African values of community and collectivism, leading people to favor national isolationism over globalization (Gordon, 2017).

Likewise, in some US states such as California and Florida where there are a large number of bilingual and limited English speakers, employment policies have been implemented that favor people who speak English and another language fluently. While intended to support increasingly diverse communities, these policies have negative consequences for monolingual Black and White American workers (Ordway, 2017). For example, one study found that when the city of Oakland, California, implemented a bilingual employment policy, the number of English-only speaking White and in particular Black employees fell while the number of bilingual Spanish/Chinese- and English-speaking employees grew, as did the number of Asian and Pacific Islander employees who only spoke English. These results suggest that not only did the language policy negatively affect Black and White monolingual speakers, but it also had unintended group-based consequences favoring the employability of Asian and Pacific Islander employees (Sewell, 2017).

Deglobalization is used as an argument against these perceived threats which are seen by some as being caused by globalization, highlighting what is negative and motivating people to set the limits against globalization. Fear over a loss of jobs and cultural differences represent perceived threats that populist leaders use to argue why deglobalization is important, and why deglobalization has to be the solution to these perceived threats (Kinnvall & Kisić Merino, 2023). Critics argue that outsiders threaten the cultural stability of a nation and introduce a lack of control over identity changes. This perceived threat is used to justify anti-immigrant responses and policies to return to the way things were (Harell et al., 2017; Tartakovsky & Walsh, 2016).

This promise to return to the way things were, or re-globalization, is a more positive view than deglobalization. In this vision, populist leaders are seen as saviors, they are looking out for their citizens' traditions, they are championing host society traditions (Kinnvall & Kisić Merino, 2023). For example, US president Donald Trump ran in campaigns leading to presidential elections in 2016, 2020, and 2024, on a slogan, Make America Great Again (MAGA), and a strong anti-immigrant and closed-borders campaign. Support for Brexit in the United Kingdom can partly be explained by fears over a perceived invasion by Muslim immigrants in England (Moghaddam, 2019). In South Africa, post-apartheid attempts to establish a national identity have led to increased calls for nativism and anti-immigrant prejudice over fears that immigrants will receive resources and benefits that should only be allocated to citizens (Gordon, 2017).

In summary, then, critics of immigration argue it leads to (1) income reduction and job loss for native citizens, (2) greater burden on society through increased social welfare costs, and (3) the decline of traditional culture, language, and values. In the following section, we explore this backlash against migration flows, and the perceived material and culture threat.

Backlash against Immigrants in Response to Globalization

This contemporary global rise in anti-immigrant violence and widespread backlash can be tied to the fear of a "migrant invasion," such that immigrants do not share the same identity as the native citizens, and instead threaten to replace native citizens' culture, language, and values (Human Rights First, 2023; Moghaddam, 2019). In recent years, violent attacks against migrants have occurred in many countries around the world as well as an unprecedented rise in abuse and assaults against asylum seekers, particularly along EU borders and the US–Mexico border (Gentry et al., 2023; Migration Information Source, 2019; Rankin, 2022). However, this fear is not only about the cultural impact, but also the economic impact – and more importantly the perceived competition that immigrants pose to native citizens over resources and power (James, 2017).

Immigrants pose a perceived cultural threat to "our way of life" (e.g., not assimilating to the national culture and customs, not speaking the national or majority language, not sharing traditional national values, following foreign religions, increasing crime in the community) and a perceived material threat (e.g., competition over resources, power) to native citizens (Murray & Marx, 2013). In the following sections, we explore this perception that immigrants present a cultural and material threat to native citizens in the Global North and South, and the extent that these threats influence prejudice and backlash against immigrants.

Immigrants Threaten Our Way of Life

Immigrants are an unknown element that can present a threat to the majority-endorsed identity – particularly if they are believed to be too different to become integrated and truly "belong" to society (Bose, 2018). As such, across Western societies there is a preference for immigrants who are perceived as similar in appearance and culture to the native citizens (Gorodzeisky & Semyonov, 2019; López-Rodríguez et al., 2014; Osbeck et al., 1997; Salas-Schweikart et al., 2024). For example, Latin American immigrants generally are received more positively in Southern Europe due to their cultural similarities (e.g., they are Christians) and willingness to take on undesirable jobs (Peixoto, 2012). Likewise, in a series of experimental studies, Kunst et al. (2018) found that White Americans were more likely to associate photos of Latinx immigrants as assimilating to US culture when they look more phenotypically white, as opposed to photos of Latinx immigrants with darker skin. These participants were more likely to see Chinese female immigrants and male Arab immigrants as phenotypically white if they were told that these immigrants had adopted US culture.

Craig and Richeson (2017) also found that White participants feared growing ethnic diversity in the United States primarily due to the loss of prototypical American culture and values. In Israel, Stephan et al. (1998) found that Israeli citizens felt more threatened by Ethiopian immigrants as compared to Russian immigrants. Despite both immigrant groups being Jewish, the Russian immigrants' culture was perceived as more culturally similar and therefore less threatening. In line with similarity-attraction hypothesis (Osbeck et al., 1997; Salas-Schweikart et al., 2024), Bessudnov (2016) suggested that an ethnic hierarchy exists based in perceived intergroup similarity, such that Russians were slightly more favorable toward immigrants from Ukraine and Moldova whom they saw as culturally similar, and less favorable toward immigrants from the Caucasus region and Central Asia. Further, fear of immigrants was a significant predictor of negative attitudes toward immigrants in a study with East and Southeast Asian citizens from China, Japan, Malaysia, the Philippines, Singapore, South Korea, Taiwan, and Thailand, such that participants felt anxious that immigrants would violate social norms (Kawasaki & Ikeda, 2020).

This perceived threat to culture and values has also been associated with increased support for assimilation to the national culture (Danbold & Huo, 2015). For example, Mashuri et al. (2013) found that in the Netherlands Muslim immigrants who chose to assimilate by abandoning their traditional clothing and engaging in religious practices in private were perceived by native citizens as less threatening. Native citizens were more willing to help these immigrants adapt to society. In the United Kingdom, research showed that support for admitting asylum seekers increased when respondents were made aware that prospective asylum seekers would be required to partake in language and civic-education courses (Neureiter, 2022). In general, this perceived threat from immigrants is associated with greater preference for assimilation policies among host society members (Badea et al., 2018; Kil et al., 2019; Watson & Riffe, 2013).

The objective underlying assimilation policy is to promote social cohesion and maintain one shared or "common" identity by immigrants' adoption of the host culture and abandonment for their heritage culture, language, and identity (Badea et al., 2018; Callens & Meuleman, 2017; see Chapter 8 for further discussion on assimilation). In focus groups with US citizens, Paxton and Mughan (2006) found that the core of assimilation is commitment; commitment to becoming a citizen, being a hardworking and productive member of society, and to speaking English and adapting to customs, in other words, commitment to what are seen as traditional American values and culture. (See Chapter 5 in this text for further discussion on American identity.)

However, in reality, native citizens often do not see immigrants as truly committing to the host society, as sharing the same collective identity as themselves and becoming equally contributing members. Assimilation is not automatic (Paxton & Mughan, 2006). Assimilation into the host culture does not stop the discrimination of immigrants, especially if they are perceived as belonging to an ethnic minority group (Cabaniss & Cameron, 2018; Moghaddam & Perreault, 1992). For example, in a series of experimental scenarios, Hartman et al. (2014) had White American participants rate how serious an offense it was for an immigrant to display a flag other than the American flag and cheer for a non-US Olympic team. They found that Mexican immigrants were rated as committing a more serious offense than Canadian immigrants. This suggests that the more similar the immigrant is to the host society, the less of a threat the immigrant is perceived to be.

Despite attempts to adopt the host culture and assimilate, immigrants with different phenotypes and cultural characteristics from the majority do stand out and are perceived as outsiders. In the United States, for example, Latinx ethnicity remains the most important factor in perceiving whether someone is undocumented. Both Latinx US citizens and legal immigrants experience the consequences of this "Latinx-is-undocumented bias" (Hendricks, 2022; Martinez & Ortega, 2019). In their study on racial positioning in the United States Zou and Cheryan (2017) found that only White Americans are perceived as both superior and American, while Latino and Asian Americans were perceived as foreign. Though African Americans were perceived as relatively American compared to Latino and Asian Americans, they were seen as culturally inferior relative to Asian Americans. Thus, being born in the United States did not mean that African Americans were seen as equal in status to some other groups of "Americans."

Likewise, in Denmark, those who are non-Western or visibly different in appearance from the Danish majority are considered culturally incompatible compared with immigrants from Western countries and Danes. In fact, since the war in Ukraine, laws have been passed giving Ukrainian refugees special treatment that allows for their integration into Danish society, but this special treatment still has not been afforded to Muslim and other non-Western refugees (Khawaja et al., 2023). Throughout Europe, there are other noted instances of preferential treatment toward Ukrainian refugees as opposed to non-Ukrainian refugees, due to the perception of people from Ukraine as white and Christian (Esposito, 2022). Further, a study examining asylum applications in France from 1976 to 2016 found that Christian applicants were more likely to be granted asylum compared to Muslim applicants (Emeriau, 2022; see Chapter 6 in this text for further discussion of Islamophobia in Europe).

These differences in characteristics and values are often seen as harmful to society. While there is little objective basis for the assertion that immigrants commit more crimes than native-born citizens (Cervantes et al., 2018; Dube, 2019; Hummel, 2016), their perceived criminality is pervasive. This perception serves to support justifications given for restrictive and punitive immigration measures against the immigrant population (Gemignani & Hernandez-Albujar, 2015; Stupi et al., 2016). In the United States, immigrants have been blamed for the ongoing fentanyl crisis even though data shows that most of the fentanyl has been brought into the country by US citizens (Bier, 2022).

Due to these biased misperceptions of immigrants (particularly those perceived as more dissimilar), isolated events such as violent attacks by ethnic minority members can have widespread effects on immigrant populations and those communities perceived to be connected. For example, the 2016 terror attacks in Nice, France, by Tunisian immigrant Mohamed Lahouaiej-Bouhlel, and in Würzburg and Ansbach, Germany, by asylum seekers led to an increase in discrimination and prejudice against refugees across Germany (Frey, 2021). The September 11 terror attacks in the United States led to increased restrictive immigration policies affecting all immigrants and those seeking legal pathways into the country (Cervantes et al., 2018). Likewise, in his first term Donald Trump issued an executive order banning refugees from several predominantly Muslim countries due to national security concerns (Immigration History, n.d.). The so-called Muslim Travel Ban eventually ended when President Biden took office in 2021 (Watson & Hudak, 2023).

Finally, in South Africa, foreigners are often blamed for crime (Dube, 2019). Seen as culturally inferior compared to the elite South Africans, black African immigrants in particular are stereotyped as criminals and are often the target of violent attacks (Dube, 2017; Ngobeni, 2022). South Africa is one of the leading African countries in politics and the economy, and as such is one of the top immigrant-receiving destinations for African immigrants (Abidde & Matambo, 2021), who are more likely to migrate to South Africa compared to Europe or North America (Whitaker, 2020).

Beginning in 2008, many xenophobic attacks by South Africans against black African immigrants occurred (Abidde & Matambo, 2021). However, "Afrophobia," the concept that Black South Africans are more hostile toward Black African immigrants relative to other groups, is suggested to be driven not by xenophobia, but instead by perceptions of criminal activity and other factors such as economic competition (Dube, 2019). In line with Frustration-Aggression Hypothesis (Dollard et al., 1939), African immigrants are often blamed for South Africans' life dissatisfaction, frustration with the post-apartheid government, and poor economic prospects (Hatungimana, 2023; Mlambo, 2021). African immigrants are seen as a burden on resources and as taking jobs away from other South Africans (Abidde & Matambo, 2021). In this next section, we further explore backlash against immigrants due to a perceived threat of material resources.

Immigrants Are Our Competition

Realistic conflict theory and other materialist theories propose that prejudice arises when groups perceive or are in actual competition over resources, power, and status (Campbell, 1965; Moghaddam, 2008; Sherif, 1966). In general, research has found that people with lower felt-or-perceived socioeconomic statuses (SES) are more threatened by the perceived competition with immigrants over resources and jobs (O'Neil & Tienda, 2010), whereas those with higher felt or perceived SES are more threatened by the group itself – immigrants – and the impact on their power and status in society (Dambrun et al., 2006).

The former can be linked to relative deprivation theory: People who perceive themselves to be relatively worse off in society compared to others feel greater prejudice toward immigrants because they see these immigrants as stealing their jobs and unfairly taking their already limited resources (Moghaddam, 2008). For example, Neureiter's (2022) study in the United Kingdom found that support for admitting asylum seekers increased when participants were told that the asylum seekers would only have limited access to social welfare. This effect was especially strong for individuals with low SES and conservatives who are more likely to view immigrants as a material threat. Baerg et al. (2014) too suggest that perceived social welfare costs and the tax burden brought by an increase in undocumented immigrants in the United States over time motivated bias against undocumented immigrants (see also Murray & Marx, 2013), driving US citizens to become more fiscally conservative.

On the other side of the ladder, individuals who already perceive themselves as better off in society are not as concerned with immigrants taking lower paid and less desirable jobs or resources. Instead, they feel greater prejudice toward immigrants they see as potential competitors for power (Dambrun et al., 2006) and their nation being overtaken by a dissimilar group. In line with system justification theory, these individuals are satisfied with their place in society and do not want to disrupt it (Jost et al., 2004). Results from a survey of 19 European countries found that racial prejudice in attitudes toward immigrants tends to increase with the relative size of the non-European racial minority population in the country (Gorodzeisky & Semyonov, 2019). Similarly, Bessudnov (2016) found a positive correlation between the size of the immigrant population from the Caucasus region and Central Asia among different regions in Russia and anti-immigrant sentiments.

Likewise, Alba et al. (2005) found that non-Hispanic White Americans who believed White people were becoming a minority in the United States were more supportive of restrictions on legal immigration. They also suggested that a threat hierarchy exists in these distorted perceptions, such that Latinx immigrants received the most restrictions, followed by Asian immigrants, while restrictions against European immigrants received the least support. In line with these studies, Pedroza (2019) found that the size of the Hispanic population influenced US counties' compliance with the Secure Communities program, which allows local law enforcement to get involved with immigration investigations (Chand & Schreckhise, 2015). Counties either below 20 percent or above 40 percent Hispanic were most compliant, suggesting that the Hispanic population was too small to influence the community in these low concentration areas and too much of a visible threat in these highly concentrated areas (Pedroza, 2019). Pedroza (2019) proposed that sizeable, but not too populated, counties were more likely to have Hispanic grass roots organizations and coalitions to influence the county officials to use discretion in favor of less deportations.

However, there are some exceptions to the trend of intergroup similarity-attraction among host and immigrant groups. For example, a few studies conducted in Europe suggest that native citizens who see immigrants as a tangible threat and competition for resources prefer immigrants with a different ethnic or cultural background because these dissimilar immigrants are perceived as unskilled and less economically competitive

(Ben-Nun Bloom et al., 2015; Hellwig & Sinno, 2017). For example, Hellwig and Sinno (2017) found that British participants were more willing to accept Muslim immigrants than East European immigrants when they perceived economic decline. The East European immigrants were also associated with abusing the welfare system and stealing jobs from British workers.

However, other studies have found that economic competition is related to cultural differences. In the United States, Latinx immigrants are often associated with job and resource competition (Brader et al., 2008; Valentino et al., 2013). In particular, Valentino et al. (2013) found that Latinx immigrants and immigrants of an unspecified ethnic origin caused the most economic concern for their White American participants, followed by East Asian immigrants. African and Eastern European immigrants were perceived as significantly less concerning, likely due to the perception that White and Black Americans are more "American" than Asian and Hispanic Americans (Zou & Cheryan, 2017). In contrast to the European studies, these findings suggest that economic threat is related to ethnic and cultural differences between Latinx immigrants and the White majority group in the United States. Ramsay and Pang (2017) also found that Singaporean attitudes were most prejudiced against Chinese immigrants in comparison to South Asian, Filipino, and Western immigrants despite their cultural similarities. Chinese immigrants may be perceived as most threatening due to their increased population in Singapore, but also due to stereotypes characterizing Chinese immigrants as unfriendly.

The size of the dissimilar outgroup is not the only factor influencing attitudes toward them. There is also a fairly large psychological literature on attitudes toward demographic rate change (e.g., Danbold & Huo, 2015; Enos, 2017; Hopkins, 2010), such that the perceived rate of an incoming immigrant population to an area leads to more negative responses and is more threatening than the number of immigrants already living in that area. According to Moghaddam (2008), there is greater danger of negative reactions from the host society associated with rapid "invasions" of and "sudden contact" with dissimilar others. Joncs-Correa (2011) described that within two years of the influx of Latinx immigrants in 2008 to Fremont, Nebraska, the town passed several laws that restricted the rights of and opportunities for undocumented immigrants. Hood III and Morris (1998) also found that as undocumented immigration rapidly increased in the 1990s, White Americans' support for legal immigration decreased and people developed more negative feelings toward immigrants. In line with these findings on demographic rate change, Hangartner et al.

(2019) examined the impact of a large increase in refugees arriving from Turkey and passing through the small Greek island communities along the Aegean Sea. Despite the temporary status of the refugee population living on the island, researchers found a lasting increase in anti-refugee and anti-Muslim attitudes, as well as support for restrictive immigration policies.

Finally, public opinion research suggests that perceptions of the health of the national economy generally influence attitudes toward immigration, such that anti-immigrant attitudes increase during economic downturns (Paxton & Mughan, 2006). Similarly, Pecoraro and Ruedin (2020) found that labor shortages increased positive attitudes toward immigrants in Switzerland among native citizens who welcomed the economic support. The opposite was true though for workers who worked alongside immigrants, as they felt they were in economic competition with their colleagues.

In another study examining Swiss university students' evaluations of Swiss, and second-generation Spanish and Kosovo Albanian job applicants, researchers found that the students were only prejudiced against the Kosovo Albanian applicants, an ethnic group in Switzerland that faces a lot of discrimination. However, this prejudice against the Kosovo Albanian applicants was only apparent for those applying for a job requiring high interpersonal skills and not for a job requiring high technical skills. This suggests that the students had the greatest prejudice against this ethnic group when they had to interact with them (Krings & Olivares, 2007), or when competition was in a nontechnical domain and the criteria for competence were ambiguous and debatable. When the immigrants came with needed technical skills, there was less prejudice against them.

Previous research in the United States has focused on proximity to the US/Mexico border as an important indicator of threat and support for policies targeting immigrants (Binder et al., 1997; Branton et al., 2007; Gravelle, 2018). Branton et al. (2007) and Gravelle (2018) found that both US liberal democrats and right-wing conservatives increase support for restrictive immigration policies, such as building a border wall, as the distance to the border with Mexico decreases. Likewise, Binder et al. (1997) found that White residents living near the border in Texas were more supportive of restrictive policies targeting undocumented immigrants. Gravelle (2018) suggests that border proximity increases perceptions of threat from undocumented immigrants because these residents are more likely to come into contact with border fences, border patrol, and hear about unauthorized immigration on the local news. This research on proximity seems to go against the broad assessment that intergroup contact leads to positive outcomes irrespective of the conditions in which contact takes place (see Pettigrew & Tropp, 2006 for a meta-analytic study on contact theory). The implication is that the conditions Allport (1954) set for the positive outcomes of intergroup contact are still relevant (see Chapter 10 in this book for further discussion on contact).

Concluding Comment

In this chapter we examined the backlash against immigrants in response to globalization, as well as the global move toward deglobalization. We explored the perception that immigrants present a cultural threat to native citizens' traditions, identity, language, and values, and material threat in the form of job competition, resource scarcity, and power. The consequences of these perceived threats have led to a preference for immigrant assimilation, restrictions on accepting asylees and refugees from certain countries, violence against immigrants, and restrictive policies regarding immigrants' rights in the host country. Another consequence of these perceived threats is increased support for extremist White Nationalist movements in Europe and in North America, as well as extremist nationalist movements in some non-Western countries (such as South Africa).

Note that this chapter focused on the *trend* toward deglobalization. Globalization is a complex process encompassing the economy, culture, technology, conflict, disease, politics, and social movements broadly. However, in the twenty-first century it may be impossible for a nation to fully deglobalize and eliminate all outside influences (Paul, 2023). Yet, nationalist policies, such as calls for a return to isolationism and a nativist identity in several African countries (Gordon, 2017), and protectionist policies, such as Brexit and attempts to stem global trade and increase internal production in the United States, continue to be popular (Paul, 2023). Immigration is at the forefront of these globalization fears and the anti-globalization movement as backlash against immigrants due to economic and cultural repercussions clash with population decreases, a need for laborers, and push factors such as climate change and political instability. In the preceding chapters we have reviewed how identity, trust, and the influence of other cultures through globalization affects attitudes against immigrants. In this next section of chapters we examine this conflict between deglobalization, identity, and immigration further by focusing on specific regions and nations.

REFERENCES

Abidde, S. O., & Matambo, E. K. (Eds.). (2021). *Xenophobia, nativism and pan-Africanism in twenty-first century Africa: History, concepts, practice and case study*. Springer.

Al-Rawashdeh, M. S. (2014). The impact of globalization on the political culture of the Arab youths. *Journal of Middle Eastern and Islamic Studies (in Asia)*, *8*(4), 81–120. https://doi.org/10.1080/19370679.2014.12023250

Alba, R., Rumbaut, R. G., & Marotz, K. (2005). A distorted nation: Perceptions of racial/ethnic group sizes and attitudes toward immigrants and other minorities. *Social Forces*, *84*(2), 901–919. https://doi.org/10.1353/sof.2006.0002

Allport, G. W. (1954). *The nature of prejudice*. Addison-Wesley.

Arau, S. (Director). (2004, May 14). *A day without a Mexican* [Comedy]. Eye On The Ball Films, Instituto Mexicano de Cinematografía, Jose and Friends Inc., Plural Entertainment, RTG Productions.

Ariely, G. (2021). State of nationalism (SON): Nationalism and globalization. *Studies on National Movements*, *8*, 1–14.

Badea, C., Iyer, A., & Aebischer, V. (2018). National identification, endorsement of acculturation ideologies and prejudice: The impact of the perceived threat of immigration. *International Review of Social Psychology*, *31*(1), 14. https://doi.org/10.5334/irsp.147

Baerg, N. R., Hotchkiss, J. L., & Quispe-Agnoli, M. (2014). *Unauthorized immigration, fiscal conservatism, and partisan support for the republicans* [MPRA Paper No. 64839,]. https://mpra.ub.uni-muenchen.de/id/eprint/64936

Ben-Nun Bloom, P., Arikan, G., & Lahav, G. (2015). The effect of perceived cultural and material threats on ethnic preferences in immigration attitudes. *Ethnic and Racial Studies*, *38*(10), 1760–1778. https://doi.org/10.1080/01419870.2015.1015581

Bessudnov, A. (2016). Ethnic hierarchy and public attitudes toward immigrants in Russia. *European Sociological Review*, *32*(5), 567–580. https://doi.org/10.1093/esr/jcw002

Bier, D. J. (2022, September 14). Fentanyl is smuggled for US citizens by US citizens, not asylum seekers [Cato Institute]. *Cato at Liberty*. www.cato.org/blog/fentanyl-smuggled-us-citizens-us-citizens-not-asylum-seekers

Binder, N. E., Polinard, J. L., & Wrinkle, R. D. (1997). Mexican American and Anglo attitudes toward immigration reform: A view from the border. *Social Science Quarterly*, *78*(2), 324–337.

Bongiorno, J. (2024, April 30). Canada is scaling back temporary foreign workers. Critics say the program needs an overhaul. *CBC News*. www.cbc.ca/news/canada/montreal/temporary-foreign-workers-reduction-rights-permanent-status-1.7155233

Bose, P. S. (2018). Welcome and hope, fear, and loathing: The politics of refugee resettlement in Vermont. *Peace and Conflict: Journal of Peace Psychology*, *24*(3), 320–329. https://doi.org/10.1037/pac0000302

Boundless Immigration. (2022, November 30). Migrant worker controversy behind the scenes of Qatar's World Cup: Boundless dives into the migrant workforce controversy surrounding the World Cup. *Boundless Immigration.* www.boundless.com/blog/qatar-world-cup-migrant-workers/#:~: text=Qatar%27s%20population%20also%20increased%20by,country% 20to%20fill%20open%20positions.

Brader, T., Valentino, N. A., & Suhay, E. (2008). What triggers public opposition to immigration? Anxiety, group cues, and immigration threat. *American Journal of Political Science, 52*(4), 959–978. https://doi.org/10.1111/j.1540-5907.2008.00353.x

Branton, R., Dillingham, G., Dunaway, J., & Miller, B. (2007). Anglo voting on nativist ballot initiatives: The partisan impact of spatial proximity to the US-Mexico border. *Social Science Quarterly, 88*(3), 882–897.

Cabaniss, E. R., & Cameron, A. E. (2018). Toward a social psychological understanding of migration and assimilation. *Humanity & Society, 42*(2), 171–192. https://doi.org/10.1177/0160597617716963

Callens, M.-S., & Meuleman, B. (2017). Do integration policies relate to economic and cultural threat perceptions? A comparative study in Europe. *International Journal of Comparative Sociology, 58*(5), 367–391. https://doi.org/10.1177/0020715216665437

Campbell, D. T. (1965). Ethnocentrism and other altruistic motives. In D. Levine, (Eds.), *Nebraska symposium on motivation* (Vol. 13, pp. 283–311). University of Nebraska Press.

Cervantes, A. G., Alvord, D., & Menjívar, C. (2018). "Bad hombres": The effects of criminalizing Latino immigrants through law and media in the rural Midwest. *Migration Letters, 15*(2), 182–196. https://doi.org/10.33182/ml.v15i2.368

Chand, D. E., & Schreckhise, W. D. (2015). Secure communities and community values: Local context and discretionary immigration law enforcement. *Journal of Ethnic and Migration Studies, 41*(10), 1621–1643. https://doi.org/10.1080/1369183X.2014.986441

Craig, M. A., & Richeson, J. A. (2017). Information about the US racial demographic shift triggers concerns about anti-White discrimination among the prospective White "minority." *PLOS ONE, 12*(9), e0185389. https://doi.org/10.1371/journal.pone.0185389

Daghrir, W. (2013). Globalization as Americanization? Beyond the conspiracy theory. *IOSR Journal of Applied Physics, 5*(?), 19–24.

Dambrun, M., Taylor, D. M., McDonald, D. A., Crush, J., & Méot, A. (2006). The relative deprivation–gratification continuum and the attitudes of South Africans toward immigrants: A test of the V-curve hypothesis. *Journal of Personality and Social Psychology, 91*(6), 1032–1044. https://doi.org/10.1037/0022-3514.91.6.1032

Danbold, F., & Huo, Y. J. (2015). No longer "All-American"? Whites' defensive reactions to their numerical decline. *Social Psychological and Personality Science, 6*(2), 210–218. https://doi.org/10.1177/1948550614546355

Diaz, J., & Zirkel, S. (2012). Globalization, psychology, and social issues research: An introduction and conceptual framework. *Journal of Social Issues, 68*(3), 439–453.

Dollard, J., Bood, L., Miller, N., Mowrer, O., & Sears, R. (1939). *Frustration and aggression*. Yale University Press.

Dube, G. (2017). Levels of othering: The case of Zimbabwean migrants in South Africa. *Nationalism and Ethnic Politics, 23*(4), 391–412. https://doi.org/10.1080/13537113.2017.1380458

(2019). Black South Africans' attitudes toward African immigrants between 2008 and 2016. *Nationalism and Ethnic Politics, 25*(2), 191–210. https://doi.org/10.1080/13537113.2019.1602372

Emeriau, M. (2022). Learning to be unbiased: Evidence from the French asylum office. *American Journal of Political Science, 67*(4), 1117–1133. https://doi.org/10.1111/ajps.12720

Enos, R. D. (2017). *The space between us: Social geography and politics*. Cambridge University Press.

Esposito, A. (2022, September 14). The limitations of humanity: Differential refugee treatment in the EU. *Harvard International Review*. https://hir.harvard.edu/the-limitations-of-humanity-differential-refugee-treatment-in-the-eu/#:~:text=How%20are%20Ukrainian%20and%20non,no%20official%20asylum%20approval%20necessary.

Frey, A. (2021). Getting under the skin: The impact of terrorist attacks on native and immigrant sentiment. *Social Forces, 101*(2), 943–973. https://doi.org/10.1093/sf/soab135

Gelfand, M. J., Lyons, S. L., & Lun, J. (2011). Toward a psychological science of globalization. *Journal of Social Issues, 67*(4), 841–853.

Gemignani, M., & Hernandez-Albujar, Y. (2015). Hate groups targeting unauthorized immigrants in the US: Discourses, narratives and subjectivation practices on their websites. *Ethnic and Racial Studies, 38*(15), 2754–2770. https://doi.org/10.1080/01419870.2015.1058967

Gentry, B., Daukei, R., Sotelo, L., & Chambers, S. N. (2023). *Out of sight and out of mind: An interpretative human rights report on US-Mexico border violence under MPP and Title 42*. Indigenous Alliance without Borders, Center for Mexican Studies, Latin American Institute. www.indigenousalliance.org/_files/ugd/7c2cd7_a4025398ffce42aca2dacc06fc6e995d.pdf

Gordon, S. (2015). Xenophobia across the class divide: South African attitudes toward foreigners 2003–2012. *Journal of Contemporary African Studies, 33*(4), 494–509. https://doi.org/10.1080/02589001.2015.1122870

(2017). A desire for isolation? mass public attitudes in South Africa toward immigration levels. *Journal of Immigrant & Refugee Studies, 15*(1), 18–35. https://doi.org/10.1080/15562948.2016.1151096

Gorodzeisky, A., & Semyonov, M. (2019). Unwelcome immigrants: Sources of opposition to different immigrant groups among Europeans. *Frontiers in Sociology, 4*, 1–10. https://doi.org/10.3389/fsoc.2019.00024

Gravelle, T. B. (2018). Politics, time, space, and attitudes toward US–Mexico border security. *Political Geography, 65*, 107–116. https://doi.org/10.1016/j.polgeo.2018.05.012

Hangartner, D., Dinas, E., Marbach, M., Matakos, K., & Xefteris, D. (2019). Does exposure to the refugee crisis make natives more hostile? *American Political Science Review, 113*(2), 442–455. https://doi.org/10.1017/S0003055418000813

Harell, A., Soroka, S., & Iyengar, S. (2017). Locus of control and anti-immigrant sentiment in Canada, the United States, and the United Kingdom. *Political Psychology, 38*(2), 245–260. https://doi.org/10.1111/pops.12338

Hartman, T. K., Newman, B. J., & Scott Bell, C. (2014). Decoding prejudice toward Hispanics: Group cues and public reactions to threatening immigrant behavior. *Political Behavior, 36*(1), 143–163. https://doi.org/10.1007/s11109-013-9231-7

Hatungimana, W. (2023). Expectation and disconfirmation: Dissatisfaction influence on attitude toward immigrants in South Africa. *Ethnic and Racial Studies*, 1–27. https://doi.org/10.1080/01419870.2023.2248295

Hellwig, T., & Sinno, A. (2017). Different groups, different threats: Public attitudes toward immigrants. *Journal of Ethnic and Migration Studies, 43*(3), 339–358. https://doi.org/10.1080/1369183X.2016.1202749

Hendricks, M. J. (2022). National identity and immigration: Threat from undocumented immigrants in the United States. In F. M. Moghaddam & M. J. Hendricks (Eds.), *Contemporary immigration: Psychological perspectives to address challenges and inform solutions*. American Psychological Association.

Hood III, M. V., & Morris, I. L. (1998). Give us your tired, your poor, ... but make sure they have a green card: The effects of documented and undocumented migrant context on Anglo opinion toward immigration. *Political Behavior, 20*(1), 1–15. https://doi.org/10.1023/A:1024839032001

Hopkins, D. J. (2010). Politicized places: Explaining where and when immigrants provoke local opposition. *American Political Science Review, 104*, 40–60. https://doi.org/doi:10.1017/S0003055409990360

Human Rights First. (2023). *Extremism fact sheet: Xenophobia and anti-immigrant extremism: From fringe to mainstream*. Human Rights First. https://humanrightsfirst.org/wp-content/uploads/2023/03/FINAL-Xenaphobia-2023.pdf

Human Rights Watch. (2023, June 16). *Qatar: Six months post-World Cup, migrant workers suffer: FIFA/Qatari authorities paid no compensation, silent on wage theft*. Human Rights Watch. www.hrw.org/news/2023/06/16/qatar-six-months-post-world-cup-migrant-workers-suffer

Hummel, D. (2016). Immigrant-friendly and unfriendly cities: Impacts on the presence of a foreign-born population and city crime. *Journal of International Migration and Integration, 17*(4), 1211–1230. https://doi.org/10.1007/s12134-015-0464-7

Immigration History. (n.d.). *Muslim travel ban*. Immigration History. https://immigrationhistory.org/item/muslim-travel-ban/

James, H. (2017). *Deglobalization as a global challenge* (135; CIGI Papers, pp. 1–11). Centre for International Governance Innovation.

Jones-Correa, M. (2011). *All immigration is local: Receiving communities and their role in successful immigrant integration* [Reports]. Center for American Progress. https://search.proquest.com/docview/1820700383?accountid=11091

Jost, J. T., Banaji, M. R., & Nosek, B. A. (2004). A decade of system justification theory: Accumulated evidence of conscious and unconscious bolstering of the status quo. *Political Psychology*, *25*(6), 881–919. https://doi.org/10.1111/j.1467-9221.2004.00402.x

Kawasaki, R. K., & Ikeda, Y. (2020). Network analysis of attitudes toward immigrants in Asia. *Applied Network Science*, *5*(1), 85. https://doi.org/10.1007/s41109-020-00315-w

Khawaja, I., Christensen, T. W., & Lerche Mørck, L. (2023). Dehumanization and a psychology of deglobalization: Double binds and movements beyond radicalization and racialized mis-interpellation. *Theory & Psychology*, *33*(2), 249–265. https://doi.org/10.1177/09593543221138541

Kil, H., Noels, K. A., Vargas Lascano, D. I., & Schweickart, O. (2019). English Canadians' cultural stereotypes of ethnic minority groups: Implications of stereotype content for acculturation ideologies and immigration attitudes. *International Journal of Intercultural Relations*, *70*, 104–118. https://doi.org/10.1016/j.ijintrel.2019.03.005

Kinnvall, C., & Kisić Merino, P. (2023). Deglobalization and the political psychology of white supremacy. *Theory & Psychology*, *33*(2), 227–248. https://doi.org/10.1177/09593543221138535

Krings, F., & Olivares, J. (2007). At the doorstep to employment: Discrimination against immigrants as a function of applicant ethnicity, job type, and raters' prejudice. *International Journal of Psychology*, *42*(6), 406–417. https://doi.org/10.1080/00207590701251721

Kunst, J. R., Dovidio, J. F., & Dotsch, R. (2018). White lookalikes: Mainstream culture adoption makes immigrants "look" phenotypically White. *Personality and Social Psychology Bulletin*, *44*(2), 265–282. https://doi.org/10.1177/0146167217739279

Levinson-King, R. (2022, November 22). *Canada: Why the country wants to bring in 1.5m immigrants by 2025*. BBC News. www.bbc.com/news/world-us-canada-63643912

López-Rodríguez, L., Navas, M., Cuadrado, I., Coutant, D., & Worchel, S. (2014). The majority's perceptions about adaptation to the host society of different immigrant groups: The distinct role of warmth and threat. *International Journal of Intercultural Relations*, *40*, 34–48. https://doi.org/10.1016/j.ijintrel.2014.02.001

Martinez, L. M., & Ortega, D. M. (2019). Dreams deterred: The collateral consequences of localized immigration policies on undocumented Latinos in Colorado. *Law & Policy*, *41*(1), 120–141. https://doi.org/10.1111/lapo.12118

Mashuri, A., Burhan, O. K., & Van Leeuwen, E. (2013). The impact of multiculturalism on immigrant helping. *Asian Journal of Social Psychology, 16*(3), 207–212. https://doi.org/10.1111/ajsp.12009

Merle, R. (2018, September 10). A guide to the financial crisis—10 years later. *The Washington Post.* www.washingtonpost.com/business/economy/a-guide-to-the-financial-crisis-10-years-later/2018/09/10/114b76ba-af10-11e8-a20b-5f4f84429666_story.html

Migration Information Source. (2019). *Top migration issues of 2019.* Migration Policy Institute. www.migrationpolicy.org/programs/migration-information-source/top-10-migration-issues-2019

Mlambo, D. N. (2021). South Africa and the challenge of xenophobia post-democratisation: A united Africa deterred. *African Journal of Peace and Conflict Studies, 10*(1), 33–50. https://doi.org/10.31920/2634-3665/2021/v10n1a2

Moghaddam, F. M. (2008). *Multiculturalism and intergroup relations: Psychological implications for democracy in global context.* American Psychological Association.

(2019). *Threat to democracy: The appeal of authoritarianism in an age of uncertainty.* American Psychological Association.

Moghaddam, F. M., & Perreault, S. (1992). Individual and collective mobility strategies among minority group members. *The Journal of Social Psychology, 132*(3), 343–357. https://doi.org/10.1080/00224545.1992.9924710

Murray, K. E., & Marx, D. M. (2013). Attitudes toward unauthorized immigrants, authorized immigrants, and refugees. *Cultural Diversity and Ethnic Minority Psychology, 19*(3), 332–341. https://doi.org/10.1037/a0030812

Neureiter, M. (2022). The effect of immigrant integration policies on public immigration attitudes: Evidence from a survey experiment in the United Kingdom. *International Migration Review, 56*(4), 1040–1068. https://doi.org/10.1177/01979183211063499

Ngobeni, M. (2022). Narratives of xenophobia at a South African university. *Communication, 48*(3), 43–60. https://doi.org/10.1080/02500167.2022.2143835

O'Neil, K., & Tienda, M. (2010). A tale of two counties: Natives' opinions toward immigration in North Carolina. *International Migration Review, 44*(3), 728–761. https://doi.org/10.1111/j.1747-7379.2010.00823.x

Ordway, D.-M. (2017, February 15). The consequences of bilingual employment policies. *The Journalist's Resource.* https://journalistsresource.org/economics/bilingual-employment-policies-spanish-black-people/

Osbeck, L. M., Moghaddam, F. M., & Perreault, S. (1997). Similarity and attraction among majority and minority groups in a multicultural context. *International Journal of Intercultural Relations, 21*(1), 113–123. https://doi.org/10.1016/S0147-1767(96)00016-8

Paul, T. V. (2023). The specter of deglobalization. *Current History, 122*(840), 3–8.

Paxton, P., & Mughan, A. (2006). What's to fear from immigrants? Creating an assimilationist threat scale. *Political Psychology, 27*(4), 549–568.

Pecoraro, M., & Ruedin, D. (2020). Occupational exposure to foreigners and attitudes towards equal opportunities. *Migration Studies*, *8*(3), 382–423. https://doi.org/10.1093/migration/mnz006

Pedroza, J. M. (2019). Deportation discretion: Tiered influence, minority threat, and "secure communities" deportations. *Policy Studies Journal*, *47*(3), 624–646. https://doi.org/10.1111/psj.12300

Peixoto, J. (2012). Back to the south: Social and political aspects of Latin American migration to southern Europe. *International Migration*, *50*(6), 58–82. https://doi.org/10.1111/j.1468-2435.2009.00537.x

Pettigrew, T. F., & Tropp, L. R. (2006). A meta-analytic test of intergroup contact theory. *Journal of Personality and Social Psychology*, *90*(5), 751–783. https://doi.org/10.1037/0022-3514.90.5.751

Pruitt, S. (2023, June 6). *How the Columbian Exchange brought globalization—And disease*. History.Com. www.history.com/news/columbian-exchange-impact-diseases

Ramsay, J. E., & Pang, J. S. (2017). Anti-immigrant prejudice in rising East Asia: A stereotype content and integrated threat analysis. *Political Psychology*, *38*(2), 227–244. https://doi.org/10.1111/pops.12312

Rankin, J. (2022, December 8). Migrants face 'unprecedented rise in violence' in EU borders, report finds. *The Guardian*. www.theguardian.com/law/2022/dec/08/migrants-face-unprecedented-rise-in-violence-in-eu-borders-report-finds

Salas-Schweikart, R., Hendricks, M. J., Boychuck, M., & Moghaddam, F. M. (2024). Similarity-attraction across ethnic, religious, and political groups: Does celebrating differences or similarities make a difference?. *The Journal of Social Psychology*, *122*, 1–20.

S&P Global. (n.d.). *The evolution of deglobalization*. S&P Global. www.spglobal.com/en/enterprise/geopolitical-risk/evolution-of-deglobalization/

Sewell, A. A. (2017). The (un)intended consequences of bilingual employment policies: Ethnoraciality and labor market segmentation in Alameda County, CA. *Du Bois Review: Social Science Research on Race*, *14*(1), 117–143. https://doi.org/10.1017/S1742058X16000345

Sherif, M. (1966). *Group conflict and cooperation: Their social psychology*. Routledge & Kegan Paul.

Stephan, W. G., Ybarra, O., Martinez, C. M., Schwarzwald, J., & Tur-Kaspa, M. (1998). Prejudice toward immigrants to Spain and Israel: An integrated threat theory analysis. *Journal of Cross-Cultural Psychology*, *29*(4), 559–576.

Stupi, E. K., Chiricos, T., & Gertz, M. (2016). Perceived criminal threat from undocumented immigrants: Antecedents and consequences for policy preferences. *Justice Quarterly*, *33*(2), 239–266. https://doi.org/10.1080/07418825.2014.902093

Tartakovsky, E., & Walsh, S. D. (2016). Testing a new theoretical model for attitudes toward immigrants: The case of social workers' attitudes toward asylum seekers in Israel. *Journal of Cross-Cultural Psychology*, *47*(1), 72–96. https://doi.org/10.1177/0022022115613860

Valentino, N. A., Brader, T., & Jardina, A. E. (2013). Immigration opposition among U.S. Whites: General ethnocentrism or media priming of attitudes about Latinos? *Political Psychology*, *34*(2), 149–166. https://doi.org/10.1111/j.1467-9221.2012.00928.x

Watson, B. R., & Riffe, D. (2013). Perceived threat, immigration policy support, and media coverage: Hostile media and presumed influence. *International Journal of Public Opinion Research*, *25*(4), 459–479. https://doi.org/10.1093/ijpor/eds032

Watson, K., & Hudak, Z. (2023, July 7). *Trump says he'd bring bag "travel ban" that's "even bigger than before."* CBS News. www.cbsnews.com/news/trump-bring-back-travel-ban-muslim-countries/

Whitaker, B. E. (2020). Refugees, foreign nationals, and Wageni: Comparing African responses to Somali migration. *African Studies Review*, *63*(1), 18–42.

Zou, L. X., & Cheryan, S. (2017). Two axes of subordination: A new model of racial position. *Journal of Personality and Social Psychology*, *112*(5), 696–717. https://doi.org/10.1037/pspa0000080

PART II

The Immigration Challenge and National Identity

Introduction to Part II

Immigration and National Identity: A Global Challenge

June 20th is recognized as World Refugee Day and is celebrated across multiple countries all over the world in honor of people who have left their homes to escape conflict and persecution, to seek refuge in another nation (UNHCR US, 2024). On June 20th, 2024 a special celebration for World Refugee Day took place at the Department of Homeland Security, United States Citizenship and Immigration Services (DHS/USCIS) Agency Headquarters that included a naturalization ceremony at which 15 refugees and asylees took the oath of allegiance to become citizens of the United States. The Deputy Director of USCIS Jennifer Higgins (a former refugee officer herself) was in attendance. Following these newest citizens' pledge, Deputy Director Higgins gave a speech where she recognized these former refugees and asylees (and newest citizens) as her fellow Americans. Thereby proclaiming their national identity.

National identity is defined as a collective identity that groups people together (Guibernau, 2001). It is often exclusive and determined by the majority or dominant group in society (see Chapter 2 in this book for a discussion on the majority dominance over national identity). Yet, national identity is also dynamic. As discussed in Chapter 4, globalization and migration can lead to increased backlash against immigrants and a call for deglobalization and return to "the way things were." Globalization highlights the differences and similarities between cultures; hardening boundaries between nations, peoples, and cultures (Bast & Orgad, 2017). Contact with other cultures and new groups of immigrants can reinforce the importance of national identity, and also contribute to its evolution (Ariely, 2021).

Social identity theory posits that the value and status of the social group that an individual identifies with is in part based on comparisons with other social groups. Individuals who are satisfied with the status of their social identity will strive to keep it that way (Tajfel & Turner, 1979). As such, globally there is a preference for immigrants who are perceived as similar in appearance and culture to the native citizens (Moghaddam, 2012), immigrants who will not change or alter the national identity, but who will instead fit in. Ultimately, national identity provides a sense of belonging, but importantly also determines *who* belongs and *who* does not (Doty, 1996).

Boundaries of Belonging
Citizenship is often tied to national identity. Being a citizen of a certain country is included on most questionnaires assessing people's attitudes and beliefs about national identity, and is considered an important item (Hendricks, 2022; Sheppard, 2015). Yet, being a citizen of a country either through birth or via naturalization does not always equal national belonging or lead to the perception of such, by oneself or others. Naturalization ceremonies (at least in the United States) such as the one described above usually include cultural or symbolic components. The ceremonies often take place on a special holiday like World Refugee Day, World Immigration Day, or Independence Day, or highlight an aspect of their new national culture, with a ceremony taking place during a sports game or in front of a national monument. In every ceremony, the Pledge of Allegiance to the United States is recited, the national anthem is performed, and a speech is always given where the administrator who leads the oath of allegiance proclaims the new citizens as their fellow Americans. While legally this is true, simply gaining citizenship does not mean that everyone (including oneself) will see these citizens as true Americans. Ultimately, there are legal ties that can bind you to a nation, that can give you rights and duties, based on birthplace, ancestry, or naturalization, but one's national identity is subjective and based on both a collective and individual sense of belonging (Ariely, 2021). Belonging is often based outside of legal status and documentation, and instead relies on factors much harder to obtain.

Beyond legal status, national identity is often determined or defined by ethnicity (phenotype), language, and religion, all of which can be highly visible in society. It is also based on common values, customs, traditions, and culture – societal norms that guide the nation (Hendricks, 2022; Sheppard, 2015). As Native American historian David Treuer stated,

"We with our fixation on blood have forgotten that bending to a common purpose is more important than coming from a common place" (2011). However, values have often been established by the majority ethnic group in power and thus are hard to disentangle from ethnicity and other visible indicators. In South America, White Europeans largely colonized the continent, and thus established the dominant culture, which is often at ends with the Indigenous populations there (see Chapter 7). The United States national identity was also largely formed on the values of White Protestants of European descent (Schildkraut, 2014). Experimental research studies have generally found that White Americans are seen as more American than other ethnic groups in the United States (e.g., Huynh et al., 2015; Kunst et al., 2018; Schachter, 2016).

Yet, national identity is continuously evolving. These boundaries of belonging are not impermeable for some. In fact, in the United States Americans of Irish and German descent are perceived as being White, as part of the dominant majority group of Americans (Zou & Cheryan, 2017), the first anti-immigrant group in the United States, the "Know Nothing" party, was formed with prejudice against Catholics, primarily Irish and German immigrants. Founding Father Benjamin Franklin too felt the arrival of large numbers of "swarthy" German immigrants would threaten the American colonial culture and language (Lee, 2021). The need to control diversity and maintain a homogenous culture, can lead to greater inclusion, such as the broadening of the "White" ethnic category in the United States to include people of German, Irish, Italian, Polish, and Russian heritage (del Mar Farina, 2018), but it can also lead to backlash and greater exclusion as discussed in Chapter 4. While these "White" immigrants were accepted and became naturalized American citizens (Lee, 2021), others have not been so fortunate and are still less accepted today (see Chapter 5 for a review on perceptions and acceptance of Latinx immigrants and citizens in the United States). As new groups of seemingly dissimilar immigrants arrive, they must conform to the host society's norms if they are to be seen to belong.

Control Immigration, Control the National Identity
When you control immigration, you control national identity. The contemporary global rise in nationalism and anti-immigrant sentiment can be tied to the fear that the current immigrants arriving in host countries do not share the same identity as the native citizens, nor are they able to fully integrate and adapt to the national identity and culture (Moghaddam, 2019).

There are several methods nations use to attempt to control immigration. Some methods involve limiting who is able to immigrate, this is often done through national quotas or caps, for example, the United States limits the number of immigrants from any one country that can receive lawful permanent residency (i.e., green cards) or certain employment-based and family-sponsored visas (Gelatt, 2019). Australia, Canada, and New Zealand use a points-based system, whereby prospective immigrants are awarded points based on factors like professional skills, work experience, education, and language proficiency. Those with the most points are considered most likely to successfully integrate and support the economy (Papademetriou & Hooper, 2019).

Further policies have been set that prevent immigrants from certain countries immigrating to the United States entirely, such as the "Muslim Travel Ban" under the Trump administration. Other methods involve giving temporary visas to certain immigrants, essentially preventing them from receiving citizenship and becoming permanent members of society, such as Canada's temporary foreign worker program (see Chapter 4 in this book). Further, countries in Europe have policies of forced assimilation to ensure they can fit in with societal norms before they can become citizens, in some cases requiring assimilation tests (see Chapter 6). We examine the impact of immigration on national identity, attempts to control national identity and attitudes towards immigrants in the context of changing identity in the following three chapters through the lens of the United States, Europe, and South America.

Though there are typically a set of common ideals and traditions from which people form their national identity, how someone describes their national identity can vary from person to person. Through an experimental study, Chapter 5 explores the division in American national identity and the impact this has on attitudes towards undocumented immigration, which is not controlled by traditional legal immigration pathways. We find that while some participants had a more open view of what it means to be American, others endorsed a more traditional view. Importantly, these differences in opinion over American identity influenced opinions on undocumented immigrants, suggesting there is division in the majority opinion over who belongs.

While the American identity appears to be divided, the European identity could be described as under construction. The European identity is made up of many individual nation states with their own national identities which creates conflict with a broader European national identity as well as opinions over how to manage immigration. The increased diversity and increase in ethnic minority immigrants are changing what "European" is, not only in terms of changing demographics but how native citizens wish to deal with diversity brought on from the immigrant population – embrace or rebel.

Finally, Chapter 7 discusses identity and immigration management in South America. South American countries have largely been shaped by European colonization and the continued European immigration into the twentieth century. Currently, however, migration in South America is intraregional, with most immigrants arriving from neighboring countries. This chapter discusses the impact this has on immigrant integration, and the identity of the continent. The increase in intraregional migration has led the countries to adopt multicultural policies, thus embracing and acknowledging diversity inherent in their collective identity. Yet, far from equal, many countries struggle with ethnic and economic inequality. Further, still many face discrimination and high levels of anti-immigrant sentiment.

Concluding Comment

Managing and maintaining national identity is a global challenge that is not going away anytime soon. Immigration policies and immigrant integration have both been shaped by perceptions of national identity and has influence over national identity. We explore this interaction further in the following three chapters through the lens of the United States, Europe, and South America, before discussing past and recent policies and theories to immigrant integration broadly.

REFERENCES

Ariely, G. (2021). State of nationalism (SON): Nationalism and globalization. ' *Studies on National Movements, 8*, 1–14.

Bast, J., & Orgad, L. (2017). Constitutional identity in the age of global migration. *German Law Journal, 18*(7), 1587–1594. https://doi.org/10.1017/S2071832200022446

del Mar Farina, M. (2018). *White nativism, ethnic identity and US immigration policy reforms: American citizenship and children in mixed status, Hispanic families*. Routledge.

Doty, R. L. (1996). Immigration and national identity: Constructing the nation. *Review of International Studies, 22*, 235–255.

Gelatt, J. (2019, April). *Explainer: How the U.S. legal immigration system works*. Migration Policy Institute. www.migrationpolicy.org/content/explainer-how-us-legal-immigration-system-works

Guibernau, M. (2001). Globalization and the nation-state. In M. Guibernau & J. Hutchinson (Eds.), *Understanding nationalism* (pp. 242–268). Cambridge University Press.

Hendricks, M. J. (2022). *The undocumented immigrant challenge to American identity* [Doctoral Dissertation, Georgetown University]. http://hdl.handle.net/10822/1064704

Huynh, Q.-L., Devos, T., & Altman, H. R. (2015). Boundaries of American identity: Relations between ethnic group prototypicality and policy attitudes. *Political Psychology, 36*(4), 449–468. https://doi.org/10.1111/pops.12189

Kunst, J. R., Dovidio, J. F., & Dotsch, R. (2018). White lookalikes: Mainstream culture adoption makes immigrants "look" phenotypically White. *Personality and Social Psychology Bulletin, 44*(2), 265–282. https://doi.org/10.1177/0146167217739279

Lee, E. (2021). *America for Americans: A history of xenophobia in the United States*. Basic Books. 2nd ed.

Moghaddam, F. M. (2012). The omnicultural imperative. *Culture & Psychology, 18*(3), 304–330. https://doi.org/10.1177/1354067X12446230

(2019). *Threat to democracy: The appeal of authoritarianism in an age of uncertainty*. American Psychological Association.

Papademetriou, D. G., & Hooper, K. (2019). *Competing approaches to selecting economic immigrants: Points-based vs. demand-driven systems*. Migration Policy Institute.

Schachter, A. (2016). From "different" to "similar": An experimental approach to understanding assimilation. *American Sociological Review, 81*(5), 981–1013. https://doi.org/10.1177/0003122416659248

Schildkraut, D. J. (2014). Boundaries of American identity: Evolving understandings of "us." *Annual Review of Political Science, 17*(1), 441–460. https://doi.org/10.1146/annurev-polisci-080812-144642

Sheppard, J. (2015). *Australian attitudes towards national identity: Citizenship, immigration and tradition* (18; ANUPOLL, pp. 1–15). Australian Centre for Applied Social Research Methods, Anu College of Arts and Social Sciences. https://csrm.cass.anu.edu.au/sites/default/files/docs/ANUpoll-national-identity-042015_0.pdf

Tajfel, H., & Turner, J. C. (1979). An integrative theory of intergroup conflict. In W. G. Austin & S. Worchel (Eds.), *The Social Psychology of Intergroup Relations* (pp. 33–47). Brooks/Cole.

Treuer, D. (2011, December 20). How do you prove you're an Indian? *The New York Times.* www.nytimes.com/2011/12/21/opinion/for-indian-tribes-blood-shouldnt-be-everything.html

UNHCR US. (2024). *World Refugee Day*. UNHCR The UN Refugee Agency. www.unhcr.org/us/world-refugee-day

Zou, L. X., & Cheryan, S. (2017). Two axes of subordination: A new model of racial position. *Journal of Personality and Social Psychology, 112*(5), 696–717. https://doi.org/10.1037/pspa0000080

CHAPTER 5

Immigration and American Identity
The Undocumented Challenge

In the twenty-first century immigration is seen as a major force of disruption and change, even in historically immigrant-receiving societies such as the United States. Public opinion toward immigrants has become increasingly divisive in recent decades (Livi-Bacci, 2012). This contemporary global rise in anti-immigrant sentiment can be tied to the fear that immigrants do not share the same identity as the native-born citizens (Moghaddam, 2019). An important part of this opposition over immigration is about controlling who is authorized to immigrate in an attempt to manage and give shape to the identity of the nation (Livi-Bacci, 2012). However, not all immigrants receive authorization to enter or live in a country. Authorized statuses include naturalized US citizens, lawful permanent residents (i.e., green card holders), temporary visa holders (e.g., foreign students), and humanitarian migrants (e.g., refugees and asylees; United States Census Bureau, 2021). Unauthorized or undocumented statuses refer to people who enter and reside in the United States without authorization. Some undocumented immigrants (approximately 30 percent) are waiting for their lawful permanent resident application to be approved, have temporary protected status, or DACA. However, most have entered the United States without authorization or overstayed the departure date on their temporary visa (Passel & Krogstad, 2024).

Chavez (2007) states that the approximately 11 million undocumented immigrants in the United States experience "simultaneous processes of inclusion and exclusion" (p. 193). Undocumented immigrants do not have the right to work in the United States, but often employers overlook this in order to take advantage of cheap and exploitable labor (De Genova, 2004; Maciel & Knudson-Martin, 2014). There are undocumented immigrants who are afforded more opportunities depending on the state they live in, such as attending college, earning money in white collar jobs, and having a driver's license (Castañeda & Melo, 2019; Valdivia, 2019). However, most undocumented workers in the United States occupy low-wage, blue-collar jobs in which they are paid under the table (De Genova, 2004; Maciel & Knudson-Martin, 2014).

Policies concerning the 11 million undocumented immigrants in the United States change in some respects with every new federal government administration. Likewise, there are differences in public opinion across the United States over undocumented immigrants' rights and enforcement decisions (Morse, 2021; Valdivia, 2019). These differing policies toward undocumented immigrants indicate the competing perspectives over undocumented immigration and their rights in the United States. The broad targeting of various aspects of these undocumented immigrants' lives reflects on a larger issue of not only who gets to be an American, but also competing beliefs about the requirements for being an American, as well as the nature of American identity.

American identity was founded not by people coming from a common place and shared bloodlines, but for a common purpose. Yet recent studies and public opinion polls have shown these shared ideals (e.g., individualism, hard work, liberty, equality of opportunity, and rule of law) are not so common across the United States (Hanson & O'Dwyer, 2019). There is polarization and division in beliefs regarding America's history, present, and future. It is important to not only examine how people feel toward an outgroup (undocumented immigrants), but also how they feel toward or associate themselves with their own group (Americans/US citizens; Wright, 2019) and the effect this has on attitudes toward undocumented immigrants.

This chapter examines the relationship between beliefs about American identity and beliefs regarding undocumented immigrants. The underlying theme is the shaping of American identity in relation to what is considered as *not* being American. In the first section, we provide an overview of undocumented immigration in the United States and the current research on attitudes toward undocumented immigrants. The second section explores the construct of American identity and the increasingly heated divisions on what exactly is national identity in the United States. Related to this, we discuss findings from a recent research study examining the relationship between prejudice against undocumented immigrants and beliefs about characteristics of true Americans and strength of American identity. The chapter concludes with a discussion of the impact of relationship between prejudice against undocumented immigrants in the United States and American identity.

Perceptions of and Attitudes toward Undocumented Immigrants in the United States

Approximately 11 million undocumented immigrants live across the United States (Passel & Krogstad, 2024). Some states and counties where undocumented immigrants live have laws that provide them with some protections, while others treat them with open hostility (Ellis et al., 2016; Hummel, 2016). Yet even in areas with hostile immigration policies and heavy enforcement of laws concerning undocumented immigrants, such as cooperative agreements between local law enforcement and the US Immigration and Customs Enforcement agency (ICE), some undocumented individuals and families continue to survive (Abrego, 2011; Ellis et al., 2016).

Individuals with limited English, low levels of formal education, and who work in the informal sector where legal documentation is often not required (Flores & Schachter, 2018; Wright et al., 2016), are highly associated with illegality. At the same time, research examining the perception of the undocumented immigrant population in the United States has found that Latinx ethnicity is the most important factor in perceiving whether someone is undocumented (Flores & Schachter, 2018). While people of Latin America do comprise the majority of the undocumented immigrant population in the United States (approximately 71 percent), they are not the only undocumented immigrants. The past three decades have seen a growing diversity of this population in the United States. For example, the number of Mexican undocumented immigrants, who make up the largest portion of undocumented immigrants, has declined by about 28 percent in the past decade. Further, undocumented immigrants of Asian origin account for 15 percent of the undocumented population, while undocumented immigrants from Europe and Canada account for 7 percent of the population (Passel & Krogstad, 2024).

Despite this growing diversity, Latinx undocumented immigrants remain the undocumented immigrant group most discriminated against by White (non-Hispanic) US citizens (Unzueta Carrasco & Seif, 2014). State and local hostile anti-immigrant policies and proposals have largely been enacted in the last two decades in areas with high rates of Latinx immigrants, regardless of individuals' legal status or citizenship (e.g., Ellis et al., 2016; Serrano-Careaga & Huo, 2019). For example, policies targeting undocumented immigrants perceived as dangerous criminals have largely been enacted in areas with large Latinx populations or near the US/Mexico border – but not in areas with high crime rates (Collingwood & O'Brien Gonzalez, 2019).

While the policies discussed above indicate the prominence of ethnicity in driving opposition toward undocumented immigrants, research examining attitudes toward undocumented immigrants of various origins suggest differing results. In considering which undocumented immigrants should be granted citizenship, Wright et al. (2016) found that most people made the decision categorically based on their own moral reasoning, either completely agreeing that they should be granted citizenship or completely disagreeing (see also Levy & Wright, 2016b). In another study assessing White Americans' attitudes toward potential neighbors, Schachter (2016) found that the legal status of the potential neighbor was most important, and White undocumented immigrants were rated as significantly less similar than White native-born and naturalized citizens, and legal immigrants.

In contrast, in a series of experimental scenarios in Hartman et al. (2014), White American participants rated how serious an offense it was for an immigrant to (1) overstay their visa, and (2) get paid under the table and not pay taxes on that income. They found that Mexican undocumented immigrants were rated as committing a more serious offense for both, compared to British undocumented immigrants, and an undocumented immigrant of unspecified national origin. These ratings also translated to more support for punitive immigration policies. Knoll et al. (2011) also found that Republican Caucus members in the state of Iowa showed greater support for punitive mass deportation policies for Mexican undocumented immigrants than illegal or undocumented immigrants. Yet, España-Nájera and Vera (2020) found no difference in support for deporting undocumented immigrants from Europe or Latin America among participants from California.

Levy and Wright (2016a) suggest that the bias against Latinx undocumented immigrants may have more to do with the stereotypes associated with Latinx people in the United States rather than a specific bias against undocumented immigrants of Latinx origin. They found that participants were equally likely to support a pathway to legalization for Chinese, German, and Mexican undocumented immigrants if it was known they could speak English and had a stable job. If these characteristics were not known, support for the Mexican undocumented immigrant was significantly lower. Their finding is in line with research by Murray and Marx (2013) suggesting that undocumented immigrants pose a perceived material (e.g., social welfare costs, job competition) and symbolic (e.g., not speaking English, not assimilating to American culture and customs) threat to the American people and their national identity, motivating bias against undocumented immigrants and prejudicial attitudes, such as hostility and rejection.

Further, research has found that participants' own values and political ideologies influence whether they support or oppose undocumented immigrants in the United States. Specifically, Wright et al. (2016) found that politically conservative participants were more likely to categorically oppose a pathway to legalization for all undocumented immigrants, while participants who were liberal and high in egalitarianism (e.g., belief in social equality for all) were more likely to categorically support a pathway to citizenship for all undocumented immigrant profiles in the study. España-Nájera and Vera (2020) too found that registered Republican participants in California were more likely to support deportation for undocumented immigrants.

Similarly, Chand and Schreckhise (2015) determined that jurisdictions engaging in the Secure Communities programs to allow local law enforcement to get involved with immigration investigations were not those with high crime rates. Instead, these communities were more likely to have greater percentages of people supporting the Republican political party and be located near the border. Further, use of the program in these highly Republican communities was generally to increase the number of deportations for undocumented immigrants.

Overall, while people of Latinx ethnicity are more likely to be perceived as undocumented, prejudicial attitudes have more to do with participants' own values and beliefs and less to do with characteristics of the undocumented immigrant. It is important to not only examine how people feel toward an outgroup (undocumented immigrants), but how they feel toward or associate themselves with their own group (Americans/US citizens; Wright, 2019) and the effect this has on attitudes toward undocumented immigrants. In the following section we review the recent research on ingroup identification and outgroup prejudice and provide an overview on the construct of American identity.

Perceptions of the Ingroup: Division in American Identity

Bias is potentially inherent in group membership. At a basic level by simply seeing oneself as belonging to a group, there is a tendency to automatically become positively biased toward the ingroup and negatively biased toward outgroups. This tendency was shown in Muzafer Sherif's (1906–88) classic field research in summer camps (Sherif, 1966), and more precisely demonstrated by Henri Tajfel (1919–1982) and his associates through the minimal group paradigm (Tajfel et al., 1971). Prejudice can often arise from even objectively trivial intergroup differences – confirming stereotypes and increasing discrimination against those considered outside of the ingroup (Cabaniss & Cameron, 2018). However, ingroup favoritism can also occur without outgroup prejudice (Brewer, 2017).

Social identity theory postulates that all individuals seek to belong to social groups that are both positive and distinct in society – as compared to other social groups (Tajfel & Turner, 1979). The idea is that identity is not just about self-categorization into a group, but about comparing your social identity (and therefore ingroup) against others. This comparison is what helps to frame the boundaries between your group's identity and other group identities (Mangum & Block Jr., 2018). Individuals who are satisfied with the status of their social identity are motivated to keep these boundaries (Tajfel & Turner, 1979). Further, research suggests these individuals who strongly identify with their ingroup will strengthen their group loyalty when they perceive threat from those outside of their group (Dovidio et al., 2016; Pérez, 2015).

Immigration is not just a potential threat to individuals but also a potential collective threat at a national level (Young et al., 2018). Empirical research has shown that native-born citizens with strong national identification are more threatened by immigrants (e.g., Badea et al., 2018; Wojcieszak & Garrett, 2018). But few studies have examined the relationship between American identity and attitudes toward undocumented immigrants. For example, Mangum and Block Jr. (2018) found that Americans who identified strongly with being American supported increased security spending to patrol the US/Mexico border in order to prevent undocumented immigration. This finding suggests that those who strongly identify as American oppose undocumented immigration.

However, this relationship of increased ingroup favoritism and outgroup prejudice (or derogation) is not always reciprocal. In her review, Marilynn Brewer (2017) argues that other relationships exist. Ingroup favoritism can occur without outgroup derogation, and outgroup derogation can also occur alone without ingroup favoritism. For example, exposure to national symbols and the desecration of national symbols has been associated with increased ingroup identification and favoritism (Kemmelmeier & Winter, 2008; Wohl et al., 2010), and increased prejudice against outgroups (Becker et al., 2012), but this outgroup derogation is dependent on perceptions of the specific outgroup (Marinthe et al., 2020). Specifically, Marinthe et al. (2020) examined native-born French citizens' reactions to the desecration of their national flag in an experimental scenario by either Irish or German citizens prior to an actual football game against an Irish or German team. They found that reactions were dependent on the outgroup being considered. In the Irish context participants showed only an increase in positive bias toward French citizens, while in the German context participants also showed greater prejudice against non-French citizens, suggesting that perceptions of symbolic threat by German citizens elicited a stronger response.

Hamley et al. (2020) found additional relationships in their study of ethnically European New Zealanders' feelings of warmth toward other ethnically European New Zealanders (ingroup) and feelings of warmth toward Māori New Zealanders (outgroup): Moderate warmth in favor of both the ingroup and outgroup, and low warmth in favor of both the ingroup and outgroup. While they did not examine these biases in response to an experimental scenario manipulating threat to the ingroup, their findings have implications for considering biases under normal conditions. Crucially, Hamley et al. suggest that ingroup warmth is not always inversely related to outgroup warmth, such that positive feelings toward one's ingroup must be associated with negative or neutral feelings toward the outgroup. Instead, for some people, positive feelings for one's ingroup can actually exist alongside positive feelings toward the outgroup.

These variations in ingroup and outgroup relationships with research by Wright et al. (2016) and others finding that participants' own values and political ideals influenced whether they support or oppose undocumented immigrants in the United States. Importantly, research on the construct of American identity has also noted this increasing political divide, such that the traditional values and ideals associated with constructs of American identity may not be characteristic of every American (e.g., Hanson & O'Dwyer, 2019; Schildkraut, 2007). In the next section, we examine common constructs of American identity and the need to consider political ideology, patriotism, and to think beyond the American Creed.

Defining American Identity

Not bound by common bloodlines and shared history, the American national identity was socially constructed on the basis of shared values of liberty, justice, and equal opportunity. Historically, the United States has been promoted as a nation of immigrants, open to all people with diverse cultures, religions, and ethnic backgrounds. Yet, recent research suggests this dominant understanding of American identity is less inclusive of all Americans, and Anglo-Protestant values of being independent and working hard have played a large role in shaping American identity (e.g., Hanson & O'Dwyer, 2019; Schildkraut, 2014).

Research on American identity typically focuses on an individual's attachment or strength of identification as American, and the content or characteristics of what it means to be American (Schildkraut, 2014). Studies that measure strength of identification often consider how important someone's American identity is to how they see themselves personally; how central being American is to their life (Schildkraut, 2007, 2014). In social identity theory terms, the question is about the role of social (in this case national) identity in personal identity (Tajfel & Turner, 1979).

Research on the content of American identity generally includes multiple dimensions. Most scholars examining samples of predominantly White participants distinguish between one or more ascriptive or ethnocultural dimensions that relate to the exclusivity of American identity (e.g., born in the United States, US citizenship, and shared language and culture) and civic dimensions (e.g., civic creedal beliefs and values, such as independence and freedom of choice, and civic republican items emphasizing rights and duties of citizenship, such as voting; Mangum & Block Jr., 2018). While studies have found that the majority of people prefer to see American identity as based on civic values and are more likely to endorse civic items of American identity (Huddy & Khatib, 2007), ethnocultural items have been implicitly associated with being a true American (Schildkraut, 2014; Wright et al., 2012).

Some measures also include affective dimensions of patriotism and nationalism (e.g., Li & Brewer, 2004; Schildkraut, 2014). In terms of liberal values, patriotism is viewed as positive, referring to a love for one's country, while nationalism is generally seen as negative, referring to an attitude of superiority about one's country (Adorno et al., 1950; Hanson & O'Dwyer, 2019). Items reflecting patriotism are more commonly included and endorsed by Americans than nationalism (Wright et al., 2012), and are associated with White US citizens who strongly identify as American (Schildkraut, 2014).

Recently, however, questions have been raised as to whether these constructs adequately capture how US citizens identify as American. Empirical results have been largely inconsistent in differentiating between dimensions (e.g., Mangum & Block Jr., 2018; Schildkraut, 2014; Wright et al., 2012). Likewise, these constructs do not account for current political issues and context (Huddy & Khatib, 2007). For example, within their sample of White Americans, McDaniel et al. (2016) found that the perceived threat to the public and the nation following the September 11 terror attacks heightened preferences for a nativist view of what it means to be an American (i.e., being born in the United States, being Christian, and having lived in the United States their whole life), over an assimilationist view (i.e., speaking English, feeling American, and US citizenship).

Similarly, despite the explicit endorsement of civic items of American identity over ethnocultural items, recent research has noted the increasing political divide in the United States and in (mostly White) Americans' beliefs about characteristics of American identity (Hanson & O'Dwyer, 2019; Schildkraut, 2007). Further, typical constructs of American identity that include civic items based on Creedal values (i.e., individualism, hard work, liberty, equality of opportunity, and rule of law; Schildkraut, 2014) and patriotism items based on pride (e.g., pride in America), and symbolic patriotism (e.g., revering the American flag; Hanson & O'Dwyer, 2019; Mangum & Block Jr., 2018) may be more associated with the conservative political ideology and less inclusive of all Americans (Hanson et al., 2021). Conservative ideology has also been associated with prejudice toward undocumented immigrants and anti-immigrant policies in general (e.g., Wright et al., 2016).

In their model of American national identity based on a sample of mostly White but politically diverse participants, Hanson and O'Dwyer (2019) found two dimensions that fall along left/right political lines. The liberal or "for the people" dimension describes true Americans as supportive of greater equality and civic engagement, while the conservative or "for the nation" dimension values equal opportunity and constitutional ideals. Importantly, they include a dimension of American patriotism that highlights criticism toward the government as an act of love for one's country (i.e., constructive patriotism), finding that these items are more associated with how liberal individuals show patriotism and define their American identity than conservatives. Conservative individuals are more likely to endorse items associated with symbolic patriotism and pride, which are more commonly found in measures of American identity (see Mangum & Block Jr., 2018). There is need to consider how the increasing polarization in the United States is impacting beliefs about the characteristics of true Americans as this might also affect US citizens' attitudes toward undocumented immigrants. We examine this in the following section through an empirical study.

American Identity and Prejudice against Undocumented Immigrants

Previous research on ingroup bias and outgroup derogation, and the influence of political polarization on American identity supports the idea that (1) people who strongly identify as American may not all be more prejudiced against undocumented immigrants (Hamley et al., 2020), and (2) differences in beliefs in the characteristics of what it means to be a true American may influence prejudice against undocumented immigrants (e.g., Hanson & O'Dwyer, 2019; Wright et al., 2016). Next, we discuss the findings from a recent study conducted by one of us (Hendricks, 2022) that examined the extent that prejudice against undocumented immigrants is predicted by White Americans' strength and differences in beliefs about American identity (see Hendricks, 2022 for the full study).

Study Methodology

In total, 649 participants (74 percent female, $M_{age} = 30.42$, $SD_{age} = 13.36$) completed the study using the online survey site Qualtrics in late summer 2021. All participants identified as native-born White Caucasian (non-Hispanic or Latinx) US citizens, and currently lived in the United States. Participants were highly educated, with a majority having completed at least a bachelor's degree (52 percent). Additionally, participants identified with a variety of political parties in the United States, but most were self-reported as Democrat (41 percent), Republican (29 percent), and Independent (23 percent).

Participants completed a series of measures to test this relationship between American identity and prejudice against undocumented immigrants. American identity was captured through a measure ranking their beliefs about characteristics of true Americans and a three-item measure to capture their strength of identification as American. Participants completed two different measures of prejudice against undocumented immigrants. One measure captured explicit prejudice through a self-report instrument assessing participant's social distance toward unauthorized immigrants. Social distance has been well-established as a behavioral form of prejudice and captures how close participants feel toward outgroups in society and how willing they would be to accept members of these outgroups into their lives (Halperin et al., 2007). The other measure implicitly assessed prejudice through the implicit association test (IAT), which captured participants' implicit prejudicial attitudes toward the outgroup ("unauthorized immigrants") relative to the ingroup ("Americans"). Prejudice was measured both implicitly and explicitly to account for the likelihood that participants may have masked their prejudice on the self-report (explicit) measure in an effort to give a socially desirable answer (Brauer et al., 2000).

Capturing American Identity

Q-methodology (Q) was utilized to identify the different dimensions underlying how groups of people identify as American. Participants ranked statements about their beliefs about characteristics of true Americans relative to one another based on how much they agree or disagree with them, then were grouped together based on common rankings. The thirty-four statements which participants ranked were related to commonly endorsed civic constructs of American identity such as civic creedal (e.g., "A true American is independent and self-reliant") and civic republican ("A true American votes in elections"), but also included relational and affective constructs of patriotism such as constructive patriotism ("A true American questions policy decisions"), pride ("A true American is proud of America's fair and equal treatment of all groups in society"), and symbolic patriotism ("A true American stands when the Star-Spangled Banner is played"), and ascriptive/ethnocultural statements that relate to the exclusivity of American identity ("A true American speaks English"). The results of the Q analysis revealed three distinct factors describing how participants view American identity: *Be the Change* ($n = 321$), *Proud to be an American* ($n = 69$), and *United, but Independent* ($n = 259$). I briefly describe these factors below before discussing the main findings of the study.

Most participants in *Be the Change* (77 percent female, $M_{age} = 28.36$, $SD_{age} = 12.07$) identified as Democrat (67 percent), and were fairly left-wing and liberal. Additionally, participants' average strength of American identity indicated there was considerable variation among participants in how central being an American was to them. This factor emphasizes looking forward and the need to make America better over praising the past. Participants support policy and societal change as a civic duty. Overall, *Be the Change* represents individuals who view true Americans as having a responsibility to make America better and more equitable for everyone in society.

On the opposing side, most participants in *Proud to be an American* (57 percent female, $M_{age} = 39$, $SD_{age} = 16.19$) belonged to the Republican Party (84 percent), and were fairly right-wing and conservative. Participants' strength of American identity indicated there was little variation among participants; most participants strongly identified as American. This factor emphasizes freedom, honoring traditions and symbols like standing for the national anthem, and love for one's country. Overall, *Proud to be an American* represents individuals who view true

Americans as taking pride in their country, showing respect for traditions, and not criticizing America, while also valuing their personal independence and freedoms.

In *United, but Independent* (74 percent female, $M_{age} = 30.68$, $SD_{age} = 13.17$), there was more diversity in participants' political identity, with participants identifying as Republican (48 percent), Independent (29 percent), and Democrat (17 percent). Participants' strength of American identity indicated there was some variation among participants in this group, but a majority of participants identified strongly as American. Like those in *Be the Change*, participants in this factor emphasized equality and respect for others, but also placed high importance on personal liberty, freedom of speech, and taking pride in being American. Overall, *United, but Independent* prioritizes a united America where all are treated equally and given a voice, but not to the detriment to individual liberties.

Discussion: American Identity and Prejudice against Undocumented Immigrants

To determine the extent that native-born White Caucasian US citizens' implicit and explicit prejudice against undocumented immigrants was predicted by differences in their beliefs about characteristics of true Americans and strength of American identity, a series of OLS regression analyses were computed. Overall, the findings indicated that participants' American identity beliefs and strength of American identity were strong predictors of implicit and explicit prejudice. In particular, participants who weakly identified as American and who held less traditional beliefs about what it means to be American (*Be the Change*) were least prejudiced against undocumented immigrants. These findings have important implications for how we consider the role of identity on prejudice against undocumented immigrants.

First, research on social identity and national belonging suggests that immigrants present a threat to the majority-endorsed national identity if they are believed to be too different to become integrated and truly "belong" to society (Bose, 2018, also see Chapter 5 in this book). Undocumented immigrants in particular present a major challenge to a nation's ability to successfully manage the identity of the country (Drouhot & Nee, 2019). Likewise, recent research suggests there is a divide in American national identity, such that there might not be one majority identity in the United States (e.g., Hanson & O'Dwyer, 2019; Schildkraut, 2007). In the study reported above, three distinct views of

American identity were identified. Participants in *Be the Change*, which represents individuals who view true Americans as having a responsibility to make America better and more equitable for everyone in society, were least prejudiced against undocumented immigrants. This is supported in part by research by Wright et al. (2016), which found that participants who were high in egalitarianism (e.g., belief in social equality for all) were more likely to support a pathway to citizenship for undocumented immigrants. Further, while the majority of participants reported at least some explicit prejudice against undocumented immigrants and implicitly favored Americans over undocumented immigrants, there were 115 participants whose implicit bias scores suggested that they favored undocumented immigrants over Americans. A logistic regression was run to determine the odds of a participant favoring the outgroup over their ingroup. This analysis indicated that participants in the *Be the Change* group had the greatest odds of favoring undocumented immigrants over Americans. Likewise, as participants' strength of American identity increased, they were less likely to favor undocumented immigrants over Americans.

Second, participants who did not strongly identify as Americans were least prejudiced and had greater odds of being in favor of undocumented immigrants over Americans. While this is in line with research by Mangum and Block Jr. (2018) examining support for increased funding to preventing undocumented immigrants from entering the United States without authorization, this contradicts one line of research on ingroup bias and outgroup derogation suggesting that people can feel strongly toward their group without feeling prejudice against outgroup members (e.g., Brewer, 2017). However, an examination of prejudice among participants who identified strongly as American but held different American identity beliefs did indicate differences in explicit prejudice. *Be the Change* participants who strongly identified as American were significantly less explicitly prejudiced than *Proud to be an American* and *United, but Independent* participants. Within *Be the Change* though, participants who strongly identified as American were more implicitly prejudiced than those weakly and moderately identified as American. These results suggest that overall strong identification is associated with greater prejudice, but beliefs may matter more when considering explicit prejudice. Ultimately, not all participants view what it means to be a true American in the same way; the results of this study suggest that their beliefs about their ingroup (American identity) and their strength of identification with the ingroup are important in determining prejudice against undocumented immigrants.

Concluding Comment

In the United States, there continues to be heated debate about the millions of undocumented immigrants in the country. Decisions continue to be made about undocumented immigrants rights in the United States, such as eligibility for deportation and detention by immigration enforcement, the continuance of Deferred Action for Childhood Arrivals, and granting a pathway to citizenship for all who live in the United States without authorization (Barros, 2021). These decisions have major consequences not only for immigration policy in the context of American political polarization (Gidron et al., 2020), but also for American national identity.

By examining how Americans' perceptions of undocumented immigrant are influenced by their own perceptions of what it means to be American, the recent research discussed in this chapter contributes to the larger literature on intergroup relations and the importance of national identity on immigration attitudes. How someone feels and identifies with their ingroup affects their attitudes toward the outgroup. Results from this research suggest that US citizens are thinking less about the characteristics of the undocumented immigrant and more about their own identity. Though most constructs of American identity have focused on Creedal values (i.e., individualism, hard work, liberty, equality of opportunity, and rule of law), recent research suggests these traditional ideals do not reflect the identity of all Americans. Instead, there exists a divide in how people view American identity (Hanson et al., 2021; Schildkraut, 2014). While some have a more open view of what it means to be American, others endorse a more traditional view. These differences in opinion over American identity influence opinions on undocumented immigrants; creating a challenge for how we think about diversity and inclusion in what it means to be American and who we consider to be American. In the next chapters we continue to explore this challenge that immigration and increasing diversity present to identity and belonging in Europe and South America.

REFERENCES

Abrego, L. J. (2011). Legal consciousness of undocumented Latinos: Fear and stigma as barriers to claims-making for first- and 1.5-generation immigrants. *Law & Society Review*, 45(2), 337–370. https://doi.org/10.1111/j.1540-5893.2011.00435.x

Adorno, T., Frenkel-Brunswik, D. J., & Nevitt, R. (1950). *The authoritarian personality* (Vol. xxxiii). Harpers.

Badea, C., Iyer, A., & Aebischer, V. (2018). National identification, endorsement of acculturation ideologies and prejudice: The impact of the perceived threat of immigration. *International Review of Social Psychology*, *31*(1), 14. https://doi.org/10.5334/irsp.147

Barros, A. (2021, December 27). Biden's first year brings modest change to immigration policy. *Voice of America News*. www.voanews.com/a/biden-s-first-year-brings-modest-changes-to-immigration-policy/6367512.html

Becker, J. C., Enders-Comberg, A., Wagner, U., Christ, O., & Butz, D. A. (2012). Beware of national symbols: How flags can threaten intergroup relations. *Social Psychology*, *43*(1), 3–6. https://doi.org/10.1027/1864-9335/a000073

Bose, P. S. (2018). Welcome and hope, fear, and loathing: The politics of refugee resettlement in Vermont. *Peace and Conflict: Journal of Peace Psychology*, *24*(3), 320–329. https://doi.org/10.1037/pac0000302

Brauer, M., Wasel, W., & Niedenthal, P. (2000). Implicit and explicit components of prejudice. *Review of General Psychology*, *4*(1), 79–101. https://doi.org/10.1037/1089-2680.4.1.79

Brewer, M. B. (2017). Intergroup discrimination: Ingroup love or outgroup hate? In C. Sibley & F. Barlow (Eds.), *The Cambridge handbook of the psychology of prejudice* (pp. 90–110). Cambridge University Press.

Cabaniss, E. R., & Cameron, A. E. (2018). Toward a social psychological understanding of migration and assimilation. *Humanity & Society*, *42*(2), 171–192. https://doi.org/10.1177/0160597617716963

Castañeda, H., & Melo, M. A. (2019). Geographies of confinement for immigrant youth: Checkpoints and immobilities along the US/Mexico border. *Law & Policy*, *41*(1), 80–102. https://doi.org/10.1111/lapo.12115

Chand, D. E., & Schreckhise, W. D. (2015). Secure communities and community values: Local context and discretionary immigration law enforcement. *Journal of Ethnic and Migration Studies*, *41*(10), 1621–1643. https://doi.org/10.1080/1369183X.2014.986441

Chavez, L. R. (2007). The condition of illegality. *International Migration*, *45*(3), 192–196. https://doi.org/10.1111/j.1468-2435.2007.00416.x

Collingwood, L., & O'Brien Gonzalez, B. (2019). Public opposition to sanctuary cities in Texas: Criminal threat or immigration threat? *Social Science Quarterly*, *100*(4), 1182–1196. https://doi.org/10.1111/ssqu.12632

De Genova, N. (2004). The legal production of Mexican/migrant "illegality." *Latino Studies*, *2*, 160–185. https://doi.org/10.1057/palgrave.lst.8600085

Dovidio, J. F., Gaertner, S. L., Ufkes, E. G., Saguy, T., & Pearson, A. R. (2016). Included but invisible? Subtle bias, common identity, and the darker side of "we". *Social Issues and Policy Review*, *10*(1), 6–46. https://doi.org/10.1111/sipr.12017

Drouhot, L. G., & Nee, V. (2019). Assimilation and the second generation in Europe and America: Blending and segregating social dynamics between immigrants and natives. *Annual Review of Sociology*, *45*(1), 177–199. https://doi.org/10.1146/annurev-soc-073117-041335

Ellis, M., Wright, R., & Townley, M. (2016). State-scale immigration enforcement and Latino interstate migration in the United States. *Annals of the American Association of Geographers*, *106*(4), 891–908. https://doi.org/10.1080/24694452.2015.1135725

España-Nájera, A., & Vera, D. (2020). Attitudes toward immigration: Ethnicity trumps skills but not legality? *Social Science Quarterly*, *101*(2), 545–557. https://doi.org/10.1111/ssqu.12758

Flores, R. D., & Schachter, A. (2018). Who are the "illegals"? The social construction of illegality in the United States. *American Sociological Review*, *83*(5), 839–868. https://doi.org/10.1177/0003122418794635

Gidron, N., Adams, J., & Horne, W. (2020). *American affective polarization in comparative perspective*. Cambridge University Press.

Halperin, E., Pedahzur, A., & Canetti-Nisim, D. (2007). Psychoeconomic approaches to the study of hostile attitudes toward minority groups: A study among Israeli Jews. *Social Science Quarterly*, *88*(1), 177–198. www.jstor.org/stable/42956178

Hamley, L., Houkamau, C. A., Osborne, D., Barlow, F. K., & Sibley, C. G. (2020). Ingroup love or outgroup hate (or both)? Mapping distinct bias profiles in the population. *Personality and Social Psychology Bulletin*, *46*(2), 171–188. https://doi.org/10.1177/0146167219845919

Hanson, K., & O'Dwyer, E. (2019). Patriotism and nationalism, left and right: A Q-methodology study of American national identity. *Political Psychology*, *40*(4), 777–795. https://doi.org/10.1111/pops.12561

Hanson, K., O'Dwyer, E., & Lyons, E. (2021). The national divide: A social representations approach to US political identity. *European Journal of Social Psychology*, *51*(4–5), 833–846. https://doi.org/10.1002/ejsp.2791

Hartman, T. K., Newman, B. J., & Scott Bell, C. (2014). Decoding prejudice toward Hispanics: Group cues and public reactions to threatening immigrant behavior. *Political Behavior*, *36*(1), 143–163. https://doi.org/10.1007/s11109-013-9231-7

Hendricks, M. J. (2022). *The undocumented immigrant challenge to American identity* [Doctoral dissertation, Georgetown University]. http://hdl.handle.net/10822/1064704

Huddy, L., & Khatib, N. (2007). American patriotism, national identity, and political involvement. *American Journal of Political Science*, *51*(1), 63–77. https://doi.org/10.1111/j.1540-5907.2007.00237.x

Hummel, D. (2016). Immigrant-friendly and unfriendly cities: Impacts on the presence of a foreign-born population and city crime. *Journal of International Migration and Integration*, *17*(4), 1211–1230. https://doi.org/10.1007/s12134-015-0464-7

Kemmelmeier, M., & Winter, D. G. (2008). Sowing patriotism, but reaping nationalism? Consequences of exposure to the American flag. *Political Psychology*, *29*(6), 859–879. https://doi.org/10.1111/j.1467-9221.2008.00670.x

Knoll, B. R., Redlawsk, D. P., & Sanborn, H. (2011). Framing labels and immigration policy attitudes in the Iowa caucuses: "Trying to out-Tancredo Tancredo." *Political Behavior, 33*(3), 433–454. https://doi.org/10.1007/s11109-010-9141-x

Levy, M. E., & Wright, M. (2016a). Re-examining group-centrism in American public opinion: The case of anti-Latino sentiment and immigration policy attitudes. *SSRN Electronic Journal.* https://doi.org/10.2139/ssrn.3022187

(2016b, June 9). *Americans aren't biased against Latino immigration. Here's what they actually fear.* Washington Post. www.washingtonpost.com/news/monkey-cage/wp/2016/06/09/americans-arent-biased-against-latino-immigration-heres-what-they-actually-fear/

Li, Q., & Brewer, M. B. (2004). What does it mean to be an American? Patriotism, nationalism, and American identity after 9/11. *Political Psychology, 25*(5), 727–739. https://doi.org/10.1111/j.1467-9221.2004.00395.x

Livi-Bacci, M. (2012). *A short history of migration.* Polity Press.

Maciel, J. A., & Knudson-Martin, C. (2014). Don't end up in the fields: Identity construction among Mexican adolescent immigrants, their parents, and sociocontextual processes. *Journal of Marital and Family Therapy, 40*(4), 484–497. https://doi.org/10.1111/jmft.12044

Mangum, M., & Block Jr., R. (2018). Social identity theory and public opinion towards immigration. *Social Sciences, 7*(3), 41. https://doi.org/10.3390/socsci7030041

Marinthe, G., Falomir-Pichastor, J. M., Testé, B., & Kamiejski, R. (2020). Flags on fire: Consequences of a national symbol's desecration for intergroup relations. *Group Processes & Intergroup Relations, 23*(5), 744–760. https://doi.org/10.1177/1368430219853352

McDaniel, E. L., Nooruddin, I., & Shortle, A. F. (2016). Proud to be an American?: The changing relationship of national pride and identity. *The Journal of Race, Ethnicity, and Politics, 1*(1), 145–176. https://doi.org/10.1017/rep.2015.7

Moghaddam, F. M. (2019). *Threat to democracy: The appeal of authoritarianism in an age of uncertainty.* American Psychological Association.

Morse, A. (2021). *Report on state immigration laws, 2020.* National Conference of State Legislatures. www.ncsl.org/Portals/1/Documents/immig/Immigration-Policy-2020_v02_web.pdf

Murray, K. E., & Marx, D. M. (2013). Attitudes toward unauthorized immigrants, authorized immigrants, and refugees. *Cultural Diversity and Ethnic Minority Psychology, 19*(3), 332–341. https://doi.org/10.1037/a0030812

Passel, J. S., & Krogstad, J. M. (2024). *What we know about unauthorized immigrants living in the U.S.* Pew Research Center. www.pewresearch.org/short-reads/2024/07/22/what-we-know-about-unauthorized-immigrants-living-in-the-us/

Pérez, E. O. (2015). Xenophobic rhetoric and its political effects on immigrants and their co-ethnics. *American Journal of Political Science, 59*(3), 549–564. https://doi.org/10.1111/ajps.12131

Schachter, A. (2016). From "different" to "similar": An experimental approach to understanding assimilation. *American Sociological Review*, *81*(5), 981–1013. https://doi.org/10.1177/0003122416659248

Schildkraut, D. J. (2007). Defining American identity in the twenty-first century: How much there is there? *The Journal of Politics*, *69*(3), 597–615. https://doi.org/10.1111/j.1468-2508.2007.00562.x

(2014). Boundaries of American identity: Evolving understandings of "us." *Annual Review of Political Science*, *17*(1), 441–460. https://doi.org/10.1146/annurev-polisci-080812-144642

Serrano-Careaga, J., & Huo, Y. J. (2019). "Illegal" by association: Do negative stereotypes divide or unite Latinxs in the United States? *Analyses of Social Issues and Public Policy*, *19*(1), 204–223. https://doi.org/10.1111/asap.12182

Sherif, M. (1966). *Group conflict and cooperation: Their social psychology*. Routledge & Kegan Paul.

Tajfel, H., Flament, C., Billig, M. G., & Bundy, R. F. (1971). Social categorization and intergroup behaviour. *European Journal of Social Psychology*, *1*, 149–177.

Tajfel, H., & Turner, J. C. (1979). An integrative theory of intergroup conflict. In W. G. Austin & S. Worchel (Eds.), *The social psychology of intergroup relations* (pp. 33–47). Brooks/Cole.

United States Census Bureau. (2021, December 3). *About the foreign-born population*. United States Census Bureau. www.census.gov/topics/population/foreign-born/about.html

Unzueta Carrasco, T. A., & Seif, H. (2014). Disrupting the dream: Undocumented youth reframe citizenship and deportability through anti-deportation activism. *Latino Studies*, *12*(2), 279–299. https://doi.org/10.1057/lst.2014.21

Valdivia, C. (2019). Expanding geographies of deportability: How immigration enforcement at the local level affects undocumented and mixed-status families. *Law & Policy*, *41*(1), 103–119. https://doi.org/10.1111/lapo.12119

Wohl, M. J. A., Branscombe, N. R., & Reysen, S. (2010). Perceiving your group's future to be in jeopardy: Extinction threat induces collective angst and the desire to strengthen the ingroup. *Personality and Social Psychology Bulletin*, *36*(7), 898–910. https://doi.org/10.1177/0146167210372505

Wojcieszak, M., & Garrett, R. K. (2018). Social identity, selective exposure, and affective polarization: How priming national identity shapes attitudes toward immigrants via news selection. *Human Communication Research*, *44*(3), 247–273. https://doi.org/10.1093/hcr/hqx010

Wright, M. (2019). Identity and immigration: What we think we know, and why we might not actually know it. *Nations and Nationalism*, *25*(2), 467–477. https://doi.org/10.1111/nana.12518

Wright, M., Citrin, J., & Wand, J. (2012). Alternative measures of American national identity: Implications for the civic-ethnic distinction. *Political Psychology*, *33*(4), 469–482. https://doi.org/10.1111/j.1467-9221.2012.00885.x

Wright, M., Levy, M., & Citrin, J. (2016). Public attitudes toward immigration policy across the legal/illegal divide: The role of categorical and attribute-based decision-making. *Political Behavior*, *38*(1), 229–253. https://doi.org/10.1007/s11109-015-9311-y

Young, Y., Loebach, P., & Korinek, K. (2018). Building walls or opening borders? Global immigration policy attitudes across economic, cultural and human security contexts. *Social Science Research*, *75*, 83–95. https://doi.org/10.1016/j.ssresearch.2018.06.006

CHAPTER 6

Immigration and European Identity

> Within EU member states, immigration has become a "hot topic"....
> Conflicts over immigration have become salient in national elections;
> they play a salient role in national referenda (most consequentially in
> the "Brexit" campaign); and they have had a significant impact on the
> political agendas of governments.
>
> Grande et al. (2019, p. 1445)

The European Union (EU) slowly rose out of the ashes of Europe while it was recovering from the Second World War (1939–1945), as plans were developed and implemented to create a Europe that would be democratic, united, interdependent, and peaceful. Two highly destructive world wars began in Europe in the twentieth century, and the merging of European countries into one highly interconnected and integrated unit was expected to lower the possibility of future wars starting in Europe. A common economic and labor market was created through the *Treaty of Rome* in 1957 (extending to the entire economy, the 1951 *Treaty of Paris* agreement on labor market mobility, which only covered the coal and steel industries), with Belgium, France, Italy, Luxembourg, the Netherlands, and West Germany as members. The subsequent political, cultural, educational, and economic unification of the nation states that make up the EU now, with thirty-one member states and expected to further expand eastward over the next few decades, represents impressive progress, as indicated by Amato et al. (2019, quoted above). However, the EU – and Europe more broadly (which has a population of about 500 million, when the United Kingdom is included) – continues to face enormous challenges. Probably the most pressing of these challenges is how to develop and implement a cohesive common policy on immigration and refugees, a topic that has become a "political hot potato" (as indicated by Grande et al., 2019, quoted above).

But why do immigrants and refugees move to Europe, and are they needed or do they represent an unnecessary burden on European societies? We address these questions in the first section of this chapter, with particular reference to demographic trends in Europe and other parts of the world (this discussion builds on the theme of demographic trends, first examined in Chapter 1). In the second section, we discuss the attitudes of European host society populations toward immigrants. As suggested by the idea that immigration is a "political hot potato" in Europe, there are widely divergent and intensely conflicting views on this topic. If there is a danger of the EU disintegrating in the future, the most probable immediate cause is disagreements on immigration policy (probably the major factor which led to Brexit). The main focus in the third section of this chapter is on integration trends among immigrant groups, as well as government policies in this area. In the fourth section, we explore European identity, including changes in European identity since the late twentieth century. Finally, we look ahead to the future of Europe.

We raise two preliminary points, which serve as a launching pad for the main discussion. First, European consciousness has its roots in the Renaissance and predates the EU by about half a millennium (Delanty, 2019). More recently, Napoleon Bonaparte (1769–1821) conquered most of Europe and "... his vision for a unified Europe lay the foundations for much that is declared as being associated with European unity today, and specifically with the European Union" (Triandafyllidou & Gropas, 2023, p. 52). Thus, European identity has deep and ancient roots. Second, European identity is in some respects dynamic, changing, and shaped in important ways by global events. For example, Russia's invasion of Ukraine in 2014 served to strengthen a sense of European identity in opposition to Russian aggression, especially for those countries that are geographically closer to Russia (Gehring, 2021). Thus, we should consider European identity as evolving over the long term, through interaction with changes in the larger global context.

Why Do Immigrants Move to Europe, and Are They Needed There?

Immigrants move to Europe for a number of compelling reasons, the most important being, first, to escape extremely difficult conditions in their country of origin, including political repression and/or violent conflicts and/or, second, to escape difficult economic conditions that prevent them from developing their talents and achieving a satisfactory standard of living. These "push factors" are extremely powerful and have propelled tens of millions of people to move from low-income countries of Africa, Asia, and South America to Europe since the 1960s. (There is also migration within Europe and from other high-income societies, but these are less controversial because they typically involve White Christian migrants, who are seen as highly assimilable.) Much of the population movement from low-income societies has been a result of sudden and unexpected violent conflicts, such as the Israel–Palestine war (which erupted again in 2023), still simmering war in Syria (starting from around 2015), and the Arab Spring Revolutions (in the early 2010s), which resulted in millions of Syrians and other Near and Middle Easterners (mostly Muslims) being displaced to Europe. Political repression in Iran and Afghanistan, where the mullahs and the Taliban rule with iron fists smashing down particularly on women who are treated as third-class citizens in their own countries, has also resulted in millions of refugees from these countries, with Europe being a major destination. The backlash to these massive and sometimes sudden population movements has been to nurture a "bunker mentality" among European populations, and attempts to build stronger walls to keep out non-Europeans. As Anna Triandafyllidou and Ruby Gropas have commented, "It is usually contended that the EU lowered its internal borders at the expense of strengthening or raising its external ones" (2023, p. 143).

But there is a third (perhaps even more important) factor leading to large-scale migration of people from low-income societies to Europe, and this has to do with demographic trends since the second half of the twentieth century. The world population continues to grow, although for the first time since 1950 the rate of growth has declined to less than 1 percent per annum (United Nations, 2022). For most low-income societies, the share of the working age population (aged between 25 and 64 years) has been increasing, but for Europe it has been decreasing. While about two-third of the world population now lives in countries or regions where lifetime fertility is below 2.1 births per woman, just about all of Europe is in this situation and is now forced to rely on immigration to try to increase or at least maintain population levels (Parr, 2023). For high-income societies around the world, between the years 2000 and 2020, the balance of birth over death was 66.2 million, which was surpassed by the 80.5 million gains made through international migration (United Nations,

2022). But for a number of reasons, Europe is even more dependent on international migration than many other high-income countries and regions. Indeed, for the foreseeable future, migration (rather than the balance of births over deaths) will be the main source of population growth in Europe.

Europe has an aging and declining population, with decreasing numbers of working-age people. Even in Catholic European countries, such as Italy and Spain, where one might expect traditional family values to influence population changes, in the last few decades the total fertility rate has reached well below 2.1 births per woman (for more detailed information on population trends in Europe, see Eurostat, 2023). An exploration of demographic scenarios for the EU from 2015 to 2060 predicts that population aging and a smaller labor force will mean that European workers will need to support more dependents in the future (Lutz et al., 2019). Unless other major changes are made, this could result in stagnation or even a drop in the standard of living in Europe. Possible remedies for this situation include 2–4 million migrants coming into Europe every year (Lutz et al., 2019). Of course, other possible remedies could be increased fertility in the host European populations, as well as dramatically increased productivity by the European native population – but neither of these are likely to be achieved at a high enough level and in a timely way to compensate for the outcome of current population trends, particularly the declining labor force (Lutz et al., 2019).

The decline in birth rates in Europe is associated with foundational changes in the role of women in European societies. As European women have made advances in education and larger numbers of them have gained university degrees, the number of children they have has declined. Similarly, immigrant women in Europe have a lower number of children when they benefit from higher education (Kulu et al., 2019). More advanced education gives women the power to do better in the employment market, and to achieve greater financial independence. Women have now held the highest posts in the EU, for example, Ursula von der Leyen, president of the European Commission, and Christine Lagarde, president of the European Central Bank. Although there is still no gender parity in Europe, particularly at the highest levels of business and politics where men are still dominant, European women have made tremendous advances in all sectors of European society (Muller & Tommel, 2022). Associated with these professional advances are lower birth rates, resulting in a need to import labor to fill the urgent needs of the European economy.

Given that 2–4 million additional immigrants are needed each year in Europe (Lutz et al., 2019), where will they come from? To address this question, we need to consider world population growth trajectories (see section 6 in Lutz et al., 2019). The trajectories predict that possible world population growth could reach between 8.9 billion and 11 billion by 2060. The region of highest population growth is predicted to be Africa, which could reach a total population ranging between 2 billion and 3.1 billion by 2060. Although there are differences between fertility rates across African countries and regions, with some fertility rates reaching as high as 6 to 7 births per woman, in general the fertility rate in Africa is well above the 2.1 "replacement" level and is closer to 3.5–4.0 (currently, Sub-Saharan Africa has the youngest population in the world). A solution to this rapid population increase is to invest heavily in education for women, which generally results in lower fertility rates (births per woman decrease among immigrants to Europe for those women with higher education, Kulu et al., 2019). However, this is a long-term solution, which is not at present being adopted in a wholehearted way. Consequently, there is a high likelihood that it is in Africa that there will be the highest "surplus labor," which could serve as the source to fill the gap in labor shortages, which will continue to be experienced in Europe for the foreseeable future.

In summary, Europe is highly dependent on immigrants to maintain or try to grow its population, in order to meet economic and other needs. Without immigration, the European population will further age and decline in total size. With respect to the populations already in place in Europe, it is the foreign-born population that is the main determinant of population changes in Europe (Bagavos, 2022). But as immigrant women arrive and integrate, and more of them and their female offspring benefit from higher education, their birth rate also declines to become similar to that of host-population females. Consequently, because of low birth rates among Europeans, the European need for immigrants will continue for some decades, at least.

Attitudes of European Host Society Populations toward Immigrants

There are now daily and hourly new mass media images and reports of immigrants arriving in Europe, as well as Europeans protesting against (and sometimes for) immigration. The Brexit vote that pulled the UK out of the EU also reflects a divided Europe, for and against immigration (Hobolt, 2016). The success of European far-right political movements in the early twenty-first century is in part because of broader opposition to immigration (Halikiopoulou & Vlandas, 2020). The research literature on the attitudes of Europeans toward immigrants has become extensive (e.g., Cavaille & Marshall, 2019; Heath et al., 2020; Martin & Indelicato, 2023; Stockemer & Halikiopoulou, 2022). In this section, we briefly examine this research literature to answer the question: Which Europeans oppose immigration? But first, we frame this question through psychological theories.

We can conceptualize European opposition to immigration as stemming from two sets of factors, material and psychological. (This builds on our earlier discussions in Chapters 2 and 4.) Realistic conflict theory, resource mobilization theory, and other theories that assume material factors to be the driving force shaping intergroup behavior, lead us to focus on competition for material resources, and on Europeans opposing immigration because they fear increased competition, especially in employment, housing, health, and educational services (see Moghaddam, 2024, chapter 2). On the other hand, social identity theory and other theories that give priority to psychological factors as drivers of intergroup behavior propose that European opposition to immigration stems from perceived threats to national identity, traditional values, and other characteristics of what is perceived as "our nation" (see Moghaddam, 2024, chapter 3). Our argument is that underlying both perspectives are psychological processes, because even material factors are interpreted and ascribed meaning through psychological processes. For example, Heinz's sense of how well-off he is and how new immigrants moving to his neighborhood will impact his standard of living are influenced by the outcomes of relative deprivation and social comparison processes, which are subjectively derived and psychological in nature.

The power of psychological factors becomes clear when we consider that research reveals opposition to immigration to be highest among those who have *less* contact with immigrants (Green, 2007; Pettigrew et al., 2007). Weber (2015) found that a greater influx of immigrants to a European country is associated with more anti-immigrant attitudes, but not in areas where the immigrants settle. Drazanova and Gonnot (2023) showed that people who have more contact with immigrants are less anti-immigrant, but anti-immigrant sentiment rises in general when there is a sudden influx of immigrants to a region. Consequently, anti-immigrant sentiments seem in part to arise from stereotypes, perceived threats, and broadly what people feel and think about immigrants, rather than direct contact with and knowledge of immigrants.

Further highlighting the importance of psychological factors is a study of seventeen European societies, which showed that opposition to immigration is also associated with an exaggeration of the size of the immigrant population (Gorodzeisky & Semyonov, 2020). The same trend of overestimation of the size of immigrant population among opponents of immigration was found in an earlier study of twenty countries (Sides & Citron, 2007). In short, people who see immigrants as a threat and who oppose immigration, perceive there to be more immigrants than there actually are. They exaggerate the size of the immigrant population. But in terms of individual characteristics, what types of people are more likely to hold such anti-immigrant attitudes and experience such threats from immigrants? These individuals are more likely to be older, less educated, higher on right-wing authoritarianism and social dominance orientation, and politically right-wing. A more recent trend among these individuals is high perceived threat from Islamic fundamentalism (Araujo et al., 2019).

To sum up, the sudden arrival of millions of non-White, non-Christian immigrants to Europe in the early twenty-first century has met with some opposition, particularly from lower-educated, older, conservative individuals. This opposition is also reflected in the rise of far-right political movements and leaders, supported by individuals who are high on authoritarianism. Opposition to immigration is driven by psychological factors, such as perceived threats to ingroup identity (discussed further below), rather than objective, rational assessments of economic interests. When the situation in Europe is assessed on the basis of rational and objective criteria, millions of immigrants are needed annually because of the labor needs of the European economy.

Integration Trends among Immigrant Groups and Government Policies

> ... an increasing number of Western European countries mandate tests of prospective immigrants' assimilability, or ability to integrate culturally, before they even arrive ... this ... fuses "immigration control with immigrant integration concerns."
>
> FitzGerald et al. (2017)

Among European governments, the selection of who can enter a territory (immigration policy) has become intertwined with how to integrate immigrants (integration policy). Greater efforts are being made by governments to prevent the entry of those who are deemed low in assimilability. These efforts are driven primarily by cultural and political concerns, and less by market forces. For example, the contemporary immigration policies of EU governments are strongly motivated to limit Muslim immigration, based on assumptions about the low assimilability of Muslims (FitzGerald et al., 2017). The attempt to limit immigration to Europe in particular ways is not a new trend. In the past, various guest worker programs, such as those in Germany and Switzerland (Ellermann, 2013), were designed to allow workers from certain countries to temporarily participate in a country's economy without settling and integrating into the host society (similar to the *Seasonal Agricultural Worker Programs* in Canada and the United States, which have serious shortcomings, Al-Bazz et al., 2022).

But there have been substantial changes in the European context in which immigrants arrive and try to integrate. Much has been said about why we must attend to the rise of populist anti-immigrant movements and leaders (Koning, 2023). But there are also positive developments that help in the immigrant integration process, and these have received less attention. For example, higher education has expanded in Europe and 32 percent of the overall population are university graduates; but 37 percent of these are under 30 years old and only 21 percent are over 70 (Ford & Jennings, 2020). This higher education level among the younger generation is resulting in substantial changes in the European social environment, because "[t]he worldview and moral values expressed by graduates are quite different in some regards from those with lower levels of formal education" (Ford & Jennings, 2020, p. 300). For example, graduates in Europe are more positively disposed toward cultural and ethnic diversity; they are more accepting of immigrants.

Another change in the European context has been the recognition, but not necessarily acceptance by the general population, of the fact that immigrants are needed to fill the labor shortage – not as a temporary, but as a continuing policy. Guest workers were accepted in Europe during the post-Second World War era as a stopgap measure. For example, the millions of Turks who moved to West Germany were not expected to integrate, but to return to Turkey after their labor was no longer needed. But the "return to Turkey" seldom took place and there are now third-generation Turks in Germany, whose ancestry starts with guest workers.

The experiences of European countries have demonstrated that "there is nothing more permanent than temporary foreign workers" (Martin, 2001, p. 1). The "permanent" settlement of "temporary" workers has become especially challenging in Europe because the workers are generally from Africa, Asia, and South America, and dissimilar to the host population in key respects, often including in phenotype, religion, heritage, language, and culture. The positive reception given to millions of Christian and White Ukrainian refugees in the 2010s and 2020s, compared to the generally negative reception of Afghan refugees, who are Muslim and non-White, puts a spotlight on the role of similarity in the integration of newcomers in Europe (De Coninck, 2023).

Immigrants to countries like the Netherlands who were expected to stay in Europe were ". . . exposed to fierce re-education programmes aimed at acculturating them into the mainstream" (Doomernik & Bruquetas-Callejo, 2016, p. 67). The general policy of European governments toward immigrants is captured by the phrase used by FitzGerald et al., "Can you become one of us?" (2017, p. 27). This kind of assimilationist approach has transformed into controversial policies, such as the banning of religious symbols (such as the Islamic veil) in schools. On the one hand, empirical evidence suggests that banning the Islamic veil in schools has resulted in improved educational performance by female students of Muslim origin and increased mixed marriages (Maurin & Navarrete, 2023). On the other hand, the strong assimilationist policies of many European governments (including the attempt to break up ethnic neighborhoods and to geographically disperse immigrants) continue to be controversial. (For a broader discussion of integration policies in Europe, see Garces-Mascaranas & Penninx, 2016.)

In summary, the broad policy in Europe has been one of assimilation of immigrants, but this policy faces considerable challenges when the immigrants are not only economically disadvantaged, but also different from the host population in terms of culture, values, language, religion, phenotype, and other characteristics. In practice, the economic disadvantages of many immigrants result in them living in ethnic enclaves, which have cheaper housing, but at least access to some public transportation and social services. However, these geographical concentrations of the "ethnic other" in "ghetto neighborhoods" are often interpreted as a lack of assimilation and a threat to European identity. For example, in Denmark there have been strenuous government efforts to break up such "ghetto neighborhoods" and to force assimilation by separating immigrant children from their parents to better teach them "Danish values" (Salem, 2018). "Ghetto neighborhoods" have also been the target of extreme right-wing nationalist movements, who want to eradicate them and "send the immigrants back home." At the center of these developments is the issue of European identity, discussed in more detail below.

European Identity: Change and Stability

In all the forms that the idea of Europe has taken, Europe has been the "self" and the "other" bound into one. Although each of its constituent parts (countries and peoples) considers itself European and rightly claims shared ownership of Europe's history, values, and civilization, this identity is simultaneously an elusive one because the centre of power is often seen, with a certain anxiety, as being "elsewhere." In short, Europe has often been ... a constantly shifting mosaic of ideas.

(Triandafyllidou & Gropas, 2023, p. 69)

... there is ... room for optimism with respect to the possibility of the EU acquiring a psychological existence in European minds. Indeed, the EU is already behaving as an actor and is recognized as such by other actors (the United States, China, Russia, Japan, etc.). This kind of recognition took place, for the first time, at the level of the United Nations with Resolution 713 on Yugoslavia, in which the European Community was acknowledged as an actor independent from European nation-states...

Castano (2004, p. 53)

There is already recognition of the EU as an independent political entity (as pointed out by Castano, 2004, quoted above), but psychological identification with Europe is constantly changing and context-dependent (as suggested by Triandafyllidou & Gropas, 2023, quoted above). A simple interpretation of European identity is "identification as a European" (Cram, 2012). The issue of "how European people in Europe feel" is of the utmost importance, because low identification with Europe and high "Euroscepticism" can result in the fragmentation of Europe. As Carl et al. (2019) argue, a weak sense of European identity contributed in key respects to Brexit, and this experience could be repeated if identification with Europe weakens in other EU member states. Ciaglia et al. (2018) have argued that, "Similar to national identity being a crucial driving factor for the emergence of the nation state, some type of European identity is seen as a precondition for the stable existence and further evolution of the European Union" (2018, p. 8). Weakening of the EU could take place in response to a number of developments, related to particular visions of European identity and the perceived threats to such visions from the perspective of different groups.

On the one hand, it is understood that European identity is to some extent flexible and "under construction." As Kohli has argued, "The discovery that national traditions have often been invented and strategically implemented ... should convince the actors of European integration that they can do it as well" (2000, p. 121). Similarly, Strath (2002) refers to European identity as an abstraction and fiction – but, of course, fictions can become very powerful. On the other hand, the very fact that European identity is "under construction" means that different, and sometimes contradictory, visions of European identity are put forward and fought over. A first issue on which competing visions of European identity are fought over concerns the relationship between European identity and national identity. What is the ideal toward which Europeans should strive with respect to the role of national identity within Europe?

A first possible ideal is for European identity to become increasingly dominant, and for national identity to weaken and become less visible. The eventual outcome of this process could be Europeans being European first, and only having weak ties to their nations. In this scenario, identity ties to nation states weaken and eventually disappear in Europe, as political, economic, and other borders disappear. A second possibility is for national identities to remain stable, but for European identity to become stronger and eventually to match national identity in prominence. The outcome of this process would be a kind of parity between European and national identity. A third possibility is for national identity to remain dominant, and perhaps become even stronger, so that national identity has a higher priority than European identity. Support for these three possibilities is associated with political orientation, so that extreme right-wing nationalists want national identity to become even stronger, and to have a much higher priority than European identity.

The actual situation in Europe at the start of the twenty-first century reflects a combination of the second and third possibilities identified above. Research using evidence from the *Eurobarometer* (https://europa.eu/eurobarometer/screen/home) casts light on this. The Eurobarometer has included questions that measure European identity; for example, the question "Please tell me how attached you feel to Europe?" has been asked since 1971 as part of the Eurobarometer surveys. This research shows that identification as a European does not necessarily increase with length of membership in the EU (Hadler et al., 2021), Europeans continue to identify more strongly with their nation states than with Europe (Ciaglia et al., 2018; Haller & Ressler, 2006), with national borders becoming more prominent again in reaction to the refugees pouring into Europe (Postelnicescu, 2016). European identity tends to change with changes in the larger context. For example, just as the "threat of migrants" has put stress on the cooperation of European nations and European identity, the economic crisis of 2007–2011 resulted in some retrenchment to traditional national interests and a move away from putting Europe first (Fligstein et al., 2012).

Research has also thrown light on the characteristics of individuals who feel more European (Garib, 2011; Haller & Ressler, 2006), and what individuals mean when they report identifying with Europe (Van Mol, 2022). As efforts are made to nurture European identity, what is the Europe that Europeans are supposed to identify with? The puzzle is captured by the book titled *What is Europe?* (Triandafyllidou & Gropas, 2023), to which question there is at present no agreed-upon answer. Individuals who identify more as European tend to be younger, have more years of education, and perceive the EU as a real entity (Castano, 2004; Tselios & Tomaney, 2019). Over time, pride in being a European has become a more important factor in shaping how Europeans relate to Europe (Garib, 2011). A wide range of activities and programs, including the *Eurovision Song Contest* (started in 1956), the *European Football Championship* (started in 1958), and *Erasmus* (the student exchange program started in 1987), serve to try to build a stronger European identity (also, see section 5.2 in Ciaglia et al., 2018). At present, among young people, the underlying European identity is a strong justice, "rights" theme (Van Mol, 2022). But this theme is challenged by controversies about how to deal with the flood of refugees coming from low-income societies. Europeans disagree as to the rights of the refugees reaching their borders (for extreme right-wing perspectives, see McMahon, 2022).

European identity is being fought over by competing political groups. In the early decades of the twenty-first century, there has been a surge in support for a vision of European identity as a historically Christian White collective (McMahon, 2022; Richards, 2022). On the other hand, ethnic minorities in Europe have become less committed to European identity (Hadler et al., 2021). While ethnic diversity is a theme in the emerging European identity, there is also some danger in what could be the eventual outcome of current developments:

> Dominant European identity narratives today turn diversity into a distinctive feature of European identity. While this view entails a risk of reifying subnational and national identities and neglecting important processes of national and regional or ethnic identity transformations, it is also promising because it remains open to diversity. However, there is a risk here that European identity becomes an empty shell and completely loses its cultural vitality. It becomes too 'thin' to matter (Triandafyllidou & Gropas, 2023, p. 121).

In summary, European identity is under construction and there are fierce fights over the direction this identity should move and the ultimate goal it should adopt. But the relationship between European identity and national identity is not zero-sum: Individuals who are strongly attached to their nation can also be strongly attached to Europe (Haller & Ressler, 2006). European identity is continually changing with changing global circumstances, and two factors that are in important ways shaping European identity are the Russian invasion of Ukraine and the increasing number of refugees entering Europe.

Concluding Comment

European governments are confronting the reality of their limited power to shape immigration and integration processes, as indicated both by their own practical experiences and by empirical evidence (Helbling et al., 2020). Europe has an aging and declining population, with birth rates that are too low to even maintain current population levels. Demographic trends mean that Europe is forced to import approximately 2–4 million immigrants a year. Given the demographic trends in the rest of the world, these millions of immigrants are most likely to come from non-Western parts of the world, particularly from Africa which is the region with the highest population increase in the world. Also, in the coming decades, climate change will probably result in higher pressures for people to move from low-income societies to Europe (see section 8 in Lutz et al., 2019).

A major question concerns the impact of immigration on the political future of Europe. Given that each year millions of mostly dissimilar others will move to Europe in the coming decades, will this trend represent a "threat" that moves European societies to the political right? Will extreme anti-immigrant nationalist leaders and groups come to political power in Europe? Will Brexit – which was greatly influenced by anti-immigrant sentiments – be followed by further weakening of ties in Europe? The answer to these questions will depend a great deal on how perceived threats, collective identities, and immigrant integration are managed in the European population over the next few decades.

REFERENCES

Al-Bazz, S. A., Béland, D., Lane, G. L., Engler-Stringer, R. R., White, J., & Vatanparast, H. (2022). Food security of temporary foreign farm workers under the seasonal agricultural worker program in Canada and the United States: A scoping review. *Advances in Nutrition*, *13*(5), 1603–1627.

Amato, G., Moavero-Milanes, E., Pasquino, G., & Reichlin, L. (Eds.) (2019). *A history of the European Union: Constructing utopia*. Oxford: Hart Publishing.

Araujo, R. C. R., Bobowik, M., Vilar, R., Liu, J. H., de Zuniga, H. G., Kus-Harbord, L., Lebedeva, N., & Gouveia, V. V. (2019). Human values and ideological beliefs as predictors of attitudes toward immigrants across 20 countries: The country-level moderating role of threat. *European Journal of Social Psychology, 50*, 534–546.

Bagavos, C. (2022). On the contribution of foreign-born populations to overall population change in Europe. *Demographic Research, 46*, 179–216.

Carl, N., Dennison, J., & Evans, G. (2019). European but not European enough: An explanation for Brexit. *European Union. Politics, 20*, 282–304.

Castano, E. (2004). European identity: A social-psychological perspective. In R. H. Hermann, T. Reise, & M. N. Brewer (Eds.), *Transnational identities: Becoming European in the EU* (pp. 40–58). Lanham, MD: Rowman & Littlefield.

Cavaille, C., & Marshall, J. (2019). Education and anti-immigrant attitudes: Evidence from compulsory schooling reforms across Western Europe. *American Political Science Review, 113*, 254–263.

Ciaglia, S., Fuest, C., & Heinemann, F. (2018). What a feeling? How to promote "European Identity." EconPol Policy Report, No. 09, info Institute-Leibnitz Institute for Economic Research at the University of Munich, Munich. www.econstor.eu/bitstream/10419/219512/1/econpol-pol-report-09.pdf

Cram, L. (2012). Does the EU need a navel? Implicit and explicit identification with the European Union. *Journal of Common Market Studies, 50*, 71–86.

De Coninck, D. (2023). The refugee paradox during wartime in Europe: How Ukrainian and Afghan refugees are (not) alike. *International Migration Review, 57*, 578–586.

Delanty, G. (2019). The renaissance and the rise of European consciousness. In G. Delanty (Ed.), *Formations of European modernity: A historical and political sociology* (pp. 109–131). Cham, Switzerland: Palgrave Macmillan.

Doomernik, J., & Bruquetas-Callejo, M. (2016). National immigration and integration policies in Europe since 1973. In B. Garces-Mascaranas & R. Penninx (Eds.), *Integration processes and policies in Europe* (pp. 57–76). Cham, Switzerland: Springer.

Drazanova, L., & Gonnot, J. (2023). *Public opinion and immigration in Europe: Can regional migration flows predict public attitudes to immigration?* Working Paper, RSC 2023/18. https://drive.google.com/file/d/1Adopnon_oKBB-DySKTDJTqVYMHMvPo9f/view

Ellermann, A. (2013). When can liberal states avoid unwanted immigration? self-limited sovereignty and guest worker recruitment in Switzerland and Germany. *World Politics, 65*, 491–538.

Eurostat (2023). Online database. Retrieved November 1, 2023. https://ec.europa.eu/eurostat/data/database

FitzGerald, D. S., Cook-Martin, D., Garcia, A. S., & Arar, R. (2017). Can you become one of us? A historical comparison of legal selection of "assimilable" immigrants in Europe and the Americas. *Journal of Ethnic and Migration Studies, 44*, 27–47.

Fligstein, N., Polyakova, A., & Sandholtz, W. (2012). European integration, nationalism, and European identity. *Journal of Common Market Studies*, *50*, 106–122.

Ford, R., & Jennings, W. (2020). The changing cleavage politics of Western Europe. *Annual Review of Political Science*, *23*, 295–314.

Garces-Mascaranas, B., & Penninx, R. (Eds.) (2016). *Integration processes and policies in Europe*. Cham, Switzerland: Springer.

Garib, G. (2011). Why do we feel European? Social mechanisms of European identity. *Journal of Identity and Migration Studies*, *5*, 108–124.

Gehring, K. (2021). Can external threats foster a European Union identity? Evidence from Russia's invasion of Ukraine. *The Economic Journal*, *132*, 1489–1516.

Gorodzeisky, A., & Semyonov, M. (2020). Perceptions and misperceptions: Actual size, perceived size, and opposition to immigration in European societies. *Journal of Ethnic and Migration Studies*, *46*, 612–630.

Grande, E., Schwarzbözi, T., & Fatke, M. (2019). Politicizing immigration in Western Europe. *Journal of European Public Policy*, *26*, 1444–1463.

Green, E. G. T. (2007). Guarding the gates of Europe: A typological analysis of immigrant attitudes across 21 countries. *International Journal of Psychology*, *42*, 365–379.

Hadler, M., Chin, L., & Tsutsui, K. (2021). Conflicting and reinforcing identities in expanding Europe from 1995 to 2019. findings revisited in an even larger Europe. *Innovation: The European Journal of Social Science Research*, *34*, 3–13.

Halikiopoulou, D., & Vlandas, T. (2020). When economic and cultural interests align: The anti-immigrations voter coalitions driving far right party success in Europe. *European Political Science Review*, *12*, 427–448.

Haller, M., & Ressler, R. (2006). National and European identity: A study of their meanings and interrelationships. *Revue française de sociologie*, *47*, 817–850.

Heath, A., Davidov, E., Ford, R., Green, E. G., Ramos, A., & Schmidt, P. (2020). Contested terrain: Explaining divergent patterns of public opinion towards immigration within Europe. *Journal of Ethnic and Migration Studies*, *46*(3), 475-488.

Helbling, M., Simon, S., & Schmid, S. D. (2020). Restricting immigration to foster migrant integration? A comparative study across 22 European countries. *Journal of Ethnic and Migration Studies*, *46*, 2603–2624.

Hobolt, S. B. (2016). The Brexit vote: A divided nation, a divided continent. *Journal of European Public Policy*, *23*, 1259–1277.

Kohli, M. (2000). The battlegrounds of European identity. *European Societies*, *2*, 113–137.

Koning, E. A. (2023). Breaking through: How anti-immigrant parties establish themselves and the implications for their study. *Journal of Elections, Public Opinion and Parties*, *33*, 519–537.

Kulu, H., Milewski, N., Hannemann, T., & Mikolai, J. (2019). A decade of life-course research on fertility of immigrants and their descendants in Europe. *Demographic Research, 40*, 1345–1374.

Lutz, W., Amran, G., Bélanger, A., Conte, A., Gailey, N., Ghio, D., ... & Stonawski, M. (2019). *Demographic scenarios for the EU: Migration, population and education.* New York: Publications Office of the European Union.

Martin, J. C., & Indelicato, A. (2023). A fuzzy-hybrid analysis of citizens' perception toward immigrants in Europe. *Quality & Quantity, 57*, 1101–1124.

Martin, P. L. (2001). There is nothing more permanent than temporary foreign workers. *Backgrounder.* Washington, DC: Center for Immigration Studies. https://cis.org/Report/There-Nothing-More-Permanent-Temporary-Foreign-Workers

Maurin, E., & Navarrete, N. (2023). Behind the veil: The effect of banning the Islamic veil in schools. *Economic Policy, 38*, 63–98.

McMahon, R. (2022). Is alt-Europe possible? Populist radical right counternarratives of European integration. *Journal of Contemporary European Studies, 30*, 10–25.

Moghaddam, F. M. (2024). *The psychology of revolution.* New York: Cambridge University Press.

Muller, H., & Tommel, I. (Eds.) (2022). *Women & leadership in the European Union.* Oxford: Oxford University Press.

Parr, N. (2023). Immigration and the prospects for long-run population decreases in European countries. *Vienna Yearbook of Population Research, 21*, 1–29.

Pettigrew, T. F., Wagner, U., & Christ, O. (2007). Who opposes immigration? Comparing German and North American findings. *Du Bois Review, 4*, 19–39.

Postelnicescu, C. (2016). Europe's new identity: The refugee crisis and the rise of nationalism. *Europe's Journal of Psychology, 12*, 203–209.

Richards, I. (2022). A philosophical and historical analysis of "generation identity": Fascism, online media, and the European new right. *Terrorism and Political Violence, 34*, 28–47.

Salem, S. (2018). Denmark's quest to socialize the "ghettos": The dark history of forced assimilation in Europe. *Discover Society.* July 3. https://archive.discoversociety.org/2018/07/03/denmarks-quest-to-socialize-the-ghettos-the-dark-history-of-forced-assimilation-in-europe/

Sides, J., & Citron, J. (2007). European opinion about immigrants: The role of identities, interests and information. *British Journal of Political Science, 37*, 477–504.

Stockemer, D., & Halikiopoulou, D. (2022). Multiple routes to immigration scepticism: The association between individual grievances and anti-immigrant attitudes in Canada, Germany, and the USA. *International Migration, 61*, 126–141.

Strath, B. (2002). A European identity: To the historical limits of a concept. *European Journal of Social Theory, 5*, 387–401.

Triandafyllidou, A. & Gropas, R. (2023). *What is Europe?* London: Routledge.
United Nations (2022). *World population prospects.* New York: United Nations Population Division. https://population.un.org/wpp/Publications/
Tselios, V., & Tomaney, J. (2019). Decentralisation and European identity. *EPA: Economy and Space, 51,* 133–155.
Van Mol, C. (2022). Intra-European student mobility and the different meanings of "Europe." *Acta Sociologica, 65,* 24–40.
Weber, H. (2015). National and regional proportion of immigrants and perceived threat of immigrants: A three-level analysis in Western Europe. *International Journal of Comparative Sociology, 56,* 116–140.

CHAPTER 7

Immigration within the Global South
Case Studies in South America

The continued growth of international migration highlights the importance of giving more attention to the challenge of managing immigration, as well as diversity within the host society (Global Migration Data Portal, 2021). For example, political repression and economic collapse in the early twenty-first century have resulted in millions of people leaving Venezuela. As a consequence, assisting Venezuelan immigrants to integrate into new host societies has been a pressing issue for neighboring Latin American countries. Similarly, following the invasion of Ukraine by Russian forces, looking after Ukrainian refugees in Europe and North America has been a pressing issue in neighboring European countries. Although the literature has distinguished between immigrants and refugees (De Haas et al., 2020), in this chapter we use immigrants as a broad term that includes refugees.

Even though migration has been extensively studied and documented, the focus has remained almost exclusively on high-income societies. Indeed, according to McAuliffe and Khadria (2019), most of the studies concentrate on the Global North countries of Europe and North America, and psychologically informed policies aimed at promoting immigrant inclusion. The goal of this chapter is to achieve a better understanding of migration management in the Global South from a psychological perspective. This remains a neglected topic in research.

Immigration in South America is significantly shaped by shared identity factors, particularly religion and language, which have deep historical roots. During the early twentieth century, Brazil and Argentina experienced substantial migration, with Catholic identities playing a prominent role. Catholic immigrants from Italy and Germany contributed to the cultural fabric of these countries. Additionally, the prevalence of Spanish as the most widely spoken language in South America facilitates migration between Spanish-speaking countries. However, not all identities contribute to immigration. South American national identities were also shaped by war. After the emancipation wars, several wars between South American countries configured the current border and national rival identities. Old national rivalries can easily turn into prejudices against immigrants. In addition, South America has a rich diversity of Indigenous peoples who preexisted the modern nation states. Their presence endowed these states with diversity, and the influx of immigrants further enriches this tapestry.

This chapter explores immigration management in South America, examining the interplay of psychological and sociological factors. Through this analysis, the chapter aims to contribute to a comprehensive understanding of immigration management in South America, from a social and psychological perspective. We begin by providing an overview of migration in the region, highlighting migration trends since 2010. In addition, the chapter includes an investigation of the relationship between gender and migration in South America. Subsequently, the paper delves into the evolution of immigration policies in South America, underscoring how contextual factors shape immigration management practices. Next, we examine how multiculturalism has been influenced by legislation in South America. We consider cases where countries explicitly incorporate multiculturalism as part of legislation. Finally, the chapter addresses anti-immigrant sentiment in South America, exploring the drivers behind it and the potential implications for immigration policies and practices. In the conclusion, the chapter reflects on issues of contingent urgency in immigration management, offering policy implications and highlighting future research agendas.

Migration in South America

To effectively manage migration within South America, it is essential to begin with a comprehensive understanding of migration patterns in the region. Migration in South America mostly involves immigrants from within the region. According to the United Nations Department of Economic and Social Affairs (UN DESA) (2020), about 80 percent of the immigrants in South America are from other Southern American countries. Moreover, in 2020, about half of the immigrants in South America came from one country: the Bolivarian Republic of Venezuela (henceforth, Venezuela). According to the same source, more than 70 percent of the immigrants in South America come from Venezuela, Colombia, and Paraguay. The data shows that South American countries with the largest number of immigrants (i.e., the receiving countries) are Argentina, Colombia, Venezuela, and Peru. As intraregional migration is

Table 7.1 *Immigration in South America in 2020*

	Immigrant population in 2020		Change in immigrants since 2010	
	Southern American immigrants	Total immigrants	Southern American immigrants	Total immigrants
Argentina	1.89 M (4.2%)	2.28 M (5.0%)	0.42 M (0.6%)	0.48 M (0.6%)
Bolivia	0.11 M (0.9%)	0.16 M (1.4%)	0.03 M (0.1%)	0.04 M (0.2%)
Brazil	0.47 M (0.2%)	1.08 M (0.5%)	0.30 M (0.1%)	0.49 M (0.2%)
Chile	1.22 M (6.3%)	1.65 M (8.5%)	0.965 M (4.8%)	1.27 M (6.4%)
Colombia	1.82 M (3.6%)	1.91 M (3.7%)	1.75 M (3.4%)	1.78 M (3.5%)
Ecuador	0.63 M (3.6%)	0.79 M (4.5%)	0.37 M (1.9%)	0.41 M (1.9%)
Guyana	0.02 M (3.4%)	0.03 M (3.9%)	0.02 M (2.8%)	0.02 M (2.9%)
Paraguay	0.15 M (2.2%)	0.17 M (2.6%)	0.00 M (−0.2%)	0.00 M (−0.2%)
Peru	1.06 M (3.2%)	1.22 M (3.7%)	1.01 M (3.0%)	1.12 M (3.4%)
Suriname	0.01 M (3.2%)	0.05 M (7.9%)	0.00 M (0.2%)	0.00 M (0.6%)
Uruguay	0.06 M (1.9%)	0.11 M (3.2%)	0.02 M (0.7%)	0.03 M (0.8%)
Venezuela	1.04 M (0.0%)	1.32 M (0.0%)	0.01 M (0.0%)	−0.03 M (0.0%)

Note. Data from UN DESA (2020).

the prevalent type of migration in South America, comprehending the migration trends within the region is fundamental to effective migration management.

Table 7.1 shows immigration statistics for all South American countries. It displays the immigrant population in 2020 and the change in immigrant population since 2010. In addition, the table differentiates between the data pertaining to immigrants from Southern America with respect to the overall immigrant population (i.e., "Total immigrants"). In 2020, Chile, Suriname, and Argentina are the countries with the highest proportion of overall immigrants compared to their populations. When it comes to South American immigrants, Chile, Argentina, Colombia, and Ecuador have the largest proportion of immigrants in relation to their populations.

To gain a deeper understanding of the profound shifts that occurred in migration patterns, we consider Table 7.1 which further provides information on the change in immigrants since 2010. According to Table 7.1, Chile, Colombia, and Peru display the highest increase in immigrants' percentage points since 2010. Changes in immigrant population since 2010 show the same trends for immigrants from South America and all immigrants (see Table 7.1). This suggests that immigration changes are driven by regional and international shifts.

The situation in Venezuela presents a notable and intricate scenario characterized by the emigration of a significant number of people, surpassing 7 million by 2023 (out of a total Venezuelan population of almost 29 million), within South America (R4V, 2023). This phenomenon underscores the strong correlation between migration and sociopolitical factors, as emphasized by McAuliffe and Khadria (2019, pp. 102–103). The deterioration of democracy, economy, and security in Venezuela has given rise to large-scale emigration, resulting in a substantial Venezuelan diaspora across Southern American countries (Bull & Rosales, 2020; De Haas et al., 2020). In Colombia, an ongoing internal crisis fueled by conflicts involving the government, left-wing guerrillas, and drug cartels has compelled numerous individuals to seek safety abroad (De Haas et al., 2020). Migration drivers such as food insecurity and violence have escalated (Morales-Muñoz et al., 2020). In the case of Paraguay, a significant proportion of migrants primarily choose Argentina as their destination country (UN DESA, 2020). The availability of employment opportunities in other countries, and the lack of such opportunities at home, serve as the primary impetus for Paraguayan migration (Cerrutti & Parrado, 2015; Parrado & Cerrutti, 2003). Thus, it becomes apparent that political and economic conditions play pivotal roles as primary drivers shaping migration dynamics within South America. The complexities of the Venezuelan situation, the internal crisis in Colombia, and the labor-driven migration from Paraguay to Argentina exemplify the multifaceted nature of migration patterns in the region.

Gender Trends in Immigration across South America

Examining the gender makeup of immigrants can provide insights into the underlying dynamics of migration patterns. The gender ratio indicates related factors that impact immigration. For example, as Gabaccia (2016) reports, a labor market that demands care workers drives a higher proportion of female immigrants, but the number of male immigrants rises when the oil industry has a shortage of workers. The gender differences in migration may indicate the need to implement specific measures. Bastia and Piper (2019) argue that immigration is theorized from a Global North and male-dominated perspective and more attention needs to be given to policies that impact women in the Global South, such as policies that prevent women's sex trafficking.

According to data from the Population Division of the UN DESA (2020) the percentage of international immigration of women to South America is 50.3 percent, which shows neglectable gender difference in the immigration stock in South America. The immigration data from the

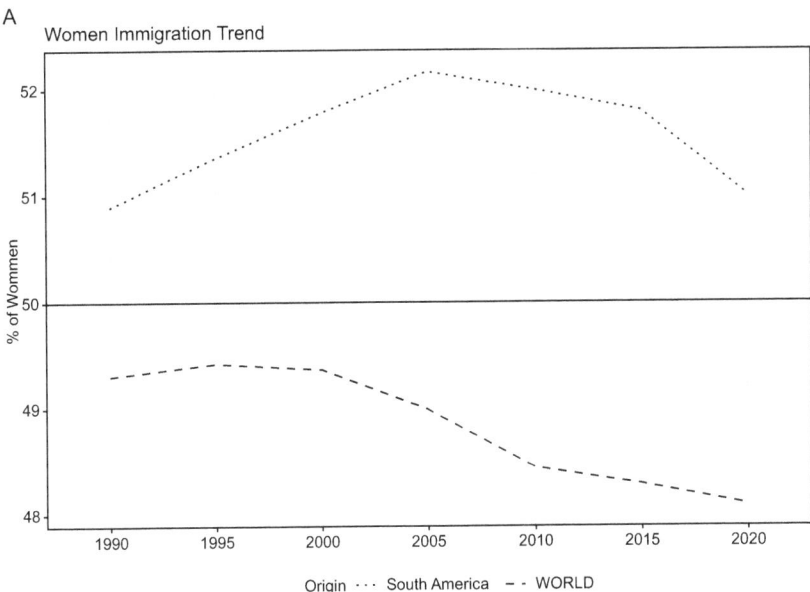

Figure 7.1a Analyzing regional immigration trends of women to South America from 1990 to 2020.

1990s to 2020 shows minimal gender differences in migration within South America over time. Specifically, as shown in Figure 7.1A, the percentage of South American immigrant women peaked in 2005 at 52 percent (dotted line), only to return to previous levels. On the other hand, immigration trends for women from other parts of the world show a significant decline since 1990, as seen in Figure 7.1A (dashed line).

Immigration within South American countries reveals variations in patterns regarding the gender composition of immigrants according to the country of origin (see Figure 7.1B). In most South American countries, the percentage of South American women exceeds the percentage of women from other parts of the world. For example, in Bolivia, Brazil, and Paraguay, there are fewer women immigrants than men over time, while Chile, Colombia, Ecuador, and Venezuela show that the trends from immigrant women from the region differ from those of immigrant women from other parts of the world. Although Argentina and Uruguay contradict this general trend, they show tendencies where immigrant women exceed immigrant men.

Political and economic instability helps to explain the trends in migration among women to some countries. A major driver of immigration is violence: Sometimes, women are forced to emigrate (De Haas, 2020).

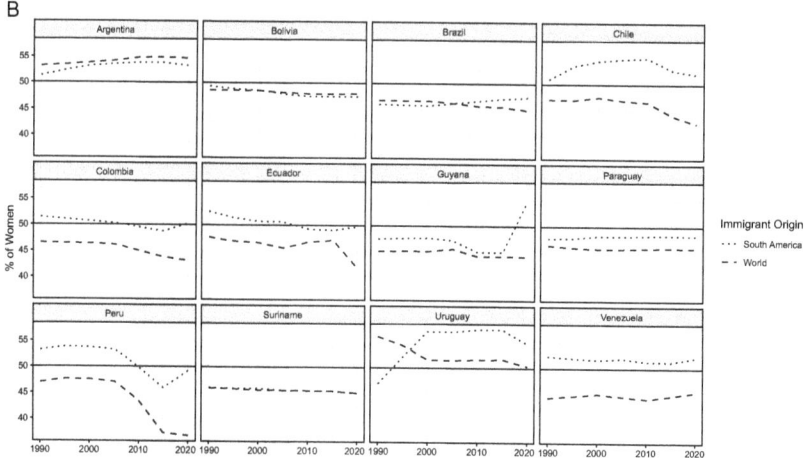

Figure 7.1b Analyzing country-level immigration trends in South America from 1990 to 2020.

Note. The percentages refer to the total immigrant population in (A) South America or (B) in the corresponding country. The dotted line represents South American women who migrated within the region, while the dashed line represents all women who migrated to South America.

In particular, violence in Colombia and Venezuela shapes women's migration: Migration is an escape from violence (Macaya-Aguirre & Espinoza, 2021). Moreover, women escaping violence often fear retribution against the remaining family members in their country of origin. Thus, women attempt to reunite the family in the new society. Women from South America migrate to countries that offer greater security. Therefore, while gender migration is not a widespread phenomenon in South America, gender does play a role in the migration of women within the region to countries that offer better living conditions.

Gender roles create barriers for women seeking to escape stereotypical roles, particularly during times of economic instability. Curtis and Pacecca (2014) described how immigrant women from Bolivia, Paraguay, and Peru who sought domestic labor in Argentina during the 2001 economic crisis, had limited power to negotiate working conditions due to the gender roles imposed by both the employer (i.e., *la patrona*) and other employees. In addition, migration within the same region offers the possibility of creating circular migratory pathways. For example, the close distances between Chile, Argentina, Peru, and Bolivia result in immigrant women combining jobs that offer better economic opportunities in a host society with a distance that facilitates a frequent return home (Guizardi & Garcés, 2013).

Evolution of Immigration Policies: South America's Shifting Landscape

South America has a rich history of immigration, and this has influenced national identities in the region. Migration to South America as we know it today is rooted in European colonization from the sixteenth and seventeenth centuries. Colonial immigrants built colonies, extracted natural resources from their original countries, and simultaneously created the foundations for the future South American republics. This section will explore the evolution in immigrant management, showing how national identity and the international political environment shaped migration. By analyzing these complex interactions, we provide a deeper understanding of the shifting relationship between national identity and immigration.

Immigration patterns in Latin America during the nineteenth and early twentieth centuries show that political leaders often used immigration policies to advance their own goals and agendas. The connections of immigration, politics, and national identity were tools used by leaders to advance their national agendas. After obtaining independence from colonial powers, Southern American countries were confronted by the challenge of securing their territory and promoting national development. Toward this goal, political leaders in South American countries relied on European immigration as a means to advance both a "civilizing" agenda and economic development, primarily centered on agricultural expansion (Acosta Arcarazo, 2017; Cano Christiny et al., 2009; Goebel, 2010; Seyferth, 2013). In pursuit of this objective, these nations actively facilitated European migration by allocating available lands for immigrant agricultural development while concurrently asserting territorial authority over previously unutilized territories.

The example of Uruguayan settlers illustrates the connection between national identity and immigration during the late 1800s and early 1900s. Uruguay also relied on the immigration and assimilation of Europeans to build the fabric of a new society. Italian and Spanish immigrants actively embraced the practices of their host nation, as evidenced by their integration into Uruguay's agricultural sector (Goebel, 2010). They readily adopted the lifestyle of the Uruguayan gauchos, immersing themselves in local traditions and rural customs. This assimilation manifested in their proficiency in cattle farming, horseback riding, and rural activities, gradually knitting them into the vibrant tapestry of gaucho culture; thus advancing the economic agenda and creating a harmonization between the gaucho way of life. This forged strong ties between Italian and Spanish immigrants with the Uruguayan community and also significantly molded the contours of modern Uruguayan identity. Moreover, granting citizenship "turned" immigrant children into Argentinians, Brazilians, and Uruguayans (Goebel, 2022), further imbricating politics, identity, and migration management.

However, later political developments created an unwelcoming environment for immigrants in South America. The identities and motives of foreign nationals, mostly Europeans, began to be viewed with suspicion in South America at the beginning of the twentieth century. As a result, policies previously designed to encourage immigration were halted, and in some cases, new policies created barriers. In effect, the political tensions caused by the First World War and the rising nativist politics – a political ideology that translates into policies that promote the native-born over immigrants – in South America raised apprehensions toward immigrants (De Haas et al., 2020; Munck & Luna, 2022).

In Southern Brazil, the presence of a significant number of German settlers led to suspicions and accusations of their alleged support for Germany during the First World War (Goebel, 2016). Additionally, the same author mentions President Getúlio Vargas's attempt to expel European immigrants during the Great Depression and shut down language schools. Thus, immigration policies were sensitive to the political context: Southern American countries adjusted their immigration policies to fit the international or national political context.

Political instability and dictatorships in South America from the 1960s to the 1980s had a significant impact on immigration patterns. During this time, South American politics were heavily influenced by the Cold War. On the one hand, the United States funded authoritarian governments and dictators and provided military support to prevent the spread of communism in South America. On the other hand, the Soviet Union and Cuba offered military training to revolutionary forces with the aim of creating revolutions and establishing communist regimes (Harmer, 2014). As a result of geopolitical tensions, emigration increased in countries that experienced revolutions.

Nationality and political views became drivers of emigration. As a consequence of the region's political instability, European immigration to South America declined. In effect, immigration was not appealing during this troubled time. However, an exception to the rule was Venezuela. Where most of the South American countries had dictators during the second half of the century, Venezuela had a relatively stable democracy. Moreover, the oil industry created a notable economic boom that created a demand for labor workers, driving immigration from neighboring countries such as Colombia (Cerrutti & Parrado, 2019). Mira (2019) shows that asylum policies promoted migration to

Venezuela in the 1960s, allowing South Americans to escape dictatorship in their homelands. Mira (2019) reports the testimony of a Chilean who entered the Venezuelan ambassador residency only to witness about two hundred people ahead in the line to seek refuge in Venezuela.

In South America, various dictatorships played a significant role in driving migration (Cerrutti & Parrado, 2015). During the time of Stroessner's dictatorship in Paraguay from 1954 to 1989, there was a noticeable increase in people migrating from Paraguay to Venezuela. Similarly, under Banzer's regime in Bolivia from 1971 to 1978, more Bolivians started migrating to Argentina. Migratory movements were not random but were influenced by political instability, dictatorships, and economic factors prevalent in South America during the 1960s to 1980s. Political instability and violent regimes led to changes in migration patterns where people escaped dictatorships.

The democratic wave of the 1990s marked a new shift in immigration trends. The end of the Cold War brought changes in South America: lower political oppression, the implementation of free trade agreements, and the widespread expansion of global markets. In this way, synergies between increased political stability in South American countries, opening economies, and commerce between Latin and South American countries created incentives for international mobility in the region. Two major agreements shaped South American migration. First, dating from 1969 the Andean Community had the objective of integration and development of a common market (Stang, 2009). However, the political tensions in South America did not help to implement the trade agreements between countries. For instance, Pinochet – Chile's dictator at the time – withdrew the country from the pact in 1976. The current members are Bolivia, Colombia, Ecuador, and Peru. The rest of the South American countries are now associate members, save for Venezuela. In 2001, the Andean Community reached agreements that promoted labor migration, prevented discrimination against migrant workers, and allowed free movement among the members of the Andean Community (Bernal et al., 2015; Stang, 2009).

The second major regional treaty is the Southern Common Market (or MERCOSUR). It is a regional trade bloc in South America that promotes economic cooperation and integration among its member countries. It includes Argentina, Brazil, Paraguay, Uruguay, and Venezuela (though Venezuela's membership has been suspended since August 5, 2017) as stable members and Bolivia, Chile, Colombia, Ecuador, Guyana, Peru, and Surinam as associate members.

MERCOSUR showed concern for the rights and security of migrants in its migration dispositions during the 2000s. The member states of the organization, while promoting labor mobility, sought to provide a legal body that would give social guarantees to migrants. In effect, MERCOSUR's residential agreement showed a favorable disposition to extend documentation to immigrants (Prieto-Rosas & Bengochea, 2022). For instance, the Residence Agreement, which was established in 2002 and includes almost every South American State, has been instrumental in promoting migration within the region and granting immigrants equal rights in labor with respect to native-born (Brumat, 2020; Cerrutti & Parrado, 2019; Prieto-Rosas & Bengochea, 2022). However, critics argue that MERCOSUR's disposition fails to balance the importance of immigrants' social rights with the importance given to labor mobility (Romano, 2009).

Following this discussion of the evolution of immigration policies in South America and the intricate relationship between national identity, politics, and migration over time, the following section will shift to explore the changes in national regulations governing immigration. This will provide insights into how South American nations implemented multiculturalism as a response to evolving migration dynamics.

Regulations, Multiculturalism, and Migration Management

The growing regional integration facilitated by agreements such as the Southern Common Market (MERCOSUR – *Mercado Común del Sur* in Spanish) and Andean Community (CAN – *Comunidad Andina* in Spanish), coupled with improved economic stability and prosperity that emerged in the 1990s, set the stage for a significant increase in intraregional migration starting in the 2000s. Concurrently, South America was influenced by global trends, particularly from the Global North, prompting the incorporation of multiculturalism into its migratory frameworks. The following section will show how some South American countries *explicitly* included the concept of multiculturalism in their formal regulations. It is worth noting that in some contexts, multiculturalism may also have been implemented without being explicitly named. Multiculturalism was implemented in different forms in South America.

Multiculturalism is the root of the linked theoretical constructs proposing the "celebration of cultural differences" of ethnic groups. Argentina explicitly framed migration management under multiculturalism. In effect, according to Argentina's Migration Law (Migration Law No. 25,781), to promote immigrant integration, the State and local governments will favor training "inspired by criteria for coexistence in a multicultural society" (art. 14). While MERCOSUR discussed migratory regulations among its members in the early 2000s, multicultural policies were specifically incorporated into migration regulation in Argentina (Soria, 2009). This led to a shift in the discourse surrounding identity differences, framing them as a valuable contribution rather than a problem. As a result, state policies began to reflect this mindset. According to Soria, educational policies were influenced by the multicultural framework to teach individuals to live in a diverse society that values and respects diversity. In addition, multiculturalism has inspired primary and secondary teachers to develop educational practices that acknowledge and appreciate the cultural differences that immigrant children bring (Beheran, 2012). Ethnographic fieldwork in Argentina by Soria has revealed the efforts of teachers to celebrate the cultural diversity brought by immigrant children's ethnicity.

Multiculturalism has also shaped Argentinian health policies; immigrants have the right to equal access to health, education, and labor, among other social rights (Argentina's Migration Law No. 25,781, art. 6). Despite this, Noy and Voorend (2016) report that immigrants face obstacles when attempting to access healthcare. In effect, the researchers found that immigration law is interpreted in different ways at different levels of the government, requiring different types of documents (e.g., national identification documents) that prevents health care access in some cases.

A second concept that developed from multiculturalism is interculturalism. In South America, Bolivia and Chile specifically use interculturalism to describe the relationship between immigrants, Indigenous people (in the case of Bolivia), and members of the host society (Migration Law 370, Bolivia, art. 2; Migration and Foreigner Law No. 21,325, Chile, art. 6). *Interculturalism* prioritizes integration and the methods utilized to accomplish it rather than emphasizing cultural differences, which is a distinct contrast to multiculturalism (Taylor, 2012). Yet, a distinctive note of interculturalism is the critical examination of colonialism and neoliberalism in Latin America (Walsh, 2008). Interculturalism aims to overcome colonialism and neoliberalism through the interactions between immigrants and native populations. Thus, interculturalism as a frame to understand immigration aims at the coexistence of different cultures that retain those differences across time while interacting with each other to overcome "oppressive structures" (Pardo, 2012, pp. 163–165).

Interculturalism impacted migration management prior to its role in migratory law. While the Chilean migration law was signed in 2021, NGO practitioners and civil servants were already implementing interculturalism in migration management before the law came into effect. Hence, interculturality was "pushed" into the Migration Law by practitioners. According to a study by Aninat and Sierra (2019), the government used accreditation processes to promote interculturality in several municipalities with many immigrants. At the federal level, the Ministry of Education introduced a policy for immigrant students that aimed to create an "intercultural school" to promote equal relationships between immigrant and native students (Agencia de Calidad de la Educación et al., 2019). This policy aimed to provide a formal solution to the numerous educational challenges that teachers attempted to solve intuitively (Martínez Rojas et al., 2021).

In Bolivia, the situation regarding interculturalism and immigration differs from Chile. As indicated in Table 7.1, Bolivia has a small immigrant population of approximately 160,000 individuals, which accounts for about 1.6 percent of the total population. In contrast, the Indigenous population constitutes about 48 percent of the population (IWGIA, 2023). Therefore, it is reasonable to assume that the lack of regulations on intercultural education for immigrants results from the small number of immigrants. In effect, the notion of interculturalism has permeated strongly in Bolivia. It shifted into the political arena, resulting in the inclusion of higher numbers of Indigenous people in Congress and in the recognition of cultural and self-government rights (Calderón & Castells, 2020; Mayorga, 2017; Munck & Luna, 2022, table 2.10). Hence, it is also reasonable to assume that intercultural practices toward Indigenous people may also affect how immigrants are managed. However, future research is needed to evaluate how interculturalism affects migration management.

Paraguay embodies another variation of multiculturalism: Pluriculturalism. Paraguay defines itself as a pluricultural state and uses this definition as a guiding principle in its Migratory Law (Migration Law 6984, art. 4). However, similar to the Chilean case, pluriculturalism was adopted and practiced informally before it was included in migration law. According to Walsh (2008), pluriculturalism is a term used to describe existing diversity in South America in contrast to new diversity created by immigration in North America. Pluriculturalism points to existing differences between native people living in the South, while multiculturalism points to the differences introduced by international immigration in North America.

South America has embraced multiculturalism in various ways, influencing immigration policies. Argentina promoted immigrant integration under multiculturalism, Chile adopted interculturalism to foster integration, and Paraguay defined itself as a pluricultural state, using this as a guide to its migration law. These diverse approaches highlight the celebration of cultural differences and promote integration, equal rights, and social inclusion in South American immigration policies, shaping the continent's evolving migration landscape.

Evidence from the Field: Empirical Research on South American Immigrants

The previous section showed how legislators use multiculturalism to frame intergroup relations between majority groups and immigrants. However, multiculturalism is also an ideology that guides how different groups should interact with each other: Activists, practitioners, and ordinary citizens can promote multiculturalism through a bottom-up approach. On the other hand, we must also consider the actions and choices immigrants make. In effect, some immigrants may adapt to the host society, leaving behind customs and traditions, thereby adopting an assimilation strategy for integration. In this section, we explore evidence from different South American countries that shows how immigrants and natives engage in assimilation or multiculturalism practices. In addition, we highlight how contextual factors shape multiculturalism and assimilation.

Immigrants' attitudes toward adaptation influence integration outcomes. Whether immigrants are inclined to adopt or reject the culture of the new society shapes their relationship with mainstream society. Empirical evidence has shown that Venezuelan immigrants in Colombia who showed a greater sense of identification with the host society had better engagement and psychological adaptation (Safdar et al., 2023). This suggests that Venezuelans in Colombia are participating in assimilation practices by adopting aspects of Colombian culture. In a similar vein, Safdar et al. (2023) underscored that having support from ingroup members (i.e., other Venezuelans, such as family members) and outgroup members (i.e., Colombian natives) predicted better adaptation and psychological well-being. This illustrates how engaging with the host society promotes better integration outcomes. Immigrants who find a balance between embracing aspects of the host culture (assimilation) and retaining their cultural heritage (multiculturalism) tend to adapt more successfully. Natives can support this process by being inclusive and open to cultural diversity, such as by promoting multicultural policies, encouraging cross-cultural interactions, and providing platforms for cultural expression.

Adaptation to the new society may also derive from *cultural intelligence*, the capacity to accurately comprehend social interactions following the prevailing norms of the host society and, subsequently, to adjust one's conduct accordingly. Because they have had more time to learn and adapt, second-generation immigrants may have higher cultural intelligence than first-generation immigrants, which might explain their higher integration. The importance of cultural intelligence was highlighted by Castro Solano and Perugini (2021, Study 4). They found that immigrants in Argentina with greater cultural intelligence achieved better adaptation and frequently interacted with Argentinians.

Social interactions with members of the new society and other immigrants can also influence assimilation and multicultural practices. Empirical research shows that close relationships influence adaptation to a new society. For example, Pavez-Soto and Chan (2018) show how second-generation children (aged 9–11) in Chile negotiate their identity when they celebrate their parents' traditions while acknowledging being Chilean citizens or when they act as cultural translators for their parents. The authors note that the children's multicultural identity challenges the idea that they should have an exclusionary identity: They argue that it is possible to be Chilean, Indigenous, and Equatorian at the same time.

The contextual factors that shape assimilation relate the surrounding environment to the existing culture. While reviewing existing literature, Espinosa et al. (2021) discovered that in Latin American nations, there was an association between right-wing authoritarianism and national identification among a higher proportion of the Mestizo/White population within each specific country. Thus, Southern American countries with higher proportions of Mestizo/White such as Argentina, Colombia, Chile, Ecuador, and Venezuela (and not in Bolivia and Paraguay), have a higher number of individuals with an authoritarian conception of the nation, which excludes immigrants. This trend was particularly strong if immigrants came from other countries in South America that had higher numbers of Indigenous or Black–African people, or if the national identity of the immigrant country highlighted the identity of Indigenous or Black-Africans.

Political leadership and culture in South American countries play a crucial role in fostering discourses about immigrants that later translate into policies or practices. Guizardi and Mardones (2021) analyzed the construction of anti-immigrant speech in the media and its consequences in Brazil by conducting ethnographic work in Foz do Iguaçu, which is a Brazilian city known for intense migration due to its proximity to Paraguay and Argentina. In a scenario where President Jair Bolsonaro (2019–2022) promoted anti-immigrant speech linking immigrants to crime, the researcher showed how anti-immigrant speech can legitimize deleterious practices against immigrants. In effect, the researchers observed how supporters embraced anti-immigrant rhetoric from their leader, President Bolsonaro, when discussing "cleansing" the country. Hence, anti-immigrant speech in South America sometimes finds support from political leaders who spread anti-immigrant sentiments among their followers.

Lay persons probably also develop anti-immigrant sentiments through the influence of mass media coverage (including electronic media) linking migration and crime. The connection between migration and crime has been a subject of ongoing debate. While assessing this link, Ousey and Kubrin (2018) found that the impact is almost negligible. Thus, according to the authors, immigration probably has no substantial effect on crime. However, transnational crime organizations exploit immigration to advance their objectives. As a result, news coverage exposing the criminal activities of these types of organizations can elicit reasonable concerns regarding immigration, particularly illegal immigration. For example, the Aragua Train (*Tren de Aragua* in Spanish) is an international crime organization originally from Venezuela that expanded its criminal activities to Colombia, Brazil, Ecuador, Peru, and Chile (Terán, 2023). The organization is based in the Tocoron Prison located in the Aragua region (Venezuela) and has local gangs exerting control over specific locations (Ford, 2020). For instance, the "Gallego clan" specialized in human, sex, and drug trafficking and neighborhood control through fear and extortion of local business owners while controlling the Peru–Chile border (Carvajal Vega & Batarce, 2023; Huamaní, 2023). Hence, the spread of criminal organizations along migration routes has heightened fear and anti-immigrant sentiments among the local population.

A study conducted by Meseguer and Kemmerling (2018) examined the emergence of anti-immigrant sentiment within Latin American countries. Drawing from data in the 2008 OECD and LAPOP datasets, the researchers sought to identify the drivers supporting such sentiments. More specifically, they examined if labor market competition or increased taxes for social welfare drove anti-immigrant sentiment. Surprisingly, their findings underscored a connection between anti-immigrant sentiment and increased taxation, particularly within countries characterized by expansive welfare states and substantial influxes of immigrants – illustrated by instances in countries such as Argentina and Uruguay. In line with Meseguer and Kemmerling's prediction, Lawrence (2011) further examined the relation between material concern and a contrasting viewpoint based on distinct datasets and methodologies. His research revealed a correlation between economic concerns and the emergence of anti-immigrant sentiment in South America. Lawrence's (2011) research uncovered that the link between worries about personal economic well-being and the rise of anti-immigrant feelings in South America could not be mitigated by Catholicism. On the contrary, South American Catholics showed less support for immigrants (Lawrence, 2011). Realistic Conflict Theory (Sherif, 1966) helps explain Lawrence's findings by suggesting that conflicts often arise when groups compete for the same resources.

Nonetheless, the surge in immigration during the mid-2010s – largely due to the influx of Venezuelans – raises questions about the persistence of previous research regarding the economic driver of anti-immigrant sentiment. The changes in the migration dynamic may have altered the validity of the research. A subsequent study sought to ascertain the significance of economic concerns in a context characterized by heightened immigration (Lawrence, 2015). Analyzing data from Chile, a country that experienced nearly double the number of immigrants from 2010 to 2015, Lawrence (2015) found that job competition remained a minimal driver of anti-immigrant sentiment. Notably, his research revealed a surprising support for high-skilled immigrant labor, even from ethnic minorities or South American countries with a high percentage of Indigenous populations (e.g., Peru). On the other hand, a significant driver of anti-immigrant sentiment is the belief that immigration leads to increased taxation (Meseguer & Kemmerling, 2018). Therefore, when immigrants tend to be lower-skilled laborers, anti-immigrant sentiments may link fear of increased taxation to accommodate the arrival of immigrants.

Psychology has illuminated the intricacies between economics and anti-immigrant sentiment. Economic conditions are key when considering individual or collective survival. In this regard, empirical studies in South America have demonstrated that valuing survival is associated with perceiving immigrants as a threat: Those who prioritize survival are more inclined to perceive immigrants as a threat (Gouveia et al., 2021). A nuanced examination of this association, however, highlights that much of the effect is mediated through individuals exhibiting high tendencies of social dominance (i.e., a high score in the Social Dominance scale) or those who prioritize authority and hierarchy (i.e., a high score in the Right-Wing Authoritarianism scale). Interestingly, Gouveia and colleagues investigated whether living in an environment with a substantial immigrant presence heightened perceived threat through survival values. Contrary to conventional assumptions, prior research suggested that a higher immigrant population does not necessarily amplify perceived threat (Schmidt et al., 2014). Furthermore, these studies demonstrated a negative correlation between increased intergroup contact – often facilitated by higher immigrant numbers – and perceived threat. These findings align with Contact Theory, reinforcing the idea that greater ethnic diversity does not inherently breed heightened perceived threats.

Concluding Comment

Immigration within the South American region offers a multifaceted landscape. In 2020, about 80 percent of immigrants in South America came from other Southern American countries, with Venezuela being the primary source. Current trends show that sociopolitical factors drive immigration. In the same way, political instability leads women to migrate within South America, resulting in an increase in women in specific countries within the region. The fact that sociopolitical factors mostly drive regional immigration underscores the need for cooperation. A regional strategy for immigration could manage migration and address underlying factors. Tailored policies could improve efficiency and foster partnerships to find sustainable solutions. Although challenging to achieve, a regional approach could provide a framework to address complexities and promote cooperation between nations. The extension of existing cooperation agreements signed by several of the South American nations (e.g., MERCOSUR, CAN) may offer potential ways to address immigration management. For example, binding agreements that manage migration may lower the chances of political leaders using anti-immigrant sentiments to further authoritarian and anti-democratic causes.

Multiculturalism plays a significant role in shaping immigration policies in South America. Argentina, Bolivia, Chile, and Paraguay explicitly adopt multicultural principles in migratory regulation. Other South American countries also have policies influenced by multiculturalism. But there needs to be greater progress in developing diversity management policies that effectively integrate Indigenous people, immigrants, and others into the nation state. One possibility is to focus on similarities between all groups; what everyone has in common simply because of their human status.

The chapter shows how individual and contextual factors can influence the adaptation of immigrants into the host society. Of notable importance is the presence of anti-immigrant sentiments, which can be influenced by political leaders and news reports, among others, about criminal organizations exploiting immigration for their objectives. Even though some people with positive views toward migration may overlook connections between immigration and crime, it is important to develop a view of migration capable of recognizing how illegal immigration can serve as an entry point for criminal organizations, a point that is often exploited by authoritarian politicians. Managing immigrants and integrating them into the host society will be improved by recognizing the perils of illegal immigration, particularly when criminal organizations are involved. Policymakers should consider emphasizing integration while addressing factors that fuel anti-immigrant sentiments, such as criminal organization involvement with immigration.

In the future, a better understanding of immigration in South America faces several challenges. First, there is a need for more empirical field research. Second, much of the existing research tends to be concentrated in South American countries with higher resources (e.g., Argentina, Colombia, and Chile) and with larger immigrant populations, potentially overlooking the experiences of migrants in countries such as Bolivia, Peru, and Ecuador. Finally, the volatile nature of South American politics and the prevalence of feelings of insecurity among migrants introduce an additional challenge. These limitations underscore the need for further research efforts to provide a more nuanced and comprehensive understanding of South American migration dynamics.

REFERENCES

Acosta Arcarazo, D. (2017). Open borders in the nineteenth century: Constructing the national, the citizen and the foreigner in south America. *SSRN Electronic Journal.* https://doi.org/10.2139/ssrn.3056287

Agencia de Calidad de la Educación, Servicio Jesuita a Migrantes, & Estudios y Consultorías Focus. (2019). *Interculturalidad en la escuela: Orientaciones para la inclusión de estudiantes migrantes*. Agencia de Calidad de la Educación. https://archivos.agenciaeducacion.cl/Interculturalidad_en_la_escuela_vf.pdf

Aninat, I., & Sierra, L. (2019). Regulación inmigratoria: Propuestas para una mejor reforma. In I. Aninat & R. Vergara (Eds.), *Inmigración en Chile: Una mirada multidimensional* (Primera edición, pp. 31–64). Fondo de Cultura Económica Chile S.A.

Carvajal Vega, J & Batarce, C. (2023, September 24). Los Gallegos: El peligroso tentáculo del Tren de Aragua que remece a Arica. La Tercera. www.latercera.com/la-tercera-sabado/noticia/los-gallegos-el-peligroso-tentaculo-del-tren-de-aragua-que-remece-a-arica/TCC7WL5YKZAUHF7H4GIH777SHQ/

Bastia, T., & Piper, N. (2019). Women migrants in the global economy: A global overview (and regional perspectives). *Gender & Development, 27*(1), 15–30. https://doi.org/10.1080/13552074.2019.1570734

Beheran, M. (2012). Migraciones y educación en la Argentina. Transformaciones y continuidades. In S. Novick (Ed.), *Migración y políticas públicas. Nuevos escenarios y desafíos* (pp. 201–226). CLACSO: Catálogos.

Bernal, N., Prada, M. A., & Urueña, R. (2015). Intra-regional mobility in South America: The Andean community and MERCOSUR. In M. Panizzon, G. Zürcher, & E. Fornalé (Eds.), *The Palgrave handbook of international labour migration* (pp. 507–534). Palgrave Macmillan UK. https://doi.org/10.1057/9781137352217_20

Brumat, L. (2020). Four generations of regional policies for the (free) movement of persons in South America (1977–2016). In G. Rayp, I. Ruyssen, & K. Marchand (Eds.), *Regional integration and migration governance in the global south* (Vol. 20, pp. 153–176). Springer International Publishing. https://doi.org/10.1007/978-3-030-43942-2_7

Bull, B., & Rosales, A. (2020). The crisis in Venezuela: Drivers, transitions, and pathways. *European Review of Latin American and Caribbean Studies, 0*(109), 1. https://doi.org/10.32992/erlacs.10587

Calderón, F., & Castells, M. (2020). The power of identity: Multiculturalism and social movements. In *The new Latin America* (pp. 105–126). Polity Press.

Cano Christiny, M. V., Contrucci, M. S., & Martínez Pizarro, J. (2009). *Conocer para legislar y hacer política: Los desafíos de Chile ante un nuevo escenario migratorio*. Naciones Unidas, CEPAL, Centro Latinoamericano y Caribeño de Demografía (CELADE) [u.a.].

Castro Solano, A., & Perugini, M. L. L. (2021). Acculturation in international students in Argentina: Factors that predict adaptation. In V. Smith-Castro, D. Sirlopú, A. Eller, & H. Çakal (Eds.), *Intraregional migration in Latin America: Psychological perspectives on acculturation and intergroup relations* (pp. 75–94). American Psychological Association. https://doi.org/10.1037/0000234-004

Cerrutti, M., & Parrado, E. (2015). Intraregional migration in South America: Trends and a research agenda. *Annual Review of Sociology, 41*(1), 399–421. https://doi.org/10.1146/annurev-soc-073014-112249

(2019). Migrations in South America. In C. Inglis, W. Li, & B. Khadria (Eds.), *The Sage handbook of international migration* (1st ed., pp. 326–341). SAGE Inc.

Courtis, C., & Pacecca, M. I. (2014). Domestic work and international migration in Latin America: Exploring trajectories of regional migrant women in domestic service in Argentina. *Women's Studies International Forum, 46*, 24–32. https://doi.org/10.1016/j.wsif.2014.01.002

De Haas, H. de, Castles, S., & Miller, M. J. (2020). *The age of migration: International population movements in the modern world* (6th ed.). Red Globe Press.

Espinosa, A., János, E., Páez, D., & Lewis, H. (2021). The relationship between political ideology and national identity in Latin America: A meta-analytical synthesis. In C. Zúñiga & W. López-López (Eds.), *Political psychology in Latin America* (pp. 151–174). American Psychological Association. https://doi.org/10.1037/0000230-008

Ford, A. (2020, December 30). GameChangers 2020: Tren de Aragua and the Exportation of Venezuelan Organized Crime. *InSight Crime*. https://insightcrime.org/news/analysis/criminal-winner-tren-de-aragua/

Gabaccia, D. R. (2016). Feminization of migration. In A. Wong, M. Wickramasinghe, R. Hoogland, & N. A. Naples (Eds.), *The Wiley Blackwell encyclopedia of gender and sexuality studies* (pp. 1–3). John Wiley & Sons, Ltd. https://doi.org/10.1002/9781118663219.wbegss732

Goebel, M. (2010). Gauchos, gringos, and Gallegos: The assimilation of Italian and Spanish immigrants in the making of modern Uruguay 1880–1930. *Past & Present, 208*(1), 191–229. https://doi.org/10.1093/pastj/gtp037

(2016). Immigration and national identity in Latin America, 1870–1930. In M. Goebel (Ed.), *Oxford research encyclopedia of Latin American history*. Oxford University Press. https://doi.org/10.1093/acrefore/9780199366439.013.288

(2022). Migration and nation in Latin America. In X. Bada, J. Durand, A. E. Feldmann, & S. Schütze (Eds.), *The Routledge history of modern Latin American migration* (1st ed., pp. 81–92). Routledge. https://doi.org/10.4324/9781003118923-8

Gouveia, V. V., Araújo, R. D. C. R., & Milfont, T. L. (2021). "They are close to us, but we are so different from them": Prejudice toward immigrants and Indigenous peoples in Brazil. In V. Smith-Castro, D. Sirlopú, A. Eller, & H. Çakal (Eds.), *Intraregional migration in Latin America: Psychological perspectives on acculturation and intergroup relations* (pp. 227–249). American Psychological Association. https://doi.org/10.1037/0000234-010

Guizardi, M. L., & Garcés, A. (2013). Circuitos migrantes: Itinerarios y formación de redes migratorias entre Perú, Bolivia, Chile y Argentina en el norte grande chileno. *Papeles de Población, 19*(78), 65–110.

Guizardi, M., & Mardones, P. (2021). The strategic production of hate: Anti-migrant discourse and xenophobic practices in Foz de Iguazú, Brazil. In M. Guizardi (Ed.), *The migration crisis in the American southern cone* (pp. 127–157). Springer International Publishing. https://doi.org/10.1007/978-3-030-68161-6_6

Global Migration Data Portal. (2021, January 20). *Migration data portal.* Migration Data Portal. www.migrationdataportal.org/international-data

Harmer, T. (2014). The cold war in Latin America. In A. M. Kalinovsky & C. Daigle (Eds.), *The Routledge handbook of the cold war* (pp. 133 148). Routledge/Taylor & Francis Group.

Huamaní, Y. (2023, September 4). *Policía de Arequipa siguen de cerca a la banda "Los Gallegos", facción del "Tren de Aragua."* Correo. https://diariocorreo.pe/edicion/arequipa/policia-de-arequipa-siguen-de-cerca-a-la-banda-los-gallegos-faccion-del-tren-de-aragua-noticia/

IWGIA – International Work Group for Indigenous Affairs. (2023). *Indigenous peoples in Bolivia.* www.iwgia.org/en/bolivia/5077-iw-2023-bolivia.html

Lawrence, D. (2011). Immigration attitudes in Latin America: Culture, economics, and the Catholic Church. *The Latin Americanist, 55*(4), 143–170. https://doi.org/10.1111/j.1557-203X.2011.01131.x

(2015). Crossing the cordillera: Immigrant attributes and Chilean attitudes. *Latin American Research Review, 50*(4), 154–177. https://doi.org/10.1353/lar.2015.0058

Macaya-Aguirre, G., & Stefoni Espinoza, C. (2021). Violence against women in the Colombian internal armed conflict: Keys for a critical reading. *Revista Punto Género, 15,* 25–46. https://doi.org/10.5354/2735-7473.2021.64397

Martínez Rojas, D., Muñoz Henríquez, W., & Mondaca Rojas, C. (2021). Racism, interculturality, and public policies: An analysis of the literature on migration and the school system in Chile, Argentina, and Spain. *SAGE Open, 11*(1), 215824402098852. https://doi.org/10.1177/2158244020988526

Mayorga, F. (2017). Estado Plurinacional e Democracia Intercultural na Bolívia. *Revista Brasileira de Ciências Sociais, 32*(94), 01. https://doi.org/10.17666/329401/2017

McAuliffe, M., James, & Khadria, B. (2019). *World migration report 2020.* International Organization for Migration.

World migration report 2022. (2021). International Organization for Migration (IOM).

Meseguer, C., & Kemmerling, A. (2018). What do you fear? Anti-immigrant sentiment in Latin America. *International Migration Review, 52*(1), 236–272. https://doi.org/10.1111/imre.12269

Mira, C. F. R. (2019). *Exiliados políticos chilenos y migración económica en la Venezuela de los setenta, 18.*

Morales-Muñoz, H., Jha, S., Bonatti, M., Alff, H., Kurtenbach, S., & Sieber, S. (2020). Exploring connections – environmental change, food security and violence as drivers of migration – a critical review of research. *Sustainability, 12*(14), 5702. https://doi.org/10.3390/su12145702

Munck, G. L., & Luna, J. P. (2022). *Latin American politics and society: A comparative and historical analysis* (1st Ed.). Cambridge University Press.

Noy, S., & Voorend, K. (2016). Social rights and migrant realities: Migration policy reform and migrants' access to health care in Costa Rica, Argentina, and Chile. *Journal of International Migration and Integration*, *17*(2), 605–629. https://doi.org/10.1007/s12134-015-0416-2

Ousey, G. C., & Kubrin, C. E. (2018). Immigration and crime: Assessing a contentious issue. *Annual Review of Criminology*, *1*(1), 63–84. https://doi.org/10.1146/annurev-criminol-032317-092026

Pardo, M. F. (2012). La inmigración y el devenir de las sociedades multiculturales: Perspectivas políticas y teóricas. In S. Novick (Ed.), *Migración y políticas públicas. Nuevos escenarios y desafíos* (pp. 153–172). CLACSO: Catálogos.

Parrado, E. A., & Cerrutti, M. (2003). Labor migration between developing countries: The case of Paraguay and Argentina. *International Migration Review*, *37*(1), 101–132. https://doi.org/10.1111/j.1747-7379.2003.tb00131.x

Pavez-Soto, I., & Chan, C. (2018). The second generation in Chile: Negotiating identities, rights, and public policy. *International Migration*, *56*(2), 82–96. https://doi.org/10.1111/imig.12410

Prieto-Rosas, V., & Bengochea, J. (2022). International migration in South America. In X. Bada, J. Durand, A. E. Feldmann, & S. Schütze (Eds.), *The Routledge history of modern Latin American migration* (1st ed., pp. 62–77). Routledge. https://doi.org/10.4324/9781003118923-6

Romano, S. (2009). Integración económica, desarrollo y migraciones en el MERCOSUR. Una aproximación crítica. In E. Domenech (Ed.), *Migración y política: El Estado interrogado. Procesos actuales en Argentina y Sudamérica* (pp. 257–290). Universidad Nacional de Córdoba.

R4V. (2023, March 29). *R4V América Latina y el Caribe: refugiados y migrantes venezolanos en la región (Marzo 2023)*. www.r4v.info/es/document/r4v-america-latina-y-el-caribe-refugiados-y-migrantes-venezolanos-en-la-region-mar-2023-0

Safdar, S., Soltan, H., Martínez-González, M. B., & Sañudo, J. E. P. (2023). Adaptation of Venezuelan refugees in Colombia: The mediating roles of acculturation orientations in influencing acculturation adaptations. *International Journal of Psychology*, *58*(3), 196–206. https://doi.org/10.1002/ijop.12901

Seyferth, G. (2013). The diverse understandings of foreign migration to the South of Brazil (1818–1950). *Vibrant: Virtual Brazilian Anthropology*, *10*(2), 118–162. https://doi.org/10.1590/S1809-43412013000200005

Schmid, K., Ramiah, A. A., & Hewstone, M. (2014). Neighborhood ethnic diversity and trust: The role of intergroup contact and perceived threat. *Psychological Science*, *25*(3), 665–674. https://doi.org/10.1177/0956797613508956

Sherif, M. (1966). *Group conflict and cooperation*. Routledge and Kegan Paul.

Soria, S. (2009). Las migraciones y el discurso multi/intercultural del Estado en Argentina. In E. Domenech (Ed.), *Migración y política: El Estado interrogado. Procesos actuales en Argentina y Sudamérica* (pp. 103–138). Universidad Nacional de Córdoba.

Stang, M. F. (2009). El dispositivo jurídico migratorio en la Comunidad Andina de Naciones. In E. E. Domenech (Ed.), *Migración y política: El estado interrogado: Procesos actuales en Argentina y Sudamérica*. Editorial Universidad Nacional de Córdoba.

Taylor, C. (2012). Interculturalism or multiculturalism? *Philosophy & Social Criticism, 38*(4–5), 413–423. https://doi.org/10.1177/0191453711435656

United Nations Department of Economic and Social Affairs, Population Division. (2020). *International Migrant Stock 2020* [dataset]. www.un.org/development/desa/pd/content/international-migrant-stock

Terán, I. (2023). *De la cárcel al barrio: El control territorial del Tren de Aragua, Venezuela*. https://doi.org/10.5281/ZENODO.8075454

Walsh, C. (2008). Interculturalidad, plurinacionalidad y decolonialidad: Las insurgencias político-epistémicas de refundar el Estado[1]; Interculturality, plurinationality and decoloniality: Political-epistemic insurgences to refound the state; Interculturalidade, plurinacionalidade e descolonização: As insurgências político-epistêmicas de re-fundar o Estado. *TABULA RASA*.

PART III

Traditional and New Solutions to Managing Diversity

Introduction to Part III

One of the most challenging issues for twenty-first-century governments is managing migration. The increasing ease of transnational travel, difficulties in regulating migration across extensive borders, and the complexity of controlling irregular immigrants who have already entered the country pose significant challenges. These challenges encompass navigating the legal entry and stay, as well as the integration of immigrants into the new society.

Managing migration is closely linked to social welfare. In effect, one area of debate in migration management involves the extension – or not – of social rights to the immigrant population, and the government's ability to uphold those rights. For instance, housing is often a contested area regarding the inclusion of immigrants in public policy. Government officials may be concerned about the struggles of recent immigrants who lack adequate housing and may experience homelessness. Consequently, policymakers may be inclined to include immigrants in housing policies. However, this inclusion could result in host society populations feeling that their housing benefits are being reduced, because scarce housing resources now have to be shared with large numbers of immigrants (Hooijer, 2021).

Migration management also involves the regulation of social relations between people with diverse backgrounds and identities. The previous chapters have shown how national identity in America, Europe, and South American countries relates to migration management. How national identity is perceived, particularly as an ideal, is associated with the host society's openness to immigrants. For example, Canada defines itself as a multicultural country. As part of its multiculturalism policy, Canada promotes the celebration of intergroup differences and the retention of immigrants' heritage cultures, offering immigrants support to adjust to the new society

(Reitz, 2011). However, attitudes toward immigrants can be influenced by individual characteristics. For example, stronger self-identification with the nation is associated with negative attitudes toward immigrants (Pinto et al., 2020).

Chapters 8 and 9 delve into the psychological foundations of different migration management strategies, focusing on assimilation, multiculturalism, and omniculturalism (Moghaddam, 2024). These strategies correspond to different public policy responses to the arrival of immigrants in the host society. Each migration management policy aims to integrate immigrants into the new society, although the meaning of integration varies across different host societies. Assimilation expects immigrants to adapt culturally and linguistically to the host society. This adaptation should lead to identity changes, where immigrants come to see themselves as citizens of the new (host) country. In contrast, multiculturalism expects immigrants to preserve some cultural, linguistic, and identity traits from their country of origin, fostering social cohesion that includes citizens with different cultural identities. Indeed, intergroup differences are highlighted, shared, and celebrated.

Acculturation refers to the psychological process of immigrants adapting to a new society. Previous research highlights the core theme of acculturation: What happens to individuals and groups when they come into prolonged contact with others from different cultural backgrounds (Berry, 1997; Sam, 2006). Acculturation affects both immigrants and the host society population. Migration management policies significantly shape this process by driving identity changes necessary for adapting to a new society. The chapters in Part III explore these changes from the perspective of the host society, including actions that range from excluding to including immigrants, and valuing or not valuing their cultural identity (Berry, 1997).

Chapter 8 explores how intergroup contact and attraction to similar others reduce prejudices and increase the willingness to interact with others, fostering conditions for assimilation. It also shows how the absence of a dominant culture, the maintenance of one's inherited culture, the positive acceptance of other cultures, and pride in one's own culture without negatively judging others, create conditions for multiculturalism. Chapter 10 explores an alternative path, omniculturalism, which begins by acknowledging that human beings are far more similar to one another than they are different. Human similarities are given highest priority and actively celebrated, but attention is also given to intergroup differences.

Social Cohesion and Migration Management Policies

Migration management policies are crucial for fostering social cohesion and national security in an increasingly globalized world. These policies play a vital role in integrating immigrants into host societies, ensuring their rights and well-being, and addressing cultural and economic needs. However, the strategies for migration management have different outcomes and understandings of social cohesion. Assimilation builds social cohesion by encouraging immigrants to adopt the identity of their new society, while multiculturalism believes that social cohesion is formed when immigrants preserve, share, and celebrate their cultural and identity heritage (Moghaddam, 2008, 2024).

Irrespective of their differences, migration management policies aim to facilitate social cohesion by promoting the integration of immigrants into their new communities, whether through adaptation, or the fostering and integration of different group identities. In this sense, effective migration management policies provide support systems that help immigrants adapt, learn the local language, and understand cultural norms. The end goal is to reduce social tensions and foster mutual respect and understanding between immigrants and native citizens, to create a more harmonious society.

Economic integration into the labor market is also essential for immigration management, in order for immigrants to contribute to the host country's growth without raising costs. Immigrants bring valuable skills, innovation, and labor. However, policymakers should design economic policies balancing immigrant participation and its consequences. Well-designed policies can facilitate immigrants' entry into the labor market, ensuring their contributions and leading to benefits for immigrants, host society populations, and the overall economy. Evidence suggests that policies that facilitate assimilation could lead to better economic outcomes for immigrants (Piracha et al., 2023). Multicultural policies aiming to reduce anti-immigrant prejudices could foster the conditions for economic integration, particularly in countries with high degrees of immigration and for immigrant populations that face discrimination (Kende et al., 2022; Platt et al., 2022). Thus, in economic integration, migration management policies foster conditions that lead to immigrant economic integration and better outcomes for the host society. However, which type of migration management policy yields the best outcomes depends highly on the immigrant population and the barriers faced for social inclusion and economic integration.

Effective migration management also bolsters national security and public safety. In effect, migration, and especially illegal immigration, cultivates security concerns in the host country population. A common (unfounded) concern regarding immigration is that it raises criminal offenses in the host society (De Haas, 2023). According to this view, immigration brings to the host society gangs, drug trafficking, and sexual offenses. Thus, effective migration management decreases these fears by steering immigrants through legal processes that can vet immigrants with criminal records. Furthermore, effective migration management can also result in secure conditions for immigrants. In effect, better regulations for immigrants' entry and stay create safer border crossing and residency in the new society by avoiding problems such as human trafficking (McAuliffe & Triandafyllidou, 2021). Policies that regulate and monitor immigration help prevent illegal entry and manage potential security risks ensuring that immigrants receive protection and that national security is not compromised.

Effective migration management policies are crucial for fostering social cohesion. This involves creating favorable living conditions for both host society populations and immigrants, ensuring economic prosperity, upholding human rights, and maintaining national security. By addressing the complexities of immigration, these policies help create inclusive, resilient, and thriving societies that benefit from the potentially rich contributions of immigrants.

In summary, the third part of the book underscores the complexity and importance of multicultural strategies (assimilation, multiculturalism, omniculturalism) and policies in shaping migration management. Anti-discrimination policies play a crucial role in fostering inclusive organizational cultures and enhancing the occupational attainment of skilled immigrants. However, the effects of anti-discrimination policies are unevenly distributed, with some members of immigrant ethnic minorities facing persistent discrimination. Labor market integration also emerges as a significant factor in providing better economic opportunities for immigrants. The reviewed literature underscores the necessity of understanding the diverse nature of immigrants and creating tailored migration policies to tackle specific challenges faced by different immigrant groups, leading to better outcomes. By combining labor market integration with robust anti-discrimination measures, policymakers can create an environment that maximizes the economic potential of immigrants, ultimately benefiting the broader society.

REFERENCES

Ajzen, I. (1974). Effects of information on interpersonal attraction: Similarity versus affective value. *Journal of Personality and Social Psychology*, *29*(3), 374–380. https://doi.org/10.1037/h0036002

Berry, J. W. (1997). Immigration, acculturation, and adaptation. *Applied Psychology*, *46*(1), 5–34. https://doi.org/10.1111/j.1464-0597.1997.tb01087.x

de Haas, H. (2023). *How migration really works: The facts about the most divisive issue in politics* (1st US ed.). Basic Books.

Hooijer, G. (2021). "They take our houses": Benefit competition and the erosion of support for immigrants' social rights. *British Journal of Political Science*, *51*(4), 1381–1401. https://doi.org/10.1017/S0007123420000150

McAuliffe, M., & Triandafyllidou, A. (Eds.). (2021). World Migration Report 2022. International Organization for Migration (IOM).

Moghaddam, F. M. (2008). *Multiculturalism and intergroup relations: Psychological implications for democracy in global context*. American Psychological Association. https://doi.org/10.1037/11682-000

(2024). *The psychology of multiculturalism, assimilation, and omniculturalism: Managing diversity in global context*. Springer Nature Switzerland. https://doi.org/10.1007/978-3-031-62597-8

Kende, J., Sarrasin, O., Manatschal, A., Phalet, K., & Green, E. G. T. (2022). Policies and prejudice: Integration policies moderate the link between immigrant presence and anti-immigrant prejudice. *Journal of Personality and Social Psychology*, *123*(2), 337–352. https://doi.org/10.1037/pspi0000376

Platt, L., Polavieja, J., & Radl, J. (2022). Which integration policies work? the heterogeneous impact of national institutions on immigrants' labor market attainment in Europe. *International Migration Review*, *56*(2), 344–375. https://doi.org/10.1177/01979183211032677

Pinto, I. R., Carvalho, C. L., Dias, C., Lopes, P., Alves, S., De Carvalho, C., & Marques, J. M. (2020). A path toward inclusive social cohesion: The role of European and national identity on contesting vs. accepting European migration policies in Portugal. *Frontiers in Psychology*, *11*, 1875. https://doi.org/10.3389/fpsyg.2020.01875

Piracha, M., Tani, M., Cheng, Z., & Wang, B. Z. (2023). Social assimilation and immigrants' labor market outcomes. *Journal of Population Economics*, *36*(1), 37–67. https://doi.org/10.1007/s00148-021-00883-w

Reitz, J. G. (2011). *Pro-immigration Canada: Social and economic roots of popular views*. Institute for Research on Public Policy.

Sam, D. L. (2006). Acculturation: Conceptual background and core components. In D. L. Sam & J. W. Berry (Eds.), *The Cambridge handbook of acculturation psychology* (1st ed., pp. 11–26). Cambridge University Press. https://doi.org/10.1017/CBO9780511489891.005

CHAPTER 8

The Psychological Foundations of Multiculturalism and Assimilation

"Our cities are being undermined," New York's Democratic mayor, Mr. Adams, said at a news conference, calling for increased federal funds to implement policies to address problems caused by immigration (Frank & Fitzsimmons, 2023). The mayor's statement highlights that even those with a positive view on immigration still encounter challenges when integrating new individuals into society. Indeed, policymakers and public officials often have to do wonders with scarce resources to cover immigrants' basic needs. However, not all the challenges regarding immigration relate directly to monetary issues, such as providing initial support for housing and food. Immigration entails challenges that transcend resources and have to do with relations between people who not only look and sound different from one another, but also think and feel differently about fundamental issues regarding living in society. This chapter is concerned with the nonmonetary challenges of managing diversity.

Increasing immigration and diversity are major challenges for societies. Moreover, they are related: increased immigration leads to increased diversity. Throughout history, societies have established fundamental agreements regarding institutions, civic behaviors, and morality. However, immigrants bring new conceptions of institutions, civic behaviors, and morality since they usually come from different cultural, linguistic, and religious traditions. Immigrants from the East may bring different religious views that challenge established civic behaviors and morals. Conversely, immigrants from the West may bring different conceptions about the State that challenge established conceptions of the relationship between the State, majority citizens, and minorities. How do societies psychologically deal with novelties brought about by the arrival of immigrants from different backgrounds? Instead of assuming that immigrant integration naturally occurs successfully over time, it should be recognized as a policy challenge.

In order to deal with the diversity brought up by immigration, societies have developed official and/or unofficial policies intended to manage increasing diversity. We can place diversity management policies on a continuum with two opposite ends. At the one end is complete assimilation, which posits that immigrants should conform to the new society, accepting societies' fundamental agreements. At the other extreme is multiculturalism, which proposes that host societies should adjust in some fundamental ways to accommodate immigrant diversity. This chapter is mainly concerned with critically assessing these diversity management policies from a psychological perspective.

The chapter is organized into four sections. First, it looks at assimilation and multiculturalism, exploring their origins, developments, and how these two diversity management policies aim to regulate diversity. Second, the chapter addresses common challenges arising from assimilation and multiculturalism as diversity management policies.

Diversity Management Policies

This section explores the contrasting immigration diversity management policies of assimilation and multiculturalism. Assimilation entails immigrants adopting the customs and practices of the host society, often leaving behind their own cultural heritage. Historically assimilation described the European migration to the United States, where European immigrants "melted" into American society and adopted a new cultural identity. For example, Italian immigrants become Americans (see also the Introduction to Part II of this book, for White European assimilation and belonging).

Multiculturalism, on the other hand, celebrates diversity and encourages the coexistence of various cultural identities within society. Following the previous example, according to the multicultural model, Italians become Italian-Americans. This model emerged as the predominant approach in developed nations characterized by substantial immigration flows, notably Canada, Australia, New Zealand, Sweden, and the Netherlands, throughout the 1970s and 1980s (De Haas et al., 2020). Canada was the first country to formally adopt multiculturalism as a national migration management policy, intended to recognize and enhance the different cultural heritages in Canada (Pier 21, n.d.). This section delves into the psychological dynamics driving both assimilation and multiculturalism, highlighting their implications and the interplay between individual-level experiences and broader societal policies.

It is worth noting that the examination of assimilation and multiculturalism policies does not imply that solely one of these psychological approaches is used in immigration management. Canada, for instance, was a major proponent of multiculturalism in the 1980s and 1990s (Berry, 2013). However, Girard and Bauder's (2007) research showed that the engineering labor market in Ontario, Canada utilized licensing procedures that created assimilation processes to introduce immigrants to the necessary cultural norms of the profession. The researchers' fieldwork revealed that employers tended to hire immigrant engineers on the basis of the necessary engineering qualifications *and* demonstrated knowledge – given by assimilation – of Canadian engineering workplace behaviors such as teamwork and dress code practices. Thus, it is more accurate to assume that countries implement a range of migration management policies, which can fall on a continuum that ranges from assimilation to multiculturalism. This includes the government's level of involvement.

Assimilation

Assimilation is one of the first policies recognized for managing immigration and diversity in contemporary societies. As early as the 1920s, *assimilation* was defined as the process through which immigrants acquired knowledge and attitudes by experience to function properly in the new society (Parks & Burguess, 1921, p. 736). Thus, assimilation involves the adaptation of immigrants to the host society (Green & Staerklé, 2013). Thereby, assimilation as an immigration management policy consists of a unilateral process where immigrants become members of the new society, sometimes leaving their customs behind to adopt the new practices.

Assimilation predicts that, over a period of time, immigrants will adopt the customs, language, and culture of the host society. Cabaniss and Cameron (2018) highlighted that while assimilation policies foster outcomes geared to the host society's customs and practices, the underlying psychological processes entail an active identity negotiation between immigrants and members of the host society. To some degree, the contact between immigrants and members of the host society is shaped by prejudice and stereotypes. People in the host society have preexisting beliefs and attitudes toward immigrants based on their group membership. Thus, when members of the host society categorize immigrants through previously formed beliefs and attitudes, immigrants try to counteract the preconceived notions through strategies that give positive meaning to their identities. Immigrants, to counteract negative attitudes toward themselves, engage in active processes of positive meaning association. Cabanis (2018) shows how undocumented youth activists, known as Dreamers, used storytelling techniques to establish themselves as a primary voice on matters of immigration reform. By doing so, they tried to position themselves as having an active role in the immigration debate, and to move away from a passive role as mere recipients of advocacy efforts by others.

In the process of assimilation, immigrants can highlight the similarities they share with members of the host society. The importance of highlighting similarities should not be undermined since research has shown that at both the individual and intergroup levels, people are attracted to similar others (Byrne, 1961; Montoya & Horton, 2013; Osbeck et al., 1997; Salas-Schweikart et al., 2024). Highlighting similarities can make immigrants more appealing to members of the host society, leading to increased acceptance. According to Safdar et al. (2020), immigrants may emphasize their adoption of cultural characteristics, such as clothing, to show their adaptation to the majority culture. According to the authors, clothing choices were used by Chinese Canadians as a way of demonstrating their adjustment to the society of their host country. However, do immigrants choose their clothing styles voluntarily?

Lewis (2021) used qualitative research to probe the extent of assimilation practices among immigrants. After conducting interviews with international students in New Zealand, the researcher discovered that the majority of participants verbally expressed support for preserving their own cultural practices while in practice adopting those of the host society. Hence, Lewis (2021) used the term *false conscientiousness* to describe the assimilation practice where immigrants in practice adopt the cultural practices of their host society without explicit verbal acknowledgement.

A criticism of assimilation is that this approach does not sufficiently give importance to the role of ethnicity in the adaptation of immigrants to the new society (Alba & Nee, 2012). In the United States context, it was found that non-White ethnic groups and their descendants fared worse than ethnic groups that shared more similarities with White Americans. Researchers have explored more constructive paths ahead. Berry (1997) discussed a form of assimilation he called integration, which he observed while studying the psychological and practical processes that immigrants undergo to adapt to a new society, also known as acculturation. Integration refers to a strategy that immigrants use, wherein they freely adopt some cultural traits of the new society while still maintaining some aspects of their original culture (Alba & Nee, 2020; Berry, 2005). However, in contrast with assimilation, integration does not necessarily lead to a decrease in cultural differences over time. Rather, it assumes a "culturally neutral" perspective.

In addition, the criticism against assimilation led to some theoretical reformulations. Portes and Zhou (1993) coined the term "segmented assimilation," which refers to the process through which immigrants integrate and adjust into a segment of the host society. For example, the authors point out that adaptation by second-generation non-White immigrants in the United States results in them being at the bottom of the status hierarchy (downward assimilation) in society, while others end up in a higher position (upward assimilation). Another distinction is between *minority assimilation*, involving the minority group changing to adopt the majority group culture, and *melting-pot assimilation*, involving the emergence of a new culture through the merging of all groups, both minority, and majority (Moghaddam, 2008). However, assimilation was soon overtaken by a new cultural diversity management policy, discussed below.

Multiculturalism

Subsequent advancements in immigration management led to the formulation of a novel policy known as the multicultural model. In contrast to assimilation, *multiculturalism* – as a migration management model – posits that immigrants should not abandon their distinctive cultural and linguistic characteristics, since that diversity enriches the host society (Kymlicka, 2005; Moghaddam, 2008, 2024). Consequently, countries with multicultural policies promote the maintenance of different minority languages, religions, customs, and other cultural characteristics (Kymlicka & Banting, 2006). It is worth mentioning that multiculturalism does not focus solely on immigrants but on all minority groups. For example, in Latin America during the 2000s, multicultural policies focusing on Indigenous people were created to recognize the long-excluded native population (Calderón & Castells, 2020; Munck & Luna, 2022).

There are two main types of multicultural policies (Moghaddam, 2008, 2024). The first is "planned" multiculturalism, which involves active government involvement in managing migration. The second is "laissez-faire" multiculturalism, which involves limited government involvement and allowing market forces to determine the survival of cultural characteristics of each ethnic group. The examples given of multicultural policies in Latin America show that the government is actively passing legislation to promote planned multiculturalism.

From a psychological standpoint, the intentional implementation of multiculturalism based on political principles or ideology is referred to as normative multiculturalism (Green & Staerklé, 2013). Normative multiculturalism refers to migration management policies that actively promote the valuing of diversity through a deliberate public policy approach.

An example of integration policies could be highlighting the culinary traditions of a particular ethnic group. Alternatively, in "laissez-faire multiculturalism", the government avoids engaging in policy planning, the integration and adaptation processes are driven by market forces and other social dynamics (Novoa & Moghaddam, 2014). For example, social networks have been reported to help immigrants to settle in the new society by providing resources and emotional support (Kindler et al., 2015; Vega et al., 1991). In this way, "laissez-faire multiculturalism" is descriptive multiculturalism, a mere observation of diversity without direct intervention.

Immigrant integration through a laissez-faire approach can create ethnic economic enclaves. This is particularly if the social ties with the community of origin are strong and the connections with the host society are weak. For example, Benenciai (2012) reports that Bolivian immigrants in Buenos Aires, Argentina, have a dominant position in the agriculture food market holding key positions in the production and commercialization of horticulture. Using a variety of formal and informal social ties, Bolivian immigrants gained influence in the agriculture sector and created distinctive labor and market spaces centered around their shared identity. However, the case of Japanese immigrants in Brazil shows that the laissez-faire approach can produce different results in time. In effect, Reichl (1995) describes how Japanese immigrants created tight bonds at the initial stages of immigration. As time passed, Japanese immigrants assimilated into Brazilian society while still maintaining their ethnic identity through involvement in voluntary groups that celebrated their culture.

Psychological Foundations of Assimilation and Multiculturalism

In the next section of this chapter, we explore the psychological foundations of assimilation and multiculturalism.

In the End, We Will Become One: Assimilation

Assimilation is the historically dominant policy for managing diversity. In this section, we examine two central psychological processes underlying assimilation, intergroup contact, and similarity-attraction.

Intergroup Contact

Contact theory is an important foundation of assimilation. The theory had one of its first formulations in Allport (1954), who pointed out that as members of different groups interact with each other, their prejudices tend to decrease, resulting in improved intergroup relations. Contact theory suggests that increased interaction between migrants and locals leads to greater understanding and knowledge of each other. This can help bridge the gaps that divide them and reduce prejudices held by the local population toward migrants. The misunderstandings and lack of knowledge that prevent the integration of migrants into the new society are addressed.

However, as we discussed in detail in Chapter 3 of this text, Allport stipulated that the contact between the migrant and local population will only lead to improved intergroup relations if it takes place under certain conditions. If these conditions are not met, intergroup conditions will not improve and immigrants will probably remain in low status positions, reminding us of "segmented assimilation." When there is unequal contact between immigrants and native citizens, the outcome could lead to immigrants always being relegated to the lower segments of that society. Indeed, contact in conditions of discrimination or in conflict contexts may end up confirming or aggravating existing prejudices toward immigrants (Kotzur et al., 2018).

On a more positive note, intergroup contact under favorable conditions has been shown to improve intergroup relations. For example, such contact is associated with increased levels of trust and forgiveness among different ethnic groups (Hewstone, 2015; Hewstone et al. 2006). Increased contact between groups also leads to a decreased perception of intergroup threat. Subsequent research has also shown that contact between groups can be improved by mediated contact. That is, contact with an ingroup member that has contact with an outgroup member can reduce prejudice. But more importantly, direct and indirect contact reduce the perception of threat, an important factor in negative attitudes toward immigrants (White et al., 2021). Bobowik et al. (2022) showed how contact between people who have social networks with greater degrees of diversity, such as greater presence of immigrants, shows a greater number of positive attitudes toward immigrants. Thus, being in contact with diverse social networks may result in positive outcomes for intergroup relations with immigrants.

Contact theory, while offering valuable insights into intergroup interactions, does have certain limitations regarding the integration of immigrants. One limitation regards the initial position of immigrants. Indeed, contact theory fails to consider the initial positions of intergroup contact. Empirical evidence has highlighted the significance of immigrants' perceptions of the host society, particularly their levels of trust in public institutions and social trust. A study conducted by Hendriks and Burger

(2020) demonstrates that immigrants with negative perceptions of the host society experience negative subjective well-being. This suggests that the process of assimilation is not a linear path and is influenced by how immigrants perceive the attitudes of the host country toward them.

Research conducted in developed European countries reveals a surprising trend. Despite objectively improving living conditions and the expectation of a "straight-line" assimilation theory, the subjective well-being of immigrants does not consistently improve with their length of stay or across generations. Politi et al. (2022) found that faltering perceptions of host-country conditions were associated with less positive subjective well-being trajectories among first-generation immigrants in developed European countries. This negative association was particularly pronounced for immigrants whose societal conditions improved substantially through migration and those who arrived in the host country after childhood. This is in line with research showing that the longer visible-minority immigrant women lived in Canada, the less they felt at home in their adopted country (Moghaddam & Taylor, 1987).

Additionally, the assimilation strategies adopted by immigrants play a crucial role in shaping their integration into the host society. There are notable differences between integrated and assimilated immigrants in their intentions regarding acquiring host-national citizenship. Integrated immigrants, despite embracing integration and assimilation, reported lower intentions to acquire host-national citizenship than assimilated immigrants (Politi et al., 2022). However, it is worth noting that assimilated immigrants were more likely to naturalize, which may contribute to maintaining asymmetric power dynamics between the national majority and immigrant minority groups.

These findings suggest that contact theory does not fully account for the complexities of immigrant assimilation. It is essential to consider the impact of immigrants' perceptions of the host society, the potential divergence between integration and naturalization intentions, and how these factors influence their overall well-being and societal participation. By acknowledging these limitations, policymakers and researchers can develop more comprehensive approaches to foster positive interactions and successful integration between immigrant and host communities.

Similarity-Attraction
Another psychological theory that provides support for assimilation is Similarity Attraction Theory. This theory provides valuable insights into how immigrants adopt the cultural characteristics or identity of their new society. This theory posits that individuals are positively attracted to others

they perceive as more similar to themselves (Ajzen, 1974; Byrne, 1961, 1971). The concept of similarity is closely linked to attraction; people often assume that if they have a close relationship with someone, they must share similarities. The implication is that the host society evaluates immigrants based on their perceived similarities. Closer relations tend to develop with immigrants who are deemed more similar to the majority culture.

How similar immigrants perceive themselves to be to the host society has also been shown to be important. Nesdale and Mak (2000) tested a model that predicted the identification of immigrants in the host country. Data was collected from immigrants in Australia from countries from Asia and New Zealand. Immigrants from New Zealand, who considered themselves to be more similar to Australia compared to immigrants from Asia, had higher levels of acceptance from Australians. This finding points to the link between identification and integration. Higher identification with the host society appears to lead to higher levels of integration, reducing the risk of marginalization within the host society. Thus, similarity shapes immigrant life by increasing the chances of immigrant integration.

Immigrants and individuals from the host society may exhibit similarities due to a shared identity. This is true for immigrants who, despite belonging to an ethnic group distinct from that of the host society, share the same religion. Ben-Nun Bloom et al. (2015) tested the effect of sharing similar religious social identity on anti-immigrant sentiment. When immigrants were of the same religion as the majority population, it led to a decrease in anti-immigrant sentiment. However, the authors also note that religious social identity can lead to increased anti-immigrant sentiments, when immigrants do not share a religion with the host population. However, when immigrants are willing to abandon their different cultural or religious heritage, this can contribute to a sense of similarity by reducing differences. Matera et al. (2020) found that Italians had a more favorable disposition toward Muslim immigrants who were perceived to be willing to abandon their heritage and become similar to Italians in culture and/or religion. Moreover, Italians were more favorable toward Arabs if the differencing factor of religion was withdrawn.

Similarly, having similar values can make the process of integration and assimilation easier, just like sharing a religion. This can result in greater social cohesion and better conditions for immigrants to thrive in the new society. According to Wolf et al. (2021), higher similarities in values such as achievement, self-enhancement, and security lead to greater well-being among immigrants. Thus, if immigrants and native populations have shared values on important societal issues like social security and fair recognition of individual achievements, it is beneficial for society overall.

One possibility is to use intergroup contact to identify, highlight, and celebrate similarities between groups (Moghaddam, 2024). This is an area where the benefits of similarity-attraction and contact theory can become additive, particularly using varieties of intergroup contact. For example, "imagined contact" with illegal immigrants had positive spillover effects on similar groups. Harwood et al. (2011) explored the effects of imagined contact with illegal immigrants, finding that imagined positive contact developed positive attitudes toward immigrants and similar groups, such as Mexican Americans and legal immigrants. The positive effects of imagined contact with one group spread to similar groups. Thus, similar immigrant groups can benefit indirectly from contact with other immigrants deemed as similar by the host population.

To conclude, in this section we have shown that contact theory plays a pivotal role in understanding immigrant assimilation: Increased interaction between immigrants and natives can (under certain conditions) diminish prejudices and foster intergroup understanding. For successful assimilation, contact should occur in an atmosphere of equality, collaboration, shared goals, and community approval. Research supports the theory, showing that positive intergroup contact reduces prejudice, builds trust, and decreases the perception of threat. However, contact theory has limitations, as it fails to consider immigrants' initial positions, perceptions of the host society, and the impact of assimilation strategies on their integration. Acknowledging these complexities can inform more effective approaches for promoting positive interactions and successful immigrant assimilation. Related to this, Similarity Attraction Theory highlights the importance of perceived similarity between immigrants and the host society in shaping integration and social interactions. Studies show that shared identity, such as on the basis of religion, can reduce anti-immigrant sentiment, and immigrants' willingness to abandon cultural heritage can foster a sense of similarity. When immigrants and natives share common values, assimilation becomes easier, leading to greater social cohesion and well-being. Imagined contact with similar immigrant groups also has positive effects on attitudes. Understanding and promoting similarity can facilitate smoother integration and foster positive intergroup relations in host societies.

We Can Become One by Accepting Our Differences: Multiculturalism

How is the attraction to diversity – the core of multiculturalism – psychologically supported? Through an analysis of original sources on multiculturalism, four key factors were identified that help us understand this concept. These include (1) the absence of a dominant culture and the ability to choose one's own cultural identity, (2) the motivation to maintain one's inherited culture, (3) the belief that embracing one's own culture leads to greater acceptance of other cultures, and (4) most importantly, taking pride in one's own culture without negatively judging others' cultures (Moghaddam, 2008, 2024). In the following section, I will analyze the four presuppositions of multiculturalism and consider empirical research that supports this drive of being attracted to diversity.

The Absence of a Dominant Culture and the Ability to Choose One's Own Cultural Identity

A key component of multiculturalism is that we live in diverse societies, where it's important to have the ability to respect and consider every culture as valuable. Every culture has the right to be heard and acknowledged. Hence, cultural humility is a crucial aspect of multiculturalism. In effect, empirical support has been shown to be positively correlated with openness to immigration and negatively associated with prejudice and (symbolic or real) threats from immigrants (Captari et al., 2019; Rullo et al., 2022).

When multicultural studies were booming in the 1990s, Tervalon and Murray-García (1998) proposed a shift in professional practices, moving practitioners toward humility – rather than competence – when dealing with people from different cultural backgrounds. The authors proposed to downplay the assumption of superiority given by Western education in clinical settings. By doing this, the authors' proposal endorsed the assumption that there is no official culture, an idea that broadly influenced multicultural policies and training programs (Abbott et al., 2019; Pham et al., 2022; Tervalon & Murray-García, 1998).

The multicultural claim is that the majority culture should not have a dominant position that leads to exclusion. Every individual and community has the right to live in accordance with their own cultural beliefs and practices. In the same vein, democratic ideals promote acceptance of diverse cultural beliefs within society. However, at the same time that democracy requires the acceptance of diversity, it also requires support for universal rights and duties (Moghaddam et al., 2023). Hence, democratic citizens are key for multiculturalism since they endorse the ideal of openness to diversity while upholding universal values in the global political community.

At an individual level, the characteristics of the democratic citizen align with intellectual humility. In effect, the democratic belief that one can be wrong and can learn from others overlaps with the core claim of intellectual humility: the skill to recognize that one is fallible (Tanesini, 2018). Moreover, empirical research has shown the association between believing that one can be wrong and openness to others (Leary et al., 2017). The same research showed that individuals with high intellectual humility were less assured of their religious beliefs and less judgmental toward other people on a religious basis. Thus, intellectual humility is a key characteristic of democratic citizenship, capable of successfully supporting a diverse society.

The Motivation to Maintain One's Inherited Culture
After immigrating to a new society, individuals are often left with the dilemma of deciding which aspects of their culture to preserve for themselves and/or for future generations. Culture is a broad concept, which can encompass language, religion, nationality, and/or ethnicity, among others. In this way, the process of preserving the culture of immigrants can range from a wide array to a limited number of beliefs and practices, depending on the specific circumstances of each case. Multiculturalism assumes that individuals are motivated to preserve and pass down their significant cultural traditions. As such, heritage is closely related to multiculturalism, as it is intertwined with cultural identity, its practices, and transmission. Moreover, the United Nations Educational, Scientific, and Cultural Organization (UNESCO) (2005) recognizes that the transmission of intangibles, such as culture and practices, is a form of inherited social capital that impacts education, health, and sustainable practices with the environment. Indeed, according to this UN agency, intangible cultural heritage is essential to maintaining cultural diversity in a globalized world.

Culture and identity are directly linked. Individuals connect their inherited cultures to their identities. When immigrants share their stories with others about their travel or about their homeland, they articulate their culture as part of their identity (László, 2014). Through this process, immigrants create a unified sense of self by linking culture and identity. Consequently, when culture is attached to personal identity, cultural inheritance is achieved through this association. However, it is also possible that culture is part of *immigrant social identity*, referring to an immigrant's membership in social groups related to their country of origin, ethnicity, language, religion, or immigrants. Social identity theory postulates that individuals want to develop social identities and belong to those groups that have positive and distinct identities (Tajfel, 1974; Tajfel et al., 1971). Consequently, this theory relates to multiculturalism and to the psychological drive to keep a distinct identity, different from that of the majority group. In effect, the drive toward "distinctiveness" and "positivity" can explain why immigrants might be motivated to keep their culture and identity while integrating into the new society. Empirical evidence has shown examples of immigrant parents who are motivated to transmit the native identity to their children (Vermeulen & Kranendonk, 2021). Children of parents with multicultural identities tend to have multicultural identities themselves. This identity development process is in line with the active self-categorization behavior of immigrants, who do not passively accept identities ascribed to them, but take the initiative and shape their own identities, in line with self-categorization theory (Turner & Reynolds, 2012).

The Belief That Embracing One's Own Culture Leads to Greater Acceptance of Other Cultures
Another central assumption of multiculturalism is that pride and confidence in the ingroup lead to positive relations with outgroups. However, this assumption contradicts a well-supported social psychological finding: Ingroup favoritism often leads to detrimental outcomes for outgroups. In effect, the tendency to favor our own group is associated with less willingness to cooperate with the outgroup and a greater tendency to discriminate against the outgroup (Balliet et al., 2014).

On a more optimistic note, the assumption that identification with the ingroup can lead to acceptance of outgroups has found some empirical support under certain conditions. For example, Yzerbyt and Cambon (2017) found that high-status ingroup members can regard members of the outgroup as warm, as long as the ingroup is well positioned in regard to something that they value more than warmth: competence. Ingroup members may acknowledge and recognize that those outside of their group have a superior ability in a certain aspect that they do not value as highly. However, they still maintain the belief that their own group holds a superior position in the aspects they highly value.

The "Multiculturalism Hypothesis" At the heart of multiculturalism policy is the so-called multiculturalism hypothesis, which proposes that by having pride and confidence in the ingroup heritage culture, ingroup members will be open and accepting toward others (Moghaddam, 2024). From a rationalist perspective, this assumption seems to make sense, because it suggests that a solid ingroup identity will enable ingroup members to have better relations with and greater tolerance toward outgroups. However, in practice, intergroup relations are often associated with irrational rather than rational psychological processes (Moghaddam, 2018). Irrational processes become particularly influential with respect to emotional ties to nations. For example, nationalism has been shown to be associated with negative outcomes for immigrants, such as pejorative views that regard their cultures and customs (Ariely, 2012).

The empirical evidence related to the multiculturalism hypothesis is mixed (Moghaddam, 2024). Green et al. (2011) found that patriotism is positively associated with individual attitudes that support immigrants, Marinthe et al. (2023) found that patriotism played no role in participants' feelings regarding immigrants when exposed to an experimental manipulation that involved the desecration of a national symbol (i.e., the burning of a national flag), and Lambert et al. (2006) found no relationship between national pride and confidence in the ingroup and acceptance of outgroups. One possible interpretation of these mixed results is to distinguish qualitatively between different types of identification with the ingroup. For example, one distinction is between *blind patriotism*, uncritical adherence to one's nation and its policies, and *constructive patriotism*, which involves a desire for positive change and a willingness to criticize the practices of one's own nation. There is some support for the idea that blind patriotism is associated with negative attitudes toward immigrants, whereas constructive patriotism is associated with positive or indifferent attitudes toward immigrants (Willis-Esqueda et al., 2017). Constructive patriotism is more in line with the multiculturalism hypothesis.

In conclusion, the manner in which individuals connect with their culture influences their attitudes toward immigrants. Positive intergroup relationships with immigrants are associated with constructive patriotism. In this context, the endorsement of multiculturalism gains support when patriotism is dissociated from nationalism, the latter often linked to adverse outcomes for immigrants. This underscores the significance of nurturing favorable intergroup relations through constructive patriotism.

Concluding Comment

Managing immigration is a major challenge faced by many contemporary societies. Most societies tackle this challenge by implementing a combination of assimilation and multiculturalism immigration management policies, which brings unique opportunities and challenges for both host societies and immigrants.

Assimilation is anchored in the notion of adaptation and integration. It assumes that immigrants will "naturally" adapt to the new society in the long run. Psychologically, assimilation is rooted in intergroup contact and similarity-attraction theories. First, it is assumed that varieties of intergroup contact between host society members and immigrants will result in constructive relations between them, thereby increasing trust. Second, Similarity Attraction Theory posits that immigrants and natives will become more similar over time, and because they come to share common traits they will be attracted to each other, creating fertile grounds for trust. Yet, assimilation has limitations. Resistance from the host society, fueled by emotional and ideological responses, often impedes genuine acceptance of immigrants. Despite the psychological underpinnings of intergroup contact and similarity attraction, societal biases and perceived threats can hinder the assimilation process.

Furthermore, the challenge of balancing diversity with a shared identity complicates assimilation efforts. Failure to strike a healthy balance risks immigrants being forced to adopt the customs of the host society at the expense of their own cultural heritage. Policymakers face the daunting task of navigating these tensions, ensuring that integration initiatives foster inclusivity without erasing immigrants' cultural identities. However, achieving this delicate equilibrium requires long-term commitment, often transcending the political tenure of policymakers.

On the other hand, multiculturalism emphasizes the significance of diversity and acknowledges the right of individuals to choose their own cultural identity. It advocates for the preservation of one's inherited culture and promotes the idea that embracing one's own culture fosters a greater acceptance of others, while also encouraging pride in one's culture without disparaging others. A central aspect of multiculturalism is the expectation that individuals from all cultures will be motivated to both preserve their unique cultural traits and be respected by others. However, multiculturalism has its own set of challenges. Establishing social cohesion while celebrating cultural differences is a formidable task. Multicultural societies must balance the need for common ground with the desire to embrace diversity. Policymakers face the challenge of devising practical strategies that promote unity amidst diversity. Moreover, the process of cultural celebration can be fraught with racialization and essentialization of identities, hindering self-determination and perpetuating stereotypes of both minority and majority groups. Resistance from the majority culture further complicates the implementation of multiculturalism policies, highlighting the need for inclusive decision-making processes that consider the perspectives of all stakeholders.

In navigating these complexities, policymakers must prioritize fostering inclusive environments where all individuals experience a meaningful sense of belonging. Embracing diversity while promoting unity requires a nuanced approach that transcends simplistic dichotomies. Evolving policies must be responsive to the changing landscape of immigration, adapting to emerging challenges while upholding fundamental principles of equity and justice. By fostering dialogue, promoting understanding, and cultivating empathy, societies can aspire to create environments that honor the richness of cultural diversity while forging common bonds of solidarity.

Ultimately, the journey toward effective immigration management is multifaceted and ongoing. It demands a commitment to equity, social justice, and human dignity. By addressing the challenges of assimilation and multiculturalism, policymakers can chart a path toward inclusive societies where every individual is valued and respected, regardless of their cultural background or immigration status. In this shared journey, collaboration and cooperation among diverse stakeholders is indispensable, so that diversity can become celebrated as a source of strength and resilience.

REFERENCES

Abbott, D. M., Pelc, N., & Mercier, C. (2019). Cultural humility and the teaching of psychology. *Scholarship of Teaching and Learning in Psychology*, *5*(2), 169–181. https://doi.org/10.1037/stl0000144

Ajzen, I. (1974). Effects of information on interpersonal attraction: Similarity versus affective value. *Journal of Personality and Social Psychology*, *29*(3), 374–380. https://doi.org/10.1037/h0036002

Alba, R., & Nee, V. (2012). Rethinking assimilation theory for a new era of immigration. In M. M. Suárez-Orozco, C. Suárez-Orozco, & D. Qin-Hilliard (Eds.), *The new immigration* (pp. 49–80). Routledge.

(2020). Assimilation. In C. Inglis, W. Li, & B. Khadria (Eds.), *The SAGE handbook of international migration* (pp. 400–417). SAGE.

Ariely, G. (2012). Globalization, immigration and national identity: How the level of globalization affects the relations between nationalism, constructive patriotism and attitudes toward immigrants? *Group Processes & Intergroup Relations*, *15*(4), 539–557. https://doi.org/10.1177/1368430211430518

Balliet, D., Wu, J., & De Dreu, C. K. W. (2014). Ingroup favoritism in cooperation: A meta-analysis. *Psychological Bulletin*, *140*(6), 1556–1581. https://doi.org/10.1037/a0037737

Benenciai, R. (2012). Predominio de inmigrantes bolivianos en los eslabones estratégicos de la cadena agroalimentaria de la horticultura en fresco de la

Argentina. *Política y Sociedad*, *49*(1), 163–178. https://doi.org/10.5209/rev_POSO.2012.v49.n1.36521

Ben-Nun Bloom, P., Arikan, G., & Courtemanche, M. (2015). Religious social identity, religious belief, and anti-immigration sentiment. *American Political Science Review*, *109*(2), 203–221. https://doi.org/10.1017/S0003055415000143

Berry, J. W. (1997). Immigration, acculturation, and adaptation. *Applied Psychology*, *46*(1), 5–34. https://doi.org/10.1111/j.1464-0597.1997.tb01087.x

(2005). Acculturation: Living successfully in two cultures. *International Journal of Intercultural Relations*, *29*(6), 697–712. https://doi.org/10.1016/j.ijintrel.2005.07.013

(2013). Research on multiculturalism in Canada. *International Journal of Intercultural Relations*, *37*(6), 663–675. https://doi.org/10.1016/j.ijintrel.2013.09.005

Bobowik, M., Benet-Martínez, V., & Repke, L. (2022). "United in diversity": The interplay of social network characteristics and personality in predicting outgroup attitudes. *Group Processes & Intergroup Relations*, *25*(5), 1175–1201. https://doi.org/10.1177/13684302211002918

Byrne, D. (1961). Interpersonal attraction and attitude similarity. *The Journal of Abnormal and Social Psychology*, *62*(3), 713–715. https://doi.org/10.1037/h0044721

(1971). *The attraction paradigm* (Vol. 462). Academic Press.

Cabaniss, E. R., & Cameron, A. E. (2018). Toward a social psychological understanding of migration and assimilation. *Humanity & Society*, *42*(2), 171–192. https://doi.org/10.1177/0160597617716963

Calderón, F., & Castells, M. (2020). The power of identity: Multiculturalism and social movements. In *The new Latin America* (pp. 105–126). Polity Press.

Captari, L. E., Shannonhouse, L., Hook, J. N., Aten, J. D., Davis, E. B., Davis, D. E., Van Tongeren, D., & Ranter Hook, J. (2019). Prejudicial and welcoming attitudes toward Syrian refugees: The roles of cultural humility and moral foundations. *Journal of Psychology and Theology*, *47*(2), 123–139. https://doi.org/10.1177/0091647119837013

De Haas, H., Castles, S., & Miller, M. J. (2020). *The age of migration: International population movements in the modern world*. Guilford.

Frank, J. D., & Fitzsimmons, E. G. (2023, January 15). Adams visits the border to step up pressure on Biden for migrant funds. *The New York Times*. www.nytimes.com/2023/01/15/nyregion/eric-adams-mexico-border-migrants.html

Girard, E. R., & Bauder, H. (2007). Assimilation and exclusion of foreign trained engineers in Canada: Inside a professional regulatory organization. *Antipode*, *39*(1), 35–53. https://doi.org/10.1111/j.1467-8330.2007.00505.x

Green, E. G. T., Sarrasin, O., Fasel, N., & Staerklé, C. (2011). Nationalism and patriotism as predictors of immigration attitudes in Switzerland: A municipality-level analysis: Nationalism, patriotism and immigration. *Swiss Political Science Review*, *17*(4), 369–393. https://doi.org/10.1111/j.1662-6370.2011.02030.x

Green, E. G. T., & Staerklé, C. (2013). Migration and multiculturalism. In L. Huddy (Ed.), *The Oxford handbook of political psychology* (2nd ed.). Oxford University Press.

Harwood, J., Paolini, S., Joyce, N., Rubin, M., & Arroyo, A. (2011). Secondary transfer effects from imagined contact: Group similarity affects the generalization gradient: Secondary transfer from imagined contact. *British Journal of Social Psychology*, *50*(1), 180–189. https://doi.org/10.1348/014466610X524263

Hendriks, M., & Burger, M. J. (2020). Unsuccessful subjective well-being assimilation among immigrants: The role of faltering perceptions of the host society. *Journal of Happiness Studies*, *21*(6), 1985–2006. https://doi.org/10.1007/s10902-019-00164-0

Hewstone, M. (2015). Consequences of diversity for social cohesion and prejudice: The missing dimension of intergroup contact. *Journal of Social Issues*, *71*(2), 417–438. https://doi.org/10.1111/josi.12120

Hewstone, M., Cairns, E., Voci, A., Hamberger, J., & Niens, U. (2006). Intergroup contact, forgiveness, and experience of "the troubles" in Northern Ireland. *Journal of Social Issues*, *62*(1), 99–120. https://doi.org/10.1111/j.1540-4560.2006.00441.x

Kindler, M., Ratcheva, V., & Piechowska, M. (2015). Social networks, social capital, and migrant integration at local level. European literature review. Institute for Research into Superdiversity, *6*.

Kymlicka, W. (2005). Liberal multiculturalims: Western models, global trends, and Asian debates. In W. Kymlicka & B. He (Eds.), *Multiculturalism in Asia*. Oxford University Press.

Kymlicka, W., & Banting, K. G. (Eds.). (2006). *Multiculturalism and the welfare state: Recognition and redistribution in contemporary democracies*. Oxford University Press.

Kotzur, P. F., Tropp, L. R., & Wagner, U. (2018). Welcoming the unwelcome: How contact shapes contexts of reception for new immigrants in Germany and the United States. *Journal of Social Issues*, *74*(4), 812–832. https://doi.org/10.1111/josi.12300

László, J. (2014). National identity. In *Historical tales and national identity: An introduction to narrative social psychology*. Routledge.

Lambert, P. (2006). Myth, manipulation, and violence: Relationships between national identity and political violence. In *Political violence and the construction of national identity in Latin America* (pp. 19–36). Palgrave Macmillan.

Leary, M. R., Diebels, K. J., Davisson, E. K., Jongman-Sereno, K. P., Isherwood, J. C., Raimi, K. T., Deffler, S. A., & Hoyle, R. H. (2017). Cognitive and interpersonal features of intellectual humility. *Personality and Social Psychology Bulletin*, *43*(6), 793–813. https://doi.org/10.1177/0146167217697695

Lewis, L. (2021). Assimilation as "false consciousness": Higher education immigrant students' acculturation beliefs and experiences. *International Journal of*

Intercultural Relations, *83*, 30–42. https://doi.org/10.1016/j.ijintrel.2021.04.012

Matera, C., Picchiarini, A., Olsson, M., & Brown, R. (2020). Does religion matter? Italians' responses towards Muslim and Christian Arab immigrants as a function of their acculturation preferences. *International Journal of Intercultural Relations*, *75*, 1–9. https://doi.org/10.1016/j.ijintrel.2019.12.002

Marinthe, G., Testé, B., & Kamiejski, R. (2023). Don't burn our flag: Patriotism, perceived threat, and the impact of desecrating a national symbol on intergroup attitudes. *Current Psychology*, *42*(5), 3780–3793. https://doi.org/10.1007/s12144-021-01696-6

Moghaddam, F. M. (2008). *Multiculturalism and intergroup relations: Psychological implications for democracy in global context*. American Psychological Association. https://doi.org/10.1037/11682-000

(2018). *Mutual radicalization: How groups and nations push each other to extremes*. American Psychological Association Press.

(2024). *The psychology of multiculturalism, assimilation, and omniculturalism*. Springer Nature.

Moghaddam, F. M., Salas-Schweikart, R., & Schneider, M. (2023). The democratic citizen, political plasticity and national development: A psychological perspective. *Psychology and Developing Societies*, *35*(2), 302–323. https://doi.org/10.1177/09713336231180961

Moghaddam, F. M. & Taylor, D. M. (1987). The meaning of multiculturalism for visible minority immigrant women. *Canadian Journal of Behavioural Science*, *19*, 121–136.

Montoya, R. M., & Horton, R. S. (2013). A meta-analytic investigation of the processes underlying the similarity-attraction effect. *Journal of Social and Personal Relationships*, *30*(1), 64–94. https://doi.org/10.1177/0265407512452989

Munck, G. L., & Luna, J. P. (2022). *Latin American politics and society: A comparative and historical analysis* (1st ed.). Cambridge University Press.

Nesdale, D., & Mak, A. S. (2000). Immigrant acculturation attitudes and host country identification. *Journal of Community & Applied Social Psychology*, *10*(6), 483–495. https://doi.org/10.1002/1099-1298(200011/12)10:6<483::AID-CASP580>3.0.CO;2-0

Novoa, C., & Moghaddam, F. M. (2014). *Policies for managing cultural diversity*. Oxford University Press. https://doi.org/10.1093/oxfordhb/9780199796694.013.009

Osbeck, L. M., Moghaddam, F. M., & Perreault, S. (1997). Similarity and attraction among majority and minority groups in a multicultural context. *International Journal of Intercultural Relations*, *21*(1), 113–123. https://doi.org/10.1016/S0147-1767(96)00016-8

Park, R. E., & Burgess, E. W. (1921). *Introduction to the science of sociology*. University of Chicago Press. Retrieved January 13, 2023, from www.gutenberg.org/files/28496/28496-h/28496-h.htm

Pham, A. V. N., Goforth, A. N., Aguilar, L., Burt, I., Bastian, R., & Diaków, D. M. (2022). Dismantling systemic inequities in school psychology: Cultural humility as a foundational approach to social justice. *School Psychology Review*, *51*(6), 692–709. https://doi.org/10.1080/2372966X.2021.1941245

Pier 21. (n.d.). *Canadian Multiculturalism Policy (1971)*. Retrieved April 30, 2025, from https://pier21.ca/research/immigration-history/canadian-multiculturalism-policy-1971

Politi, E., Bennour, S., Lüders, A., Manatschal, A., & Green, E. G. T. (2022). Where and why immigrants intend to naturalize: The interplay between acculturation strategies and integration policies. *Political Psychology*, *43*(3), 437–455. https://doi.org/10.1111/pops.12771

Portes, A., & Zhou, M. (1993). The new second generation: Segmented assimilation and its variants. *The Annals of the American Academy of Political and Social Science*, *530*(1), 74–96.

Reichl, C. A. (1995). Stages in the historical process of ethnicity: The Japanese in Brazil, 1908–1988. *Ethnohistory*, *42*(1), 31. https://doi.org/10.2307/482933

Rullo, M., Visintin, E. P., Milani, S., Romano, A., & Fabbri, L. (2022). Stay humble and enjoy diversity: The interplay between intergroup contact and cultural humility on prejudice. *International Journal of Intercultural Relations*, *87*, 169–182. https://doi.org/10.1016/j.ijintrel.2022.02.003

Safdar, S., Goh, K., & Choubak, M. (2020). Clothing, identity, and acculturation: The significance of immigrants' clothing choices. *Canadian Journal of Behavioural Science/Revue canadienne des sciences du comportement*, *52*(1), 36–47. https://doi.org/10.1037/cbs0000160

Salas-Schweikart, R., Hendricks, M. J., Boychuck, M., & Moghaddam, F. M. (2024). Similarity-attraction across ethnic, religious, and political groups: Does celebrating differences or similarities make a difference? *The Journal of Social Psychology*, 1–20. https://doi.org/10.1080/00224545.2024.2427834

Tanesini, A. (2018). Intellectual humility as attitude. *Philosophy and Phenomenological Research*, *96*(2), 399–420. https://doi.org/10.1111/phpr.12326

Tervalon, M., & Murray-García, J. (1998). Cultural humility versus cultural competence: A critical distinction in defining physician training outcomes in multicultural education. *Journal of Health Care for the Poor and Underserved*, *9*(2), 117–125. https://doi.org/10.1353/hpu.2010.0233

Tajfel, H. (1974). Social identity and intergroup behaviour. *Social Science Information*, *13*(2), 65–93. https://doi.org/10.1177/053901847401300204

Tajfel, H., Billig, M. G., Bundy, R. P., & Flament, C. (1971). Social categorization and intergroup behaviour. *European Journal of Social Psychology*, *1*(2), 149–178. https://doi.org/10.1002/ejsp.2420010202

Turner, J. C., & Reynolds, K. J. (2012). Self-categorization theory. In P. Van Lange, A. Kruglanski, & E. Higgins (Eds.), *Handbook of theories of social psychology* (pp. 399–417). SAGE Publications Ltd. https://doi.org/10.4135/9781446249222.n46

United Nations Educational, Scientific and Cultural Organization (UNESCO). (2005). Convention for the safeguarding of the intangible cultural heritage

2003. *International Journal of Cultural Property*, *12*(4), 447–458. https://doi.org/10.1017/S0940739105050277

Vega, W., Kolody, B., Valle, R., & Weir, J. (1991). Social networks, social support, and their relationship to depression among immigrant Mexican women. *Human Organization*, *50*(2), 154–162. https://doi.org/10.17730/humo.50.2.p340266397214724

Vermeulen, F., & Kranendonk, M. (2021). Intergenerational transmission of social identity: Dual identification among Turkish immigrant parents and their adult children in Western Europe. *Ethnic and Racial Studies*, *44*(16), 194–214. https://doi.org/10.1080/01419870.2021.1939090

White, F. A., Borinca, I., Vezzali, L., Reynolds, K. J., Blomster Lyshol, J. K., Verrelli, S., & Falomir-Pichastor, J. M. (2021). *Beyond* direct contact: The theoretical and societal relevance of indirect contact for improving intergroup relations. *Journal of Social Issues*, *77*(1), 132–153. https://doi.org/10.1111/josi.12400

Willis-Esqueda, C., Delgado, R. H., & Pedroza, K. (2017). Patriotism and the impact on perceived threat and immigration attitudes. *The Journal of Social Psychology*, *157*(1), 114–125.

Wolf, L. J., Hanel, P. H. P., & Maio, G. R. (2021). Measured and manipulated effects of value similarity on prejudice and well-being. *European Review of Social Psychology*, *32*(1), 123–160. https://doi.org/10.1080/10463283.2020.1810403

Yzerbyt, V., & Cambon, L. (2017). The dynamics of compensation: When ingroup favoritism paves the way for outgroup praise. *Personality and Social Psychology Bulletin*, *43*(5), 587–600. https://doi.org/10.1177/0146167216689066

CHAPTER 9

Building Commonality in Diverse Societies

In earlier chapters we identified a number of major challenges that arise in association with the arrival of new immigrants and refugees, and the resulting increased diversity in societies. For example, we discussed how increased diversity can be associated with interethnic prejudice, discrimination, conflict, and a decline in generalized trust in a population (of course, increased diversity is also associated with certain benefits, such as achieving a more culturally rich society, but our focus here is on challenges raised by diversity). The traditional policies for managing diversity provide some solutions to these challenges, but traditional policies also have some shortcomings (as discussed in Chapter 9). In the present chapter, we explore alternative solutions through projects that build commonalities and a unified collective identity in society, as well as the policy of omniculturalism, which we also critically assess in light of psychological research. Given continuing increases in migration and rising diversity in major societies in the twenty-first century, we believe the critical discussion of policies for managing diversity must be given high priority.

In the first section, we describe the policy of omniculturalism in relation to the basic challenges confronting increasingly diverse societies. In the second section, we discuss psychological research and theories on the characteristics of people who identify with all of humanity. These individuals are "omnicultural," in the sense that they give priority to common human characteristics. In the final major part of this chapter, we discuss research on superordinate goals, the common group identity model, and intergroup contact – paths for building commonalities and a shared identity in diverse societies.

Omniculturalism and Major Challenges Confronting Humankind

The policy of omniculturalism was put forward as an alternative to the more established policies of assimilation (integration) and multiculturalism, for the purpose of managing diversity in societies around the world (Moghaddam, 2010, 2012, 2024). Omniculturalism has two interconnected goals. The first goal is to manage human relationships within a generally accepted understanding derived from science that all human beings share foundational and important similarities. We humans are very similar to one another, and the contention is that our similarities are – and should be given – far more important than our differences. The second goal is to acknowledge that in some respects all humans belong to groups that to some degree differ from one another, such as in terms of the languages they speak, the religions they practice, and the colors of their skins. However, these intergroup differences are of minor importance, compared to the foundational similarities all humans share – including in terms of genetic characteristics. Humans are genetically very similar to one another; *there are more genetic variations within than between human populations* (Witherspoon et al., 2007). We can compare these intergroup differences to the tip of an iceberg that sticks out from the water and attracts attention, as opposed to the far larger, vast body of an iceberg that remains out of sight submerged under water, representing the deep and foundational characteristics shared by all humans.

Omniculturalism proposes a number of basic principles that should serve as the foundation for socializing and educating young people. These principles provide a framework for all social relationships, and especially intergroup interactions. First, the *omnicultural imperative* is proposed as the guiding principle in all human relationships: "During interactions with others, under all conditions, first give priority to the characteristics you share with other people as members of the human group" (Moghaddam, 2012, p. 318). The omnicultural imperative is strongly influenced by Kant's categorical imperative, "Act only in accordance with that maxim through which you can at the same time will that it becomes universal law" (G 4:421). In a society guided by omniculturalism, children are socialized to interact with others through priority and focus on what they have in common with others as human beings. This perceptual and motivational framework results in the inclusion rather than exclusion, and the acceptance rather than rejection, of all others.

Following a Kantian approach, human universals serve as an end in themselves, and not a means to an end. Human universals are identified through objective means and in a politically neutral manner, and not as a means to ascribe superiority to certain selected groups and inferiority to other groups. This is a supremely important point, because one of the criticisms that must be raised in relation to any effort to identify human universals relates to the question, "But who defines humanity and human universals?" (see Bilewicz & Bilewicz, 2012). Humanity and human universals have often been defined by the most powerful human groups in ways that work against the interests of minority groups. For example, the Western powers that colonized large parts of Asia, Africa, and South America used their own cultures, religions, values, and criteria in general to define what is superior and what represents humanity, including in the area of human rights (Samson, 2020). Similarly, feminists point out that in many respects men continue to design the world in their own terms, assuming men to represent humanity (Perez, 2019). Thus, we must take care to define humanity and human rights in objective ways that bring benefits to all people, and not just to some groups.

Omniculturalism that gives priority to human commonalities is also inspired by John Rawls's (1921–2002) proposition that individuals should make decisions under a "veil of ignorance" about their own group memberships (Rawls, 1971). For example, if individuals are voting to decide whether or not there should be slavery in their society, they should not know whether they will become one of the slave owners or one of the slaves. To take another example, if decisions are made about taxation levels for the rich, the middle class, and the poor, and social services for the poor, then people should cast votes without knowing whether they will be one of the rich, the middle class, or the poor. If they vote for slavery, they could become one of the slaves; if they vote for low taxes for the rich and weak social services for the poor, they might well be one of the poor and suffer the consequences. Similarly, in a society where priority is given to intergroup differences, groups that have positively valued characteristics and high status today could find themselves discriminated against tomorrow. By giving priority to human commonalities, omniculturalism places high value on all humans – because they all have valued characteristics, inherently because of their humanness.

The second proposition of omniculturalism concerns group distinctiveness, captured by the *sharing imperative*: "Actively reach out to share cultural differences, teaching others about your group's distinct characteristics and also learning about the distinct characteristics of other groups" (Moghaddam, 2012, p. 319). It is proposed that the sharing imperative must be given secondary importance, and only be introduced to children in schools (or at home, in the case of homeschooled children) around the age of fourteen years. During the first fourteen years, children must be educated in a way that gives priority to human similarities. By the age of fourteen, children are able to think abstractly (following Piaget, Marini & Case, 1994) and it will be possible for them to simultaneously consider the many foundational ways in which all humans are similar and the less important ways in which human groups differ.

Under present cultural and political conditions, it seems to be easier for people to focus on and give priority to intergroup differences, than it is for them to give priority to the characteristics that all human beings share. Whereas people need encouragement and training to give priority to human commonalities during their interactions with others, the tendency to highlight intergroup differences seems to come more naturally (at least under current sociopolitical conditions). As suggested by the need for identity distinctiveness that is central to social identity theory (Tajfel & Turner, 1979), individuals strive to belong to groups that have a distinct (and positive) identity. This need for distinctiveness often results in groups manufacturing and exaggerating intergroup differences, and this tendency is even greater in societies that "celebrate differences" as part of a multicultural approach (see Chapter 8 in this text).

The need for distinctiveness is probably influenced by evolutionarily developed strategies humans have acquired in relentless competition for vacant spaces and scarce resources. When people are in a context of competition for scarce resources, among the strategies they adopt is specialization and differentiation, which increases the probability of individuals finding more vacant spaces and resources (Moghaddam, 1997). For example, research shows that when applying for jobs, young Americans and Europeans will try to highlight how they differ from competitors in ways that make them appear to be stronger candidates (Lee et al., 2008; Lemaine, 1974). Similarly, when competing with more affluent women who could afford expensive beautification products and techniques, poor women interviewed in Brazil (a country where there is intense emphasis on female beautification) found ways to differentiate and make themselves distinct in beautification activities that relied less on money (Lee et al., 2008). The tendency to differentiate, specialize, and search for vacant spaces is ongoing and intense in academic domains, including in psychology (Moghaddam, 1989).

The social identity tradition (Tajfel & Turner, 1979; Turner et al., 1987) has emphasized the centrality of distinctiveness in how individuals construct their identities. But the motivation to be distinct is directed by the need for achieving a positive identity. Both experimental and field research demonstrate how easy it is for individuals to be biased in favor of the ingroup after a person has been categorized as a group member – even when group membership is on an objectively trivial basis (Moghaddam, 2008, chapter 5). This trend of favoring the ingroup is confirmed by a long history of research on ethnocentrism, from the early twentieth century (Sumner, 1906) to more recent times (Bizumin, 2019; Hammond & Axelrod, 2006; LeVine & Campbell, 1972). Ingroup favoritism seems to be universal and easily triggered. Thus, the implication is that (under present circumstances) whereas giving attention to group differences encompassed by the sharing imperative normally comes to life in everyday interactions, the omnicultural imperative and a focus on human commonalities can only come to fruition through programs that explicitly socialize individuals to give priority to human similarities.

Given that in the present cultural conditions, people tend to give priority to group differences and to favor the ingroup without much encouragement, what are the possibilities for the future development of omniculturalism – according to which people should give primacy to what they have in common with all other humans? In addressing this question, we begin (in the next section) by identifying the characteristics of individuals who identify with all humanity. We accept that in certain domains of behavior integral to intergroup relations, inherited characteristics can also play a part; an example is the role of genetic factors in authoritarianism (Nacke & Riemann, 2023). However, environmental conditions play an important role in the activation of genes, and research in epigenetics shows that the traditional "genes versus environment" perspective is misleading (Moore, 2003). Thus, rather than being focused on whether certain genes are present or absent, our ultimate concern (discussed in the final section of this chapter) is with the educational and socialization programs that render certain developmental and behavioral trajectories more probable (Lickliter & Witherington, 2017).

What Are the Characteristics of Omnicultural Individuals?

Omniculturalism puts forward the following ideal: In all interactions between individuals and groups, humans should give priority to the similarities they share with all other humans. These human universals have been identified scientifically (Brown, 1991), including in the area of genetics (Witherspoon et al., 2007). The ideal of identifying with all humanity is reflected in the ideas of many classical authors, as well as modern psychologists. (For a more in-depth discussion of this ideal in the work of past thinkers, see McFarland et al., 2019, and Reysen & Katzarska-Miller, 2018.) Most explicitly, in his highly influential model of self-actualization, Abraham Maslow (1954) sees the highest level of individual development being achieved by people who "... have a deep feeling of identification, sympathy, and affection for human beings in general. They feel kinship and connection, as if all people were members of a single family" (p. 138).

But according to Maslow, self-actualization is the highest and most difficult to achieve level of human development. Under present conditions, only individuals such as Mahatma Gandhi (1869–1948) and Nelson Mandela (1918–2013) self-actualize. In practice, the majority of people do not progress beyond the first few levels of Maslow's hierarchy of needs, so they are stuck at the lower levels attempting to satisfy their physiological, safety, social, esteem, and other more basic needs. Self-actualized individuals are few and far between, and they have very special characteristics. They are democratic in a deep sense; they are open to learning from all others who can teach them valuable lessons, and they give respect to any and all human beings just because of their human status. Self-actualized individuals do this irrespective of group membership (in terms of nationality, ethnicity, sex group, and so on). Indeed, self-actualized individuals do not seem to notice group memberships; in twenty-first-century terminology, they are color-blind in their cognitions and actions.

These characteristics of self-actualized individuals described by Maslow (1954) are closely related to the characteristics of democratic citizens capable of participating in and sustaining an actualized or fully developed democracy (Moghaddam, 2016). However, like the self-actualized individual, the democratic citizen is an ideal. We can add to this list of ideals the omnicultural individual, capable of identifying with all humanity. But what are the characteristics of individuals who identify with all humanity? Next, we critically assess this question in light of available empirical research.

Characteristics of the Omnicultural Individual

By outlining the characteristics of individuals who are inclined to identify with all humanity rather than just their ingroup(s), we are helping to shed light on the characteristics of the persons who can participate in and support an omnicultural society. Thus, we are helping to clarify the omnicultural ideal we should be attempting to achieve, through family, school, and community programs that are discussed in the final section of this chapter.

At the outset, we need to take note of the fast-changing context for this discussion, particularly because of the increasing role of electronic communications in the lives of young people (Szymkowiak et al., 2021). Globalization and the rapid advancement of electronic communications have meant that people have communication with many others who are not physically living close to them. In this sense, "community" has expanded for many people using electronic communications, as they acquire information about and communicate with others who they seldom or never have interaction with in person. As electronic communications play a larger role in our everyday lives, this tendency for our communities to expand will probably continue. However, it is an open research question as to whether there will be changes in the characteristics of individuals who identify with larger communities and even all of humanity.

Different terminology has been used in research exploring the characteristics of individuals who identify with all of humanity. Some examples of the different terms used are: Global citizenship (Blake et al., 2015; Reysen & Katzarska-Miller, 2013), global citizenship identification (Reysen & Katzarska-Miller, 2017), global identity (de Rivera & Carson, 2015), global social identity (Buchan et al., 2011), global identification (Ariely, 2017), cosmopolitan identity (Beros, 2016), citizen of the world (Carmona et al., 2022), world-mindedness (Der-Karabetian, 1992), identification with all humanity (McFarland et al., 2013; Reese et al., 2015), and global human identification (McFarland & Hornsby, 2015). Sampson and Smith (1957) were one of the first to develop psychological measures in this area, using the terms international-mindedness and world-mindedness. Research continues on psychological measures of identification with all humanity in the twenty-first century, particularly through cross-national studies (e.g., Hamer et al., 2021).

Despite the different terminologies and research methods used over time, the central research question in this domain has remained fairly stable: What are the psychological characteristics of individuals who are more inclined to identify with all of humanity? For example, the measure used by Hamer et al. (2021, appendix) includes the following questions for American participants (questions for participants from other nationalities would be revised accordingly).

> How close do you feel to each of the following groups? (1) People in my community (2) Americans (3) People all over the world. (Hamer et al., 2021, p. 169)
>
> How often do you use the word "we" to refer to the following groups of people? (1) People in my community (2) Americans (3) People all over the world. (Hamer et al., 2021, p. 169)
>
> How much would you say you have in common with the following groups? (1) People in my community (2) Americans (3) People all over the world. (Hamer et al., 2021, p. 169)

Although there are different conceptual approaches to, as well as measures of, identification with all of humanity, the measure developed by Hamer et al. (2021), and the representative questions provided above, captures the main theme of this research. (See the review by McFarland et al., 2019.) Underlying this research is a question that has historically been at the heart of social identity theory (Tajfel & Turner, 1979): Is there a negative correlation between identification with one's nation and identification with all of humanity? That is, does strong identification with one's nation necessarily mean weak identification with all humanity? Research on identification with all humanity shows that at least some people are identifying strongly *both* with their nations and with all of humanity (Bassett & Cleveland, 2019; McFarland et al., 2019). Bayram (2019) perhaps best captures the apparent contradiction in this type of behavior, being high on both nationalism and cosmopolitanism, through the phrase "nationalist cosmopolitanism."

But what are the characteristics of people who identify with all of humanity? In answering this question, we quickly realize that although there are some individuals who identify highly with both their nations and with all of humanity, there are many others who believe that identifying with their nations and identifying with all humanity is a contradiction. For example, this includes right-wing nationalists who support leaders such as Donald Trump, who has said that.

> There is no global anthem. No global currency. No certificate of global citizenship. We pledge allegiance to one flag and that flag is the American flag. (RealClear Politics, 2016)

The above statement could have been made by Narendra Modi about allegiance to India (see Jaffrelot, 2019), or Recep Erdogan about allegiance to Turkey (see Cagaptay, 2017), or by any of the other authoritarian leaders on the rise in different countries around the world in the twenty-first century (Moghaddam, 2019). Extensive research on authoritarian movements and the authoritarian personality since the Second World War suggest that identification with all humanity will be rejected by individuals who have authoritarian personalities. These individuals tend to be ethnocentric, categorical in thinking, low on tolerance for ambiguity, high on conspiratorial thinking and obedience to authority, punitive toward minorities and dissimilar others in general, and high on conformity to conventional values (Adorno et al., 1950; Altemeyer, 1988).

The research that is more specifically focused on individuals who endorse identification with all humanity shows them to be characterized by six groups of prosocial values, reflecting: (1) Higher intergroup empathy and (2) helping, and (3) value for diversity, (4) stronger concern with environmental sustainability and (5) social justice, and improving the state of the world (see chapter 4 in Reysen & Katzarska-Miller, 2018). Individuals who identify with all humanity have the general profile of being more worldly and accepting toward different others, being stronger supporters of human rights, and higher on the personality trait "openness to experience" (Hamer et al., 2019). Related to this, individuals with a cosmopolitan orientation (being more culturally open, having higher respect for human rights and cultural differences) tend also to behave in more pro-environment ways (Leung et al., 2015). Given that we know the general characteristics of individuals who do not and those who do identify with all humanity and look beyond their national interests, what kinds of experiences do we need to provide for individuals in order to increase the number of people who do identify with all humanity? Our working assumption is that those individuals who identify with all humanity are giving priority to what all humans have in common, and only secondarily attending to intergroup differences.

Providing Experiences for People to Identify with All Humanity

We believe that identification with all humanity can be taught, although inherited characteristics also influence how individuals react to this kind of educational training (see McFarland, 2011). We discuss education for identification with all humanity in two main sections: First, we consider broad educational issues and proposals; second, we discuss psychological research that leads to applied programs and training. Our goal is to progress beyond the experience of identification with all humanity only among an elite "global community" (Rofe, 2003). Rather, we are concerned with this experience as shared by ordinary people around the world.

Educational Issues and Proposals

The defense of authenticity is a human need, but it cannot seek to rupture the interdependence of humanity and the obvious necessity of "living together."

The above quotation from Mary Joy Pigozzi (2006, p. 1), a representative of the United Nations Educational Scientific and Cultural Organization (UNESCO), highlights the tension between allegiance to local ingroups and allegiance to humanity – a tension we earlier discussed in relation to allegiance to the nation versus allegiance to all humanity. UNESCO is among the international organizations concerned with education for global citizenship, another important one being Oxfam. According to Oxfam (n.d.), "Education for global citizenship is a framework to equip learners for critical and active engagement with the challenges and opportunities of life in a fast-changing and interdependent world. It is transformative, developing the knowledge and understanding, skills, values and attitudes that learners need both to participate fully in a globalized society and economy, and to secure a more just, secure and sustainable world than the one they have inherited" (p. 5). In order to reach this goal, Oxfam (n.d.) maps out how subject curricula and global citizenship can be developed in tandem for different age groups of students, including in subjects such as "art and design," "design and technology," "computing and ICT," and "mathematics."

Education programs for global citizenship as proposed by Oxfam, UNESCO and other international organizations are highly ambitious and expansive, and to some degree controversial in light of the ongoing right-wing backlash against liberal education (although some argue that this is exactly the time to globalize public education, Darian-Smith, 2020). For example, according to Oxfam (n.d.), science curriculum should be developed to teach students to "engage with the social, cultural, and economic contexts in which scientific inquiry takes place; explore ethical issues surrounding science and its pursuit and uses; consider the contribution of science to debates around sustainable development and climate change; develop appreciation of interdependence within the natural world and between people and planet; provide opportunities to explore the contributions of different cultures to science" (p. 13). But issues such as "climate change " and "the contributions of different cultures to science" have become politicized, with extremist right-wing groups such as *Moms for Liberty* attacking what they consider to be "far-left" education, with its "liberal biases" and "internationalism" (The Economist, 2023).

Just as globalization has been a powerful force supporting education for global citizenship, the backlash against globalization has been associated with attacks on education for global citizenship. The result is that we have two ongoing processes, moving forward in parallel. On the one hand, global citizen education continues to be a strong theme in the education systems of the United States and many other Western and non-Western countries (Dill, 2013; Hicks, 2003), in part through the influence of UNESCO, Oxfam, and other international organizations. On the other hand, rising populism and right-wing nationalist movements, often spearheaded by authoritarian strongmen such as Donald Trump, are associated with efforts to end education for global citizenship. These right-wing attacks include slogans such as "America First," "India First," and so on, and attempts to control schools and universities to meet right-wing nationalist goals (including by censorship and banning progressive books in schools, Perez, 2022). The evidence suggests that *more* education is associated with positive identification with global citizenship (Smith et al., 2017), and this seems encouraging to educators. However, critics would contend that it is only education biased by liberal values that leads to stronger identification with global citizenship; in contrast, a conservatively oriented education would lead to stronger feelings of nationalism rather than internationalism.

The same themes are apparent in university education. Evidence has accumulated to suggest that identification with all humanity is nurtured and strengthened through a university atmosphere and courses that value global awareness, knowledge, and identity (Blake et al., 2015; Reysen et al., 2012; Reysen et al., 2013). On the one hand, globalization is moving higher education in this internationalist direction, through study-abroad programs, the learning of foreign languages, the arrival of increasing numbers of foreign students, and the internationalization of curriculum. "Internationalization" is an increasingly important theme in higher education in many societies around the world (Sa & Serpa, 2020). On the other hand, a focus on what all humans have in common and identification with all humanity is under attack from two politically opposed groups: Extreme right-wing nationalists who demand to put "our country first," and extreme left-wing cultural relativists who tend to be internationalists but give priority to celebrating intergroup *differences* within their countries. There is danger that these two opposing movements will become trapped in a process of mutual radicalization, pushing each other to further extremes (Moghaddam, 2018).

Psychological Research Leading to Applied Programs and Training

In this section we examine two areas of research that lead to applied programs and training toward people giving priority to human commonalities and identifying with all humanity. The first of these research areas is part of the identity tradition, stemming from the summer camp studies of Muzafer Sherif (1906–1988) (see Sherif, 1966) and social identity theory (Tajfel & Turner, 1979). The second of these research areas centers on the theme of intergroup contact, shaped in large part by Gordon Allport's (1897–1967) seminal work *The Nature of Prejudice* (1954).

Identity and identification are at the center of Sherif's (1966) influential intergroup research in the context of summer camps (this point tends to be neglected, because Sherif's research is often only interpreted through his contributions to realistic conflict theory; Moghaddam, 2008). Sherif was the first researcher to empirically point to the consequences of mere categorization. In one of the conditions in his intergroup studies, Sherif showed that when a group of boys learned that there is a second group of boys nearby, the mere presence of this second group (without direct contact) triggered feelings of competitiveness and hostility in the first group. Later, the impact of this "mere categorization" was experimentally demonstrated through the minimal group paradigm that is integral to social identity theory (Tajfel & Turner, 1979). A second important way in which Sherif contributed to the identity tradition is through the concept of *superordinate goals*, which are goals that both groups want to achieve, but neither can reach without the cooperation of the other group.

Sherif's demonstration of the power of superordinate goals was achieved in the third and fourth stages of his summer camp studies. Over the course of the first two stages, the boys got to know one another and were placed into two different groups. During the third stage, the two groups of boys engaged in a variety of intergroup competitions, with the winning group receiving rewards. As a result of competition for scarce rewards, increasingly intense conflict arose between the two groups of boys. The attitudes and prejudices of each group of boys became fiercely negative toward the outgroup. Having created intergroup conflict, Sherif's next challenge was: How to transform the relationship between the two groups from intense fighting to peace and cooperation? Sherif achieved this goal by introducing superordinate goals. For example, the vehicle bringing food to the summer camp "broke down" (arranged by Sherif) and the two groups of boys were forced to cooperate to pull the truck into the camp, and in this way gain access to food. Through superordinate goals, the two groups of boys came to identify themselves as belonging to one large group. Superordinate goals have proved to be very useful in a number of applied domains, such as reaching agreements between groups in organizational negotiations (Swaab et al., 2021).

Sherif's concept of superordinate goals has also influenced theoretical and experimental innovation involving recategorization and achieving a "common" or superordinate identity (Gaertner et al., 1993; Lemay Jr., &

Ryan, 2021). The basic idea of the common group identity model is that when people recategorize the members of their ingroup and the members of an outgroup as belonging to one common group, this reduces prejudice, discrimination, and conflict. In essence, when people identify with a larger group that encompasses both ingroup and outgroup, "intergroup harmony" is achieved. One could argue that, just as all the boys in Sherif's summer camp studies ended up identifying with one group and thus ending the salience of the smaller groups to which they formerly belonged, in common group identity experiments recategorization and identification with one large common group diminishes the salience of smaller groups (such as ethnic and racial groups, Cunningham, 2005; Nier et al., 2001; Scheepers et al., 2014). Research shows that when majority group members of a host society identify with a common group, they are more supportive of immigrant integration, both in their attitudes and actual actions (e.g., volunteering in organizations that help immigrants; Kunst et al., 2015).

Thus, there is solid experimental evidence, from Sherif's summer camp studies in the mid twentieth century to contemporary research on the common group identity model, showing that intergroup relations improve when group members adopt a common or superordinate identity. Earlier in this chapter, we discussed research on "identification with all humanity," and the idea central to omniculturalism of individuals giving priority to what all human beings have in common. Given that "humanity" is the largest (most common) human group, what practical approaches do we have for achieving identification with all humanity? Sherif's concept of superordinate goals has inspired a tradition of applied projects (Swaab et al., 2021), and at the global level we could adopt climate change as the first challenge confronting all humanity, our primary superordinate goal, which we have to solve – or perish. A first practical path, then, is to educate people to become more cosmopolitan and to identify with all humanity, so they become more environmentally conscious and tackle the problem of climate change (following Leung et al., 2015).

Research suggests that another important practical path toward a common identity is through increased intergroup contact (Gaertner et al., 1996). The original formulation of Allport (1954) stipulated that in order for intergroup contact to improve intergroup relations, four conditions have to be met: The groups should, first, enjoy equal status; second, be in a cooperative rather than competitive relationship; third, have common goals; fourth, be supported to have contact by the larger community. An argument put forward (and backed by evidence) by Gaertner et al. (1996) is that if the conditions stipulated by Allport (1954) are met, then the groups in contact develop a common identity. Alternative interpretations suggest that contact moves groups toward better intergroup relationships, and probably more common identity, independent of the conditions stipulated by Allport (see Pettigrew, 2021). Consequently, a practical path toward strengthening people having a common identity, identifying with all humanity, and giving priority to what all humans have in common, is to increase intergroup contact. As contact increases and people develop common rituals that are shared by increasing numbers of individuals, then the sense of global community is also strengthened (De Rivera & Carson, 2015).

Concluding Comment

There is an increase both in migration and the backlash against migration. We have argued that we need to go beyond assimilation (integration) and multiculturalism in order to find better solutions for solving the challenge of migration in the twenty-first century. The solution we have critically considered is to shift to giving priority to human commonalities, and only secondarily attend to intergroup differences. This omnicultural approach is in line with research on identification with all humanity, and on the common group identity model. An inspiration for all these ideas is Sherif's concept of superordinate goals. Given current trends in climate change, it is imperative that we adopt the improvement of environmental conditions as our first global superordinate goal.

Other practical paths for reaching a behavioral style involving giving priority to human commonalities are: education and intergroup contact. The internationalization of education movement has been underway since the 1960s, but has crashed into right-wing political opposition and populist movements led by authoritarian strongmen in the twenty-first century. Intergroup contact might seem to be a more promising path for arriving at common group identities, because societies are becoming more diverse and increased intergroup contact seems inevitable. However, the contact of intergroup contact is being influenced by political trends, and hostility from extreme White nationalists is a major factor in these processes. Thus, although the research on intergroup contact seems to suggest that contact is beneficial independent of the conditions specified by Allport (1954), the hostile context created by extremist political movements is influencing the integration of migrants.

REFERENCES

Adorno, T. W., Frenkel-Brunswik, E., Levinson, D. J., & Sanford, B. W. (1950). *The authoritarian personality*. New York: Harper & Row.

Allport, G. W. (1954). *The nature of prejudice*. Cambridge, MA: Addison-Wesley.

Altemeyer, B. (1988). *Enemies of freedom: Understanding right-wing authoritarianism*. San Francisco, CA: Jossey-Bass.

Ariely, G. (2017). Global identification, xenophobia, and globalization: A cross-national exploration. *International Journal of Psychology, 52*, 87–96.

Bassett, J. F., & Cleveland, A. J., (2019). Identification with all humanity, support for refugees and for extreme counter-terrorism measures. *Journal of Social and Political Psychology, 7*, 310–334.

Bayram, A. B. (2019). Nationalist cosmopolitanism: The psychology of cosmopolitanism, national identity, and going to war for the country. *Nations and Nationalism, 25*, 757–781.

Beros, M. (2016). Cosmopolitan identity – Historical origins and contemporary relevance. *Tabula, 14*, 197–211.

Bilewicz, M., & Bilewicz, A. (2012). Who defines humanity? Psychological and cultural obstacles to omniculturalism. *Culture & Psychology, 18*, 331–344.

Bizumic, B. (2019). *Ethnocentrism: Integrated perspectives*. Oxford, UK: Routledge.

Blake, M. E., Pierce, L., Gibson, S., Reysen, S., & Katzarska-Miller, I. (2015). University environment and global citizenship. *Journal of Educational and Developmental Psychology, 5*, 97–107.

Brown, D. E. (1991). *Human universals*. Philadelphia, PA: Temple University Press.

Buchan, N. R., Brewer, M. B., Grimalda, G., Wilson, R. K., Fatas, E., & Foddy, M. (2011). Global social identity and global cooperation. *Psychological Science, 22*, 821–828.

Cagaptay, S. (2017). *The new sultan: Erdogan and the crisis of modern Turkey*. New York: I. B. Tauris.

Carmona, M., Guerra, R., & Hofhuis, J. (2022). What does it mean to be a "citizen of the world": A prototype approach. *Journal of Cross-Cultural Psychology, 53*, 547–569.

Cunningham, G. B., (2005). The importance of common ingroup identity in ethnically diverse groups. *Group Dynamics: Theory, Research, and Practice, 9*, 251–260.

Darian-Smith, E. (2020). Globalizing education in times of hyper-nationalism, rising authoritarianism, and shrinking worldviews. *New Global Studies, 14*, 47–68.

De Rivera, J. & Carson, H. A. (2015). Cultivating a global identity. *Journal of Social and Political Identity, 3*, 310–330.

Der-Karabetian, A. (1992). World-mindedness and the nuclear threat: A multinational study. *Journal of Social Behavior and Personality, 7*, 293–308.

Dill, J. D. (2013). *The longings and limits of global citizenship education: The moral pedagogy of schooling in a cosmopolitan age*. New York: Routledge.

Gaertner, S. L., Dovidio, J. F., & Bachman, B. A. (1996). Revisiting the contact hypothesis: The induction of a common group identity. *International Journal of Intercultural Relations, 20*, 271–290.

Gaertner, S. L., Dovidio, J. F., Anastasio, P. A., Bachman, B., & Rust, M. C. (1993). The common group identity model: Recategorization and the reduction of intergroup bias. *European Review of Social Psychology, 4*, 1–26.

Hamer, K., McFarland, S., & Penczek, M. (2019). What lies beneath? Predictors of identification with all humanity. *Personality and Individual differences, 141*, 258–267.

Hamer, K., Penczek, M., McFarland, S., Wlodarczyk, A., Luzniak-Piecha, M., Golinska, A., Cadena, L. M., Ibarra, M., Bertin, P. & Delouvee, S. (2021). Identification with all humanity – A test of the factorial structure and measurement invariance of the scale in five countries. *International Journal of Psychology, 56*, 157–174.

Hammond, R. A., & Axelrod, R. (2006). The evolution of ethnocentrism. *Journal of Conflict Resolution, 50*, 926–936.

Hicks, D. (2003). Thirty years of global education: A reminder of key principles and precedents. *Educational Review, 55*, 265–275.

Jaffrelot, C. (2019). *Modi's India: Hindu nationalism and the rise of ethnic democracy*. Princeton, NJ: Princeton University Press.

Kant, E. (2002[1785]). *Groundwork for the metaphysics of morals*. In A. W. Wood (Ed. & Trans.). New Haven, CT: Yale University Press..

Kunst, J. R., Thomsen, L., Sam, D. L., & Berry, J. W. (2015). "We are in this together": Common group identity predicts majority members' active acculturation efforts to integrate immigrants. *Personality and Social Psychology Bulletin, 41*, 1438–1453.

Lee, N., Lessem, E., & Moghaddam, F. M. (2008). Standing out and blending in: differentiation and conflict. In F. M. Moghaddam, R. Harré, & N. Lee (Eds.), *Global conflict resolution through positioning analysis* (pp.113–131). New York: Springer.

Lemaine, G. (1974). Social differentiation and social originality. *European Journal of Social Psychology, 4*, 17–54.

Lemay Jr., E. P. & Ryan, J. (2021). Common group identity, perceived similarity, and communal interracial relationships. *Personality and Social Psychology Bulletin, 47*, 985–1003.

Leung, A. K. Y., Koh, K., & Tam, K. P. (2015). Being environmentally responsible: Cosmopolitan orientation predicts pro-environmental behaviors. *Journal of Environmental Psychology, 43*, 79–94.

LeVine, R. A., & Campbell, D. T. (1972). *Ethnocentrism: Theories of conflict, ethnic attitudes, and group behaviour*. New York: Wiley.

Lickliter, R., & Witherington, D. C. (2017). Toward a truly developmental epigenetics. *Human Development, 60*, 124–138.

Marini, Z., & Case, R. (1994). The development of abstract reasoning about the physical and social world. *Child Development, 65*, 147–159.

Maslow, A. H. (1954). *Motivation and personality.* New York: Harper & Row. 3rd ed.
McFarland, S. (2011). The slow creation of humanity. *Political Psychology, 32,* 1–20.
McFarland, S., Brown, D., & Webb, M. (2013). Identification with all humanity as a moral concept and psychological construct. *Psychological Science, 22,* 194–198.
McFarland, S., Hacket, J., Hamer, K., Katzarska-Miller, I., Malsch, A., Reese, G., & Reysen, S. (2019). Global human identification and citizenship: A review of psychological studies. *Advances in Political Psychology, 40,* 141–171.
McFarland, S., & Hornsby, W. (2015). An analysis of five measures of global human identification. *European Journal of Social Psychology, 45,* 806–817.
Moghaddam, F. M. (1989). Specialization and despecialization in psychology: Divergent processes in the three worlds. *International Journal of Psychology, 24,* 103–116.
(1997). *The specialized society: The plight of the individual in an age of individualism.* Westport, CT: Praeger.
(2008). *Multiculturalism and intergroup relations: Psychological implications for democracy in global context.* Washington, DC: American Psychological Association.
(2010). *The new global insecurity: How terrorism, environmental collapse, economic inequalities, and resource shortages are changing our world.* Santa Barbara, CA: Praeger Security International.
(2012). The omnicultural imperative. *Culture & Psychology, 18,* 304–330.
(2016). *The psychology of democracy.* Washington, DC: American Psychological Association Press.
(2018). *Mutual radicalization: How groups and nations push each other to extremes.* Washington, DC: American Psychological Association Press.
(2019). *Threat to democracy: The appeal of authoritarianism in an age of uncertainty.* Washington, DC: American Psychological Association Press.
(2024). *The psychology of multiculturalism, assimilation, and omniculturalism.* Cham, Switzerland: Springer Nature.
Moore, D. S. (2003). *The dependent gene: The fallacy of "nature vs. nurture."* New York: Henry Holt.
Nacke, L., & Riemann, R. (2023). Two sides of the same coin? On the common etiology of right-wing authoritarianism and social dominance orientation. *Personality and Individual Differences, 207,* 112160.
Nier, J. A., Gaertner, S. L., Dovidio, J. F., Banker, B. S., Ward, C. M., & Rust, M. C. (2001). Changing interracial evaluations and behavior: The effect of a common group identity. *Group Processes & Intergroup Relations, 4,* 299–316.
Oxfam (n.d.). Education for global citizenship: A guide for schools. https://oxfamilibrary.openrepository.com/bitstream/handle/10546/620105/edu-global-citizenship-schools-guide-091115-en.pdf?sequence=11&isAllowed=y. Accessed 6:45pm July 12, 2023
Perez, A. H. (2022). Defeating the censor within. *Knowledge Quest, 50,* 34–39.

Perez, C. C. (2019). *Invisible women: Data bias in a world designed for men.* New York: Abrams Press.
Pettigrew, T. (2021). Advancing intergroup contact theory: Comments on the issue's articles. *Journal of Social Issues, 77,* 258–273.
Pigozzi, M. J. (2006). A UNESCO view of global citizenship education. *Educational Review, 58,* 1–4.
Rawls, J. (1971). *A theory of justice.* Cambridge, MA: Harvard University Press.
RealClear Politics (2016, December 1). www.realclearpolitics.com/video/2016/12/01/trump_there_is_no_global_flag_no_global_currency_no_global_citizenship_we_are_united_as_americans.html. Accessed 4:15pm July 8, 2023
Reese, G., Proch, J., & Finn, C. (2015). Identification with all humanity: The role of self-definition and self-investment. *European Journal of Social Psychology, 45,* 426–440.
Reysen, S., & Katzarska-Miller, I. (2012). College course curriculum and global citizenship. *International Journal of Development Education and Global Learning, 4,* 27–39.
(2013). Intentional worlds and global citizenship. *Journal of Global Citizenship & Equity Education, 3,* 34–52.
(2017). Media, family, and friends: Normative environment and global citizenship identification. *Journal of International & Global Studies, 9,* 38–55.
(2018). *The psychology of global citizenship: A review of theory and research.* Lanham, MD: Lexington Books.
Reysen, S., & Katzarska-Miller, I., Gibson, S. A., & Hobson, B. (2013). World knowledge and global citizenship: Factual and perceived world knowledge as predictors of global citizenship identification. *International Journal of Development Education and Global Learning, 5,* 49–68.
Reysen, S., Pierce, L., Spencer, C. J., & Katzarska-Miller, I. (2013). Exploring the content of global citizen identity. *The Journal of Multiculturalism in Education, 9,* 1–31.
Rofe, M. W. (2003). "I want to be global": Theorizing the gentrifying class as an emergent elite global community. *Urban Studies, 40,* 2511–2526.
Sa, M. J., & Serpa, S. (2020). Cultural dimensions in internationalization of the curriculum in higher education. *Education Science, 10,* 375. Doi:10.3390/educsci10120375
Samson, C. (2020). *The colonialism of human rights: Ongoing hypocrisies of western liberalism.* Cambridge, MA: Polity Press.
Sampson, D. L., & Smith, H. P. (1957). A scale to measure world-minded attitudes. *The Journal of Social Psychology, 45,* 99–106.
Scheepers, D., Saguy, T., Dovidio, J. F., & Gaertner, S. L. (2014). A shared dual identity promotes cardiovascular challenge response during interethnic interactions. *Group Processes & Intergroup Relations, 17,* 324–341.
Sherif, M. (1966). *Group conflict and cooperation: Their social psychology.* London: Routledge & Kegan Paul.

Smith, W. C., Fraser, P., Chykina, V., Ikoma, S., Levitan, J., Liu, J., & Mahfouz, J. (2017). Global citizenship and the importance of education in a globally integrated world. *Globalisation, Societies, and Education, 15*, 648–665.

Sumner, R. (1906). *Folkways*. Boston, MA: Ginn.

Swaab, R. I., Lount Jr., R. B., Chung, S., & Brett, J. M. (2021). Setting the stage for negotiations: How superordinate goal dialogues promote trust and joint gain in negotiations between teams. *Organizational Behavior and Human Decision Processes, 167*, 157–169.

Szymkowiak, A., Melovic, B., Babic, M., Jeganathan, K., Kundi, G. S. (2021). Information technology and Gen Z: The role of teachers, the internet, and technology in the education of young people. *Technology and Society, 65*, 101565.

Tajfel, H., & Turner, J. C. (1979). An integrative theory of intergroup conflict. In W. G. Austin & S. Worchel (Eds.), *The social psychology of intergroup relations* (pp. 33–47). Monterey, CA: Brooks/Cole.

The Economist (2023). MAGA mummies. July 8, p. 21.

Turner, J. C., Hogg, M. A., Oakes, P. J., Reicher, S. D., & Wetherell, M. S. (1987). *Rediscovering the social group: A self-categorization theory*. Oxford: Basil Blackwell.

Witherspoon. D. J., Wooding, S., Rogers, A. R., Marchani, E. E., Watkins, W. S., Batzer, M. A., & Jorde, L. B. (2007). Genetic similarities within and between human populations. *Genetics, 176*, 351–359.

CHAPTER 10

Looking Ahead
The Future of Immigration, National Identity, and Deglobalization

In the earlier chapters of this book, we explored how in the contemporary context the othering and marginalization of immigrants continues in different societies around the world, as part of a wider contestation about the imagined identities of nations (following Anderson, 1983). We have witnessed the same pattern of behavior across different Western and non-Western societies faced with the so-called "threat" of immigrants: The rise of ethnocentric and sometimes violent right-wing nationalist groups (such as those responsible for the riots in the United Kingdom in August 2024), and "banal radicalization " (when radicalization leads extremism to seep into everyday life and become mainstream, Moghaddam, 2024) associated with support for authoritarian, ethnocentric leaders. These leaders are usually in the "strongman" mold, but in a few instances (e.g., Italy) they are female. The same anti-immigrant and anti-minority pattern of reactions that are evident in India and South Africa, can be seen in many European and North American countries.

The idea that nations are imagined communities (Anderson, 1983) might be taken to imply that identification with one's nation is flexible and even weak, and from this perspective it seems surprising that such strong passions and violence is unleashed on the basis of nationhood. After all, the possibility of "imagining a nation" (Anderson, 1983, p. 36) is relatively recent historically and only arose after certain traditional forms of understanding the world lost their grip, such as the understanding "... that a particular script-language offered privileged access to ontological truth, precisely because it was an inseparable part of that truth ..." (Anderson, 1983, p. 36). However, despite the relatively recent development of most national identities, historical experience attests to the strength of the ties people develop with their nations; these ties are often extremely strong, resilient, and ferociously defended. This trend continues in the same way in the twenty-first century, with national identities and national cultures being defended against supposed "invasions" and "threats" from immigrants. Despite the imagined nature of nations and the socially constructed nature of national identities, they have come to serve as solid and often emotionally charged foundations for contemporary social identities. As such, nations serve as perhaps the most important group that people fight for and defend – sometimes to the death, such as in numerous wars (some of them ongoing) between nations.

From a psychological perspective, the zeal with which the imagined community of nations is guarded by people reminds us, once again, of what is often a subjective and arbitrary basis of group formation and collective identity development. A wide range of research evidence, from laboratory experiments using the minimal group paradigm (Tajfel et al., 1971) to field research with ethnic groups (Maquet, 2018), demonstrates that even arbitrary and objectively trivial differences between groups can be, and routinely are, used as a justification for intergroup bias, discrimination, and violent conflict. Differences between groups can be manufactured or newly "discovered," and objectively trivial differences can be given priority and importance, as a way to keep intact and to separate the identity of the imagined community of "our nation" from the identity of "those other(s)."

In addition to identifying and scrutinizing this pattern of "othering," we have critically discussed possible solutions, as represented by assimilation, multiculturalism, and omniculturalism (Chapters 8 and 9 in this text). We have considered the possibility that a more constructive alternative to celebrating intergroup differences is to actively celebrate human similarities, and only give attention to differences at a secondary level (Moghaddam, 2024). This is on the basis of the idea that humans share many important similarities, and are actually more similar than they are different. In this final chapter, we first critically review some central features of contemporary immigration from a psychological perspective and, second, look ahead to the future of immigration in global context, assessing alternative paths for the future development of the community of nations. We discussed in earlier chapters how low birth rates in Western countries and very high birth rates in parts of Africa, Asia, and some other parts of the world will serve as a motor for migration. The sheer power of demography (Dao et al., 2021) means that migration across national borders will continue at high rates and very probably increase in the coming decades. Consequently, it is important to look ahead and try to find better solutions to the challenges faced by both immigrants and host nations.

Key Features of Contemporary Immigration from a Psychological Perspective

In this first section of the final chapter, we highlight from a psychological perspective four central features of twenty-first-century immigration.

Immigration and the Challenge of Population Decline

Countries as different as France, Russia, Japan, Iran, Germany, China, and Italy are facing the prospect of population decline. This is because the fertility rate in these and many other countries has fallen below the replacement level; this has been the case in much of Europe for several decades, and it was the case in every European country in 2018 (Parr, 2023). The average number of children American women had decreased from 3.6 in 1960 to 1.6 in 2023 (The Economist, 2024). This decline has been sharpest among women who are younger and college-educated. Associated with the trend of population decline is the aging of populations and smaller labor forces; the result being fewer people working and supporting a retired population. Attempts by governments to use financial incentives to increase birth rates have had too little success (The Economist, 2024). The most immediate solution to this problem is through adding to the host population by accepting more immigrants, and this solution has been adopted with some modest success by Sweden, Belgium, and a number of other countries (Parr, 2023). However, in many countries, such as those of Eastern Europe, Italy, and Finland, as well as a number of non-Western countries (including China and Japan), not enough immigrants have been accepted to compensate for the low fertility rate among the host population, with the result that in some countries "... extinction would occur over the long term if net migration, fertility and mortality remain constant" (Parr, 2023, p. 22). But despite the long-term threat of extinction, the strength of ethnocentrism and the fear of dissimilar outsiders is so great that in some countries, immigration remains extremely difficult to implement as a solution to declining populations.

Another solution considered in response to the problem of low fertility rates and population declines is increased use of automation, artificial intelligence (AI), and robotics. The increased use of new technologies seems inevitable, but some authors have argued against using this approach specifically as a way to compensate for declining populations. For example, Lant Pritchett (2023) has argued that, "Raw labor power is the most important (and often the only) asset low-income people around that world have. The drive to make machines that perform roles that could easily be fulfilled by people not only wastes money but helps to keep the poorest poor" (p. 55). Despite this argument, the solution to use low-income people from around the world to meet labor needs in low-fertility countries faces a challenge we have explored in this book: The backlash from host society populations, faced with what they see to be "invasions" by dissimilar others.

Given the ongoing challenge of population decline faced by many Western and non-Western societies, and the availability of higher immigration as a solution to this problem, greater efforts need to be made to facilitate the integration of immigrants into host societies. Psychological research suggests that programs based on intergroup contact could play a constructive role in the integration of immigrants, and meta-analytic research suggests that intergroup contact has positive outcomes irrespective of the conditions in which it takes place (as we discussed in Chapter 9). However, there are two possible shortcomings with this approach. First, the conditions in which intergroup contact takes place, as first specified by Allport (1954), seem stubbornly relevant and cannot be dismissed, in part because they are directly linked to issues of justice. These include, for example, the conditions that for intergroup contact to have positive outcomes the groups need to have equal status and their interactions should be positively regarded and supported by the larger society. Second, we also need to address the increasingly urgent problem of extremist and sometimes violent right-wing nationalist reactions to rising immigration. Intergroup contact could contribute to solving this problem, but needs to be supplemented by other programs.

We have also raised questions about programs for managing diversity in societies experiencing declining populations and rising immigration. The currently dominant approach of multiculturalism, central to which is the celebration of intergroup differences, might not be the most constructive one. This is particularly because empirical evidence shows that people seek closer contact with those others who they see to be more similar to – rather than different from – themselves (Osbeck et al., 1997; Salas-Schweikart et al., 2024). By highlighting and celebrating intergroup differences, we may be influencing host society members and others to want less contact with immigrants. We must keep in mind that in the twenty-first century, immigrants are more likely to be different from the host society population in terms of ethnicity, language, religion, and cultural characteristics in general. (Consider, for example, the case of Muslim Middle Eastern migrants moving to Western Europe.)

Universality of Experiences with Immigration

There are certain commonalities in the experiences of different Western and non-Western societies in dealing with immigration. (This builds on our earlier discussions, particularly in Chapters 2–8.) The foundation for these commonalities is the basic dynamics of ingroup–outgroup relations, studied extensively by researchers, particularly since the European research movement led by Henri Tajfel (1919–1982) and others from the 1970s (Brown & Pehrson, 2020; Moghaddam, 2008). When faced with the influx of large numbers of migrants, host societies – irrespective of whether it is the United States, South Africa, Italy, or some other nation – come to see themselves and to behave as a group under threat from an outside force, and migration is interpreted as a "crisis" (Cantat et al., 2023). This perceived external threat results in predictable changes within the ingroup. For example, even though the migrants are in important respects very similar to the host society (after all, humans are far more similar to one another than they are different, Moghaddam, 2024), even objectively trivial differences between immigrants and host populations are exaggerated and used as a basis for discrimination and rejection of immigrants. Moreover, stereotypes with negative features are developed that incorporate manufactured, imagined differences between immigrants and host populations (Sánchez-Junquera et al., 2021).

The opportunity for intergroup differences to be used as a way to isolate immigrants is enhanced because at present immigrants arrive in societies dominated by multiculturalism and the "celebration of group differences." According to multicultural norms, host-population children are taught from an early age to look for ways in which they are different from immigrant groups, and to highlight and celebrate such differences. This highlighting of group differences can serve as a foundation for manufacturing intergroup differences and othering of minorities, as well as discrimination against them.

A second universal characteristic of host societies as they react to a perceived "invasion" from immigrants is greater ethnocentrism and support for authoritarian leadership. This is reflected in the political rise of leaders such as Donald Trump in the United States, Marie le Pen in France, and Michael Farage in the United Kingdom, but it is also evident in classic experimental research. For example, in Sherif's (1966) studies on intergroup behavior, when the two groups of boys moved to the stage of intense intergroup rivalry and conflict, there was greater support for more aggressive leadership. At this stage, boys who were more conciliatory lost support and status. There are also many historic examples of the rise of a different, more aggressive type of leadership during wartime, such as the "bulldog" image of Winston Churchill leading Britain during the World War Two.

The recognition of these types of common experiences in the host society arising from the arrival of large numbers of migrants in Western and non-Western societies has resulted in a more global approach being adopted by immigration researchers (Abdelaaty, 2021; Adamson & Tsourapas, 2020; Natter, 2018). This newly developed research literature blurs the lines between immigration in Western and non-Western societies (this relates to our earlier discussion on immigration within the Global South, Chapter 7).

Negative Host Society Attitudes toward Immigrants

Donald Trump, who has called migrants "animals" and "not human" (Layne et al., 2024), has come to symbolize intolerance and prejudice towards immigrants. Trump has tens of millions of supporters in the United States; well over 70 million people voted for him in the 2020 and in 2024 elections (putting him back in the White House), and many of these supporters oppose immigration in part because they feel that their own needs are not being adequately addressed, at the same time that immigrants take (what Trump and his supporters see as) unfair advantage of the system to get rewards that they have not earned. These anti-immigration sentiments are associated with systematic and large misperceptions about immigrant populations. These misperceptions are consistent across different societies. Alesina et al. (2023) point out that, "...in the US, the actual number of documented immigrants is 10% of the population, but the average perception is 36%; in Italy, the true share of immigrants is 10%, but the perceived share is 26%. Misperceptions about the size of the immigrant population are widespread among all groups of respondents across the political spectrum" (p. 2).

In addition to exaggerating the size of the immigrant population, many among the host population hold negative attitudes toward immigrants. A survey of Germany, France, Sweden, the United Kingdom, and the United States revealed that a significant number of the population believe (incorrectly) that immigrants receive twice as much government benefits on average as non-immigrants and are less educated than they are (Alesina et al., 2023). Research on attitudes toward immigrants in the United Kingdom, where immigrants are fiscal contributors, shows that nonimmigrants see immigrants to be a major cause of inequality in society, whereas in practice this effect is minimal (Dustmann et al., 2022). Research in France suggests that immigrants are influenced by politics and attitudes toward them in different municipalities, tending to congregate in areas where politics is more favorable to them (Schmutz & Verdugo, 2023). The places where immigrants feel least welcome tend to be where people experience what Twan Huijsmans (2023) refers to as *place resentment*, ". . . a perception of unjust socioeconomic, cultural and political inequality between the own area and other areas" (p. 286). These are places that people feel do not matter and are neglected by politicians, and where immigrants are pushed into.

Another negative feature of attitudes toward immigrants is the assumption that immigrants raise crime levels. Tufail et al. (2023) point out that, "In Australia, 35% of respondents claim that immigrants raise violence. The proportion was 40% in France, 64% in Germany, 72% in Japan, and 27% in the USA, while 40% in the United Kingdom" (p. 1868). But an extensive international study demonstrated that increased immigration does not increase crime (Tufail et al., 2023). These misperceptions about the association between immigration and crime are being loudly propagated by populist right-wing political leaders and are common to experiences in many different Western and non-Western countries.

Globalization and Immigration

Immigration is directly contributing to globalization (Leblang & Peters, 2022), just as globalization is contributing to immigration, and reactions to immigration are an integral part of a broader set of negative reactions to globalization. The same forces that are creating an anti-immigration movement across many different parts of the world are also resulting in an anti-globalization or deglobalization movement that spans many countries and regions. Deglobalization has taken many shapes, encompassing economic, cultural, and other factors. The economic factors are touted by populist politicians, although in practice the empirical evidence shows that economic deglobalization has not been significant (Goldberg & Reed, 2023). Despite this, populist and even relatively moderate politicians such as President Biden have been pressured to put up higher walls around their countries through increased trade tariffs. Similar protectionist actions have been taken in different countries, as a result of pressure from populist political movements (Ehrlich &

Gahagan, 2023), despite the self-harm economic isolationism tends to bring nations (Barattieri, & Cacciatore, 2023).

Given that the deglobalization movement is shown not to be very strong economically (Goldberg & Reed, 2023), what is all the "sound and fury" about? Using the case of backlash against immigration, we argue that the deglobalization movement is full of "sound and fury" because it is in foundational ways about culture and national identity. Yes, the backlash against immigrants is partly about issues such as "the immigrant threat to our jobs," "the immigrant threat to our housing and health services," and other material factors, but the backlash against immigration and the force of the deglobalization movement derives much of its power from perceived threats against "our culture," "our way of life," and "our national identity." This is not just a matter of money and other material factors, but more about a sense of the kind of nation we see ourselves to be and want to remain.

The culture-based and identity-based backlash against globalization is strong in many North American and European societies, but it is perhaps even stronger in some non-Western societies. An important example is the attacks on globalization by different groups of Islamic fundamentalists, including major fundamentalist governments such as that of Iran and numerous less centralized Islamic fundamentalist movements and groups. Salzman (2008) has noted that, "... globalization is a source of anxiety because it threatens traditional sources of meaning and value" (p. 326). For Islamic fundamentalists, globalization is a threat because they see it as "Westernization" (and "Americanization," more specifically) and the spread of Western (and American) values in sensitive areas such as gender roles and gender relations. Islamic fundamentalists attack migration particularly when it involves Westerners and those representing Western values being present in Islamic countries. One of the central demands of Islamic fundamentalists, including the terrorist leader Osama bin Laden (1957–2011), has been that Westerners and those disseminating Western cultures must leave Islamic societies.

An even more powerful group questioning the spread of Western democratic values through globalization are dictatorships, headed by China and Russia. These countries present an alternative model of societal progress to Western democracies; an alternative which they argue is more suitable for non-Western societies. Similar to fundamentalist Islamic groups, the major dictatorships are opposed to migration that spreads Western culture and democratic values. This is the main foundation on which President Xi of China and President Putin of Russia have formed their strategic alliance.

In conclusion, there are certain important themes in the psychological experience of immigration. Some of these common themes concern processes internal to nations. These include low birth rates and the threat of population decline, making the acceptance of immigration necessary for economic reasons in many Western and non-Western countries, but at the same time hostility to dissimilar outgroups arriving suddenly and in large numbers. Some other themes concern processes that are international, such as the backlash against globalization. Interestingly, anti-globalization sentiments are held by groups that are in many respects different from and opposed to one another, such as right-wing extremist nationalists in Western societies, Islamic fundamentalists in countries such as Iran, and also large dictatorships.

Alternative Future Paths

In this section, we critically discuss alternative paths for the future development of immigration in global context. To conceptualize the range of options, imagine a continuum from "borders completely closed" to "borders completely open" (see Figure 10.1).

Within the context of many countries (including those of North America and Europe), this continuum is to some degree associated with political orientation, so that the extreme political right-wing groups and individuals support positions closer to "borders completely closed," and the extreme political left-wing groups and individuals support positions closer to "borders completely open" (Karreth et al., 2015). However, this picture is too simplistic, because some politically right-wing groups also support a global economic free market, where people, goods, and services are able to move to anywhere in the global market in order to maximize profits. After all, free market economics is historically associated with the political right, and in theory businesses thrive in a borderless, free market world.

The relationship between the political left and open national borders is also complex and involves competing forces. For example, labor unions tend to be inclined to the political left and supportive of left-wing political parties, but in many contexts labor unions are opposed to open national borders because immigration can increase the labor supply and put

Borders completely closed---Borders completely open

Figure 10.1 Continuum of different levels of openness across national borders.

downward pressure on wages. In practice, then, in the context of many nations, immigration attitudes are complex (Helbling et al., 2023), and many factors intervene in the relationship between political orientation and immigrant attitudes. Most groups and individuals are positioned around the center on this continuum (Figure 10.1), somewhere between the extreme poles of "borders completely closed" and "borders completely open."

Surprisingly, surveys show that the most pro-immigration "open-borders" groups are not necessarily recently arrived immigrants. "Immigrants against immigration" is a theme in numerous countries, including affluent ones such as Switzerland (Strijbis & Polavieja, 2018), where one might imagine (wrongly, as it turns out) that greater material resources would result in more benign and open attitudes among immigrants toward immigration. In line with an "immigrants against immigration" theme, in the United States, Latinos have shifted to be more supportive of the Republican Party policies toward immigration (Leonhardt, 2024). In 2012, 29 percent of Latinos voted in support of the Republican Party, and in 2024 Latino support put Donald Trump and the Republican Party in charge of all branches of government.

There are practical reasons why the extreme poles on the continuum shown in Figure 10.1 do not represent viable solutions. To begin, consider the extreme pole of "borders completely closed." As we have discussed in earlier chapters, the birth rate in European and North American societies, as well Japan, China, Russia, and some other non-Western countries, is below replacement level. In short, without importing people, these societies will suffer a decline (and even extinction, in the long term) in total population. The most immediate economic challenge faced by these countries is a decline in their workforces. Indeed, the predicted decline of populations in Europe has been postponed in part because of immigration (Alho et al., 2006).

Of course, it is possible that advances in AI and robotics, as well as increases in the age of retirement, will be able to fill at least part of the gap in the size of the labor force. AI is boosting productivity, more work is being done through robots and automation, and people are retiring later (and living longer); all these changes help to offset the smaller labor pool in some countries. However, these are only a part of pull factors influencing immigration levels. There are also push factors, including wars, environmental disasters, over-population, political repression, and other such factors that put enormous pressure on people to flee their country of birth and seek a home in another country.

The "push" factors leading to migration are increasing rather than decreasing in strength, with the implication that a "borders completely closed" option is not viable. One set of push factors stems from the continuing violent conflicts, including those in the Middle East, in Sudan and some other parts of Africa, as well as in Ukraine. These wars result in millions of people being displaced, seeking refuge in other countries and regions of the world. The availability of more advanced transportation systems means that the average distance between refugee country of origin and country of destination has increased (Fransen & De Haas, 2022). This means that, on average, refugees are from more distant lands and tend to be less similar (in terms of language, religion, ethnicity, culture) to the host society population, and face higher hurdles for integration.

A second set of push factors stems from global warming and climate change. Indeed, in the long term, global warming will probably prove to be the most important "push" factor influencing migration. Unless there are dramatic political changes in the world, global warming will result in enormous increases in migration. As Thomas Dietz and associates (2020) summarized our predicament, "By 2017, the Earth's average temperature had increased by 1°C above preindustrial levels ... It will be difficult to limit total warming to less than 2°C, and extremely difficult to reach the goal of 1.5°C, regarded as an upper bound to avoid great risk of harm to the economy, human health and well-being, and Earth's ecosystems" (p. 136). The general consensus among scientists is that the goal of keeping global warming below 1.5°C is technically feasible, but politically extremely challenging (Jewell & Cherp 2020). Indeed, unless there are fundamental changes in political systems and behaviors in both Western and non-Western societies, global warming will drive international migration higher and higher in the next few decades (Ferris, 2020).

But neither is a "borders completely open" option viable, at least not in the present circumstances of the world. The case for a "borderless world" has been made by various authors (Bauder, 2015), and in an ideal world one could argue that national borders should not exist; humans should be able to freely move around the world. Borders are at present far more open for goods and services than they are for human beings. But a number of conditions have to be met in order for borders to become more open, or to disappear. The first is that the standard of living of countries, and the political freedoms enjoyed by citizens in different countries, should become more equal. This is one of the conditions that the EU had to establish for members, otherwise there would be a rush for people to move from low-income and politically closed countries to high-income and politically more open countries. Of course, because some level of inequality still exists in the EU, there still is a tendency for some countries (e.g., Germany) to attract people from other EU member states. Similarly, the move toward a "borderless world" would first require the achievement of a certain level of resource equality and political openness across all countries, so that there is not a rush of populations from some countries to others. In the present circumstance, we are not able to achieve even a minimum level of resource equality and political openness across all countries, so the "borderless world" is not viable within the foreseeable future. Consequently, our best option is to position ourselves somewhere between the two extremes of "borders completely closed" and "borders completely open."

But policies toward immigrants and the treatment of immigrants, particularly in education and employment, is increasingly becoming a political issue. The politicization of immigration in many parts of the world has resulted in a tug-of-war between populist political right-wing groups who want to put a stop to immigration and prevent what they see to be the favored treatment of minorities, and more left-wing groups who support immigration and policies that help minorities improve their lives – even though these policies are not always available to majority group members.

In the United States, this political tug-of-war has also infiltrated the justice system and the highest level of politics. For example, the United States Supreme Court has shifted to the political right, since three new justices were appointed by Donald Trump during his 2016–2020 term as the US President. As a result, the Supreme Court has made it far more difficult for institutions of higher education to implement affirmative action so as to accept more minority student applicants (Aaron et al., 2023). But the White House, with Democrat Joe Biden serving as the US President in 2020–2024, has moved in the opposite direction. For example, through an executive order (Executive Order on Diversity, Equity, Inclusion, and Accessibility in the Federal Workforce, 2021), President Biden provided strong support for the Diversity, Equity, Inclusion, and Accessibility (DEIA) movement. A central goal of this movement is to achieve a government workforce that accurately reflects the diversity of the American people.

The DEIA movement is highly dependent on political trends, but it has already taken deep root in the education sector, in academic research, and in some nongovernmental organizations. There are now entire handbooks that report on research on this topic (e.g., Downes et al., 2024), and critical discussions on how to best implement DEIA (e.g., Feitosa et al., 2022; Stamps & Foley, 2023), including in international business

(Newburry et al., 2022). A common underlying proposition of this research literature is that a more diverse workforce is more productive and efficient (e.g., see Hampe et al., 2024). However, a limitation of this literature is that diversity in social class is not considered; neither is representation from the poor. This may well prove to be an Achilles heel for the DEIA movement, because it is opposed by enormous populist political forces fueled in part (in the European and North American contexts) by poorer Whites who believe immigrants and minorities generally are being given unfair advantages. This trend is reflected, for example, in strong support for populist anti-immigrant politicians in the 2024 European Parliamentary elections.

Concluding Comment

In exploring plans for immigration at national and international levels, we must keep in mind that we are confronted by certain limitations. One of the most important among such limitations is the central role of irrationality. Some of the most powerful "push" factors leading to mass migration arise out of irrational processes, and these include large-scale wars and extensive environmental destruction as a result of climate change. These enormous large-scale irrational factors overwhelm individuals – even when at the individual level people are capable of thinking and acting rationally.

There are many examples of large-scale conflicts in which groups and nations push one another to extremes and engage in violent conflicts, and individuals are pushed along by the sheer force of collective irrational processes – even though at the individual level people are capable of thinking rationally and recognizing that the collective conflict should and can be avoided (Moghaddam, 2018). Similarly, while at the individual level many people can make correct choices to avoid adding to environmental pollution and climate change, as part of a collective it is far more difficult to make correct choices – as is evident from the ongoing trend of global warming. Consequently, in planning for future immigration at national and international levels, we should also take into consideration the powerful impact of large-scale irrational forces.

REFERENCES

Aaron, D. G., Bajaj, S. S., & Stanford, F. C. (2023). Supreme court cases on affirmative action threaten diversity in medicine. *Proceedings of the National Academy of Sciences*, *120*(17), e2220919120.

Abdelaaty, L. E. (2021). *Discrimination and delegation: Explaining state responses to refugees*. Oxford University Press.
Adamson, F. B., and G. Tsourapas. 2020. "The migration state in the global south: Nationalizing, developmental, and neoliberal models of migration management." *International Migration Review, 54*(3), 853–882. https://doi.org/10.1177/0197918319879057.
Alesina, A., Miano, A., & Stantcheva, S. (2023). Immigration and redistribution. *Review of Economic Studies, 90,* 1–39.
Alho, J., Alders, M., Cruijsen, H., Keilman, N., Nikander, T., & Pham, D. Q. (2006). New forecast: Population decline postponed in Europe. *Statistical Journal of the United Nations,* 1–10. https://publ.nidi.nl/output/2006/sjunece-23-01-alho.pdf
Allport, G. W. (1954). *The nature of prejudice*. Addison-Wesley.
Anderson, B. (1983). *Imagined communities: Reflections on the origin and spread of nationalism*. Verso.
Barattieri, A., & Cacciatore, M. (2023). Self-harming trade policy? Protectionism and production networks. *American Economic Journal: Macroeconomics, 15*(2), 97–128.
Bauder, H. (2015). Perspectives of open borders and no border. *Geography Compass, 9,* 395–405.
Brown, R., & Pehrson, S. (2020). *Group processes: Dynamics within and between groups*. Wiley Blackwell.
Cantat, C., Pécoud, A., & Thiollet, H. (2023). Migration as crisis. *American Behavioral Scientist, 69*(6), 627–649.
Dao, T. H., Docquier, F., Maurel, M., & Schaus, P. (2021). Global migration in the twentieth and twenty-first centuries: The unstoppable force of demography. *Review of World Economics, 157,* 417–449.
Dietz, T., Shwom, R. L., & Whitley, C. T. (2020). Climate change and society. *Annual Review of Sociology, 46,* 135–158.
Downes, P., Li, G., Van Praag, L., & Lamb, S. (Eds.) (2024). *The Routledge international handbook of equity and inclusion in education*. Routledge.
Dustmann, C., Kastis, Y., & Preston, I. (2022). Inequality and immigration. IFS Report, No. R231, ISBN 978-1-80103-109-7, Institute of Fiscal Studies (IFS), London. https://doi.org/10.1920/re.ifs.2022.0231
Ehrlich, S. D., & Gahagan, C. (2023). Multisided Threat to Free Trade: Protectionism and Fair Trade During Increasing Populism. *Politics and Governance, 11,* 223–236.
Executive Order on Diversity, Equity, Inclusion, and Accessibility in the Federal Workforce, June 25, 2021. www.whitehouse.gov/briefing-room/presidential-actions/2021/06/25/executive-order-on-diversity-equity-inclusion-and-accessibility-in-the-federal-workforce/
Feitosa, J., Hagenbuch, S., Patel, B., & Davis, A. (2022). Performing in diverse settings: A diversity, equity, and inclusion approach to culture. *International Journal of Cross-Cultural Management, 22,* 433–457.

Ferris, E. (2020). Research on climate change and migration where are we and where are we going? *Migration Studies, 8*, 612–625.

Fransen, S., & De Haas, H. (2022). Trends and patterns of global refugee migration. *Population and Development Review, 48*, 97–128.

Goldberg, P. K., & Reed, T. (2023). *Is the Global Economy Deglobalizing? And if so, why? And what is next?* (Working Paper No. 31115). National Bureau of Economic Research.

Hampe, H., Frndak, D., & Robins, A. (2024). Experiential learning in diversity, equity, inclusion, and belonging. *The Journal of Health Administration Education, Spring*, 247–260.

Helbling, M., Jäger, F., Maxwell, R., & Traunmüller, R. (2023). Broad and detailed agreement: Public preferences for German immigration policy. *International Migration Review, 0*(0). https://doi.org/10.1177/01979183231216076

Huijsmans, T. (2023). Place resentment in "the places that don't matter": explaining the geographical divide in populist and anti-immigration attitudes. *Acta Politica, 58*, 285–305.

Jewell, J., & Cherp, A. (2020). On the political feasibility of climate change mitigation pathways: Is it too late to keep warming below 1.5° C? *Wiley Interdisciplinary Reviews: Climate Change, 11*(1), e621.

Karreth, J., Singh, S. P., & Stojek, S. M. (2015). Explaining attitudes toward immigration: The role of regional context and individual predispositions. *West European Politics, 38*(6), 1174–1202. https://doi.org/10.1080/01402382.2015.1022039

Layne, N., Slattery, G., & Reid, T. (2024, April 3). Trump calls migrants "animals," intensifying focus on illegal immigration. *Reuters*. www.reuters.com/world/us/trump-expected-highlight-murder-michigan-woman-immigration-speech-2024-04-02/

Leblang, D., & Peters, M. E. (2022). Immigration and globalization (and deglobalization). *Annual Review of Political Science, 25*, 377–399.

Leonhardt, D. (2024, April 10). The Morning. *The New York Times*. https://mail.google.com/mail/u/0/#inbox/WhctKKZWmmMXQcnKSSNWpxXNXwSqxDZxFnHXgChxNqDdQMsxGRTqBTcbDvdqbjSbGlXbMlv

Maquet, J. J. (2018 [1961]). *The premise of inequality in Ruanda: A study of political relations in a central African community*. Oxford University Press.

Moghaddam, F. M. (2008). *Multiculturalism and intergroup relations: Psychological implications for democracy in global context*. American Psychological Association Press.

——— (2018). *Mutual radicalization: How groups and nations push each other to extremes*. Washington, DC: American Psychological Association Press.

——— (2024). *Mutual radicalization and the appeal of authoritarianism in an age of uncertainty*. Invited Presidential lecture delivered at the Presidential Palace, Malta.

Natter, K. 2018. Rethinking immigration policy theory beyond "Western liberal democracies". *Comparative Migration Studies, 6*(4), 1–21.

Newbury, W., Raskovic, M., Colakoglu, S. S., Gonzalez-Perez, M. A., & Minbaeva, D. (2022). Diversity, equity, and inclusion in international business: Dimensions and challenges. *AIB Insights*, *22*(3). https://doi.org/10.46697/001c.36582

Parr, N. (2023). Immigration and the prospects for long-run population decreases in European countries. *Vienna Yearbook of Population Research*, *21*, 1–29.

Pritchett, L. (2023). People over robots: The global economy needs immigration before automation. *Foreign Affairs*, March/April, 53–64.

Salas-Schweikart, R., Hendricks, M. J., Boychuck, M., & Moghaddam, F. M. (2024). Similarity-attraction across ethnic, religious, and political groups: Does celebrating differences or similarities make a difference? *The Journal of Social Psychology*, 1–20. https://doi.org/10.1080/00224545.2024.2427834

Salzman, M. B. (2008). Globalization, religious fundamentalism, and the need for meaning, *International Journal of Intercultural Relations*, *32*, 318–327.

Sánchez-Junquera, J., Chulvi, B., Rosso, P., & Ponzetto, S. P. (2021). How do you speak about immigrants? Taxonomy and stereo-immigrants dataset for identifying stereotypes about immigrants. *Applied Sciences*, *11*(8), 3610.

Schmutz, B., & Verdugo, G. (2023). Do elections effect immigration? Evidence from French municipalities. *Journal of Public Economics*, *218*, 104803.

Stamps, D. C., & Foley, S. M. (2023). Strategies to implement diversity, equity, inclusion, and belonging in the workplace. *Nurse Leader*, *21*(6), 675–680.

Strijbis, O., & Polavieja, J. (2018). Immigrants against immigration: Competition, identity, and immigrants' vote on free movement in Switzerland. *Electoral Studies*, *56*, 150–157.

The Economist (2024). Putting a price on them. Pp. 60–62. May 25–31.

Tajfel, H., Flament, C., Billig, M. G., & Bundy, R. F. (1971). Social categorization and intergroup behavior. *European Journal of Social Psychology*, *1*, 149–177.

Tufail, M., Song, L., Ali, S., Wahab, S., & Taimoor, H. (2023). Does more immigration lead to more violent and property crimes? A case study of 30 OECD countries. *Economic Research-Ekonomska Istraživanja*, *36*(1), 1867–1885. doi:10.1080/1331677X.2022.2094437

Index

acculturation, 2, 154, 162
Afrophobia, 73
American identity, 90
Americanization, 22, 67, 206
anti-immigrant, 3, 69, 143–144
artificial intelligence (AI), 201, 208
assimilation, 70, 77, 90, 135, 141–142, 160–162, 166
assimilation policy, 5–6, 70
authoritarian personality, 187
authoritarian strongmen, 2, 29, 190, 193

banal radicalization, 199
between-group differentiation, 29
birth-rates, 1, 3
borderless world, 209
Brexit, 9, 34, 68, 77, 112–113, 116, 121, 124

categorization, 8, 20, 26–28, 38, 51, 53, 98, 171, 191
Chile, 11, 131, 133–134, 137–146
citizenship, 66, 88, 90, 95, 100–101, 135, 166, 170, 189, 193
climate change, 1, 189
collective identity, 5, 71, 87, 91, 180, 200
common group identity, 6, 12, 180, 192–193
contact hypothesis, 31, 54–55
continuum of material factors and psychological factors, 32
crime, 69, 72, 97, 143, 146, 205
    criminal organizations, 143, 146
criminal activities, 132, 143, 156
criminality, 72
criminals, 72
cultural globalization, 67

decline in trust, 4
deglobalization, 2, 4, 7, 13, 65–66, 68, 77, 87, 205
discrimination, 5–6, 32, 59, 71–72, 76, 91, 98, 137, 165, 192

displacement of aggression, 25, 36
diversity, 3, 44, 46, 70, 89, 91, 95, 104, 119, 123, 129–130, 139, 141–142, 145–146, 159, 163, 211

economic competition, 73, 75–76
economics of immigration, 19
Econs, 25–26, 37
ethnocentrism, 2
Eurobarometer, 11, 122
European identity, 10, 90, 113, 120–121, 123
European Union, 66, 112, 121, 124, 209
evolutionary psychology, 34–35
explicit prejudice, 102, 104–105

false consciousness, 35
far-right, 30, 116, 118
fertility, 114–116, 201
fractured globalization, 9
free market economics, 207

gender, 22, 115, 130, 132–134, 206
Generalized trust (or social trust), 49
Gestalt, 27
global citizen education, 189
global citizenship, 186–187, 189
Global North, 11, 69, 129, 132, 138
Global South, 11, 129, 132, 204
globalization, 2, 65–66, 77, 87, 205

human rights, 156, 182, 188
human universals, 181, 184

identification with all humanity, 186–187, 190, 192–193
imagined communities, 199
imagined identities, 199
ingroup favoritism, 29, 51–52, 98, 171
integration, 5, 71, 91, 113, 118, 120, 122, 124, 135, 137, 139, 142, 146, 153, 155, 159, 164, 166, 192

215

intergroup contact, 1, 52, 54, 58, 77, 145, 154, 165, 168, 173, 180, 191–193, 202

just world theory, 37

manufacturing intergroup differences, 203
mass transportation, 1
migration management, 129, 131, 136, 139–140, 153–155, 160, 163
minimal group paradigm, 28, 98, 191, 200
mixed-ethnicity, 30
multiculturalism, 130, 138–140, 142, 145, 153, 155, 160, 170, 202
  interculturalism, 139–140
  pluriculturalism, 140
multiculturalism hypothesis, 171
Muslim Travel Ban, 72, 90
mutual radicalization, 190

national identity, 6–7, 26, 30, 46, 68, 87–88, 91, 94, 99, 104, 117, 121, 124, 135, 138, 142, 153
nationalism, vii, 100, 124, 190
need for distinctiveness, 183

omnicultural imperative, 181, 184
omnicultural individual, 185
omniculturalism, 6, 13, 154, 180, 182, 184, 192
outgroup homogeneity effect, 28

patriotism, 30, 38, 99–101, 103, 172
perceived cultural threat, 69
perceived material threat, 69
perceived threats, 25, 30, 77, 117–118, 121, 124, 145, 173, 206
percentage of immigrants, 20
polarization, 10, 57, 94, 101, 106, 108
political ideology, 99, 101, 136
political plasticity, 26, 38
politicization of immigration, 210
populism, 21, 190
populist movements, 2
prejudice, 32, 54, 69, 72–74, 76, 89, 94, 97–98, 101–102, 105, 161, 165, 169, 192
pull factors, 208
push factors, 77, 114, 208

realistic conflict, 56

realistic conflict theory, 32–33, 191
Realistic conflict theory, 52, 73, 117
relative deprivation research, 36
relative deprivation theory, 73
religious identity
  Catholic, 115, 129
  Protestants, 54, 89
resource mobilization theory, 33, 117

Secure Communities, 74, 97
self-actualization, 184
self-actualized individuals, 185
sharing imperative, 182, 184
similarity-attraction, 13, 35, 70, 74, 164, 168, 173
social classes, 2
social cohesion, 5, 43, 50–51, 58, 70, 154–156, 167–168
social identity, 3, 8, 30, 35, 37, 57, 88, 104, 117, 170, 183, 186–187
social identity theory, 190
Social identity theory, 88, 98
South Africa, 4
South American, 12, 91, 129, 131, 133, 135–138, 141, 143–146, 153
stereotypes, 8, 26, 52–53, 58, 75, 96, 98, 117, 161, 173, 203
stereotyping, 8
superordinate goals, 33, 180, 191–193
system justification theory, 36–37, 74

threat, 2, 4, 6, 19, 32–33, 58, 63, 65, 68–71, 73–74, 76–77, 98–99, 104, 118, 120, 122, 124, 206
  perceived threat, 70, 118, 145
trust, 44, 46, 53, 77

undocumented, 161
undocumented immigrants, 73, 75–76, 90, 93, 96, 99

veil of ignorance, 182
Venezuela, 129–131, 133, 136–137, 142–143, 145

working-class whites, 2

For EU product safety concerns, contact us at Calle de José Abascal, 56–1°,
28003 Madrid, Spain or eugpsr@cambridge.org.